Catholic Book of Quotations

Leo Knowles

Our Sunday Visitor Publishing Division
Our Sunday Visitor, Inc.
Huntington, Indiana 46750

13 × 841
N 56
2004
a5499901S

Catechism excerpts are taken from the *Catechism of the Catholic Church*, second edition, for use in the United States of America, copyright © 1994 and 1997, United States Catholic Conference — Libreria Editrice Vaticana. Used with permission. Every reasonable effort has been made to determine copyright holders of excerpted materials and to secure permissions as needed. If any copyrighted materials have been inadvertently used without proper credit being given in one form or another, please notify Our Sunday Visitor in writing so that future editions may be corrected accordingly. Liturgical prayer excerpts from *The Roman Missal* (England: Laverty and Sons, 1955). Prayers by Michel Quoist taken from *Prayers of Life* (Dublin: Gill & Macmillan, 1963). Other quotations gathered by the author over many years from many sources, including the Internet, books, magazine articles, word of mouth, and church documents. Every effort has been made to render the translations as accurate as possible.

Our Sunday Visitor Publishing Division
Our Sunday Visitor, Inc.
200 Noll Plaza
Huntington, IN 46750

ISBN: 1-59276-006-6
LCCN: 2003113183

Cover design by Tyler Ottinger
Interior design by Sherri L. Hoffman

PRINTED IN THE UNITED STATES OF AMERICA

In loving memory of my wife
PATRICIA KNOWLES
Born March 11, 1935
Died March 5, 2003
R.I.P.

TABLE OF CONTENTS

ACKNOWLEDGMENTS

Although they cover a wide range, the quotations in this book inevitably represent, to some extent, my own particular interests and concerns.

They are chosen from memory, from many printed sources, and from Internet web sites.

I would like to acknowledge the help of Ann Ball, Father John R. Whitley, C.S.B., Bill and Barbara Keenan, and Kristina Cooper.

LEO KNOWLES

A

ABORTION

You shall not kill an unborn child or murder a newborn infant.

> THE TEACHING OF THE APOSTLES (*2nd century*)

A woman who deliberately destroys the fetus is answerable for murder. And any fine distinction as to its being completely formed or unformed is not admissible amongst us.

> ST. BASIL (*Letters*)

We are fighting abortion by adoption. We have sent word to the clinics, to the hospitals, to the police stations: "Please do not destroy the child. We will take the child."

> BLESSED MOTHER TERESA
> (*Nobel Peace Prize Address, 1979*)

America needs no words from me to see how your decision in *Roe v. Wade* has deformed a great nation. The so-called right to abortion has pitted mothers against their children and women against men. It has sown violence and discord at the heart of the most intimate human relationships. . . . It has portrayed the greatest of gifts – a child – as a competitor, an intrusion and an inconvenience.

It has nominally accorded mothers unfettered dominion over the independent lives of their physically dependent sons and daughters. And, in granting this unconscionable power, it has exposed many women to unjust and selfish demands from their husbands or other sexual partners. Human rights are not a privilege conferred by government. They are every human being's entitlement by virtue of his humanity. The right to life does not depend, and must not be declared to be contingent, on the pleasure of anyone else, not even a parent or a sovereign.

BLESSED MOTHER TERESA
(*Wall Street Journal, February 25, 1994*)

The unborn child is not a potential life, but a life with potential.

JIM MANFORDONIA

ABSOLUTION (see also CONFESSION)

Priests have received from God a power that he has given neither to angels nor to archangels.... God above confirms what priests do here below.

ST. JOHN CHRYSOSTOM
(*Concerning the Priesthood*)

May the same God, who through the prophet Nathan forgave David when he confessed his sins, who forgave Peter when he wept bitterly, the prostitute when she washed his feet with her tears, the Pharisee and the prodigal son, through me, a sinner, forgive you both in this life and in the next and enable you to appear before his awe-inspiring tribunal without condemnation, he who is blessed for ever and ever. Amen.

BYZANTINE LITURGY (*Words of Absolution*)

Were there no forgiveness of sins in the Church, there would be no hope of life to come or eternal liberation. Let us thank God who has given the Church such a gift.

St. Augustine (*Sermons*)

In case of grave necessity recourse may be had to a *communal celebration of reconciliation with general confession and general absolution.* Grave necessity of this sort can arise when there is imminent danger of death without sufficient time for the priest or priests to hear each penitent's confession. Grave necessity can also exist when, given the number of penitents, there are not enough confessors to hear individual confessions properly in a reasonable time, so that the penitents through no fault of their own would be deprived of sacramental grace or Holy Communion for a long time. In this case, for absolution to be valid the faithful must have the intention of individually confessing their grave sins in the time required.

Catechism of the Catholic Church, 1483

ABSTINENCE

Total abstinence is easier than perfect moderation.
St. Augustine (*On The Good of Marriage*)

The right practice of abstinence is needful not only to the mortification of the flesh but also to the purification of the mind.... For the mind then only keeps holy and spiritual fast when it rejects the food of error and the poison of falsehood.

St. Leo the Great

ABUSE

We are the ones, whether through ignorance or lack of vigilance, or — God forbid — with knowledge, who allowed priest abusers to remain in ministry and reassigned them to communities where they continued to abuse.

We are the ones who chose not to report the criminal actions of priests to the authorities, because the law did not require this.

We are the ones who worried more about the possibility of scandal than in bringing about the kind of openness that helps prevent abuse.

And we are the ones who, at times, responded to victims and their families as adversaries and not as suffering members of the Church.

Our confession is matched by a heartfelt contrition.

BISHOP WILTON D. GREGORY
(*Presidential Address, United States Conference of Catholic Bishops, Dallas, Texas: June 13, 2002*)

The Church, strong in the holiness she receives from her Lord, should kneel before God and implore forgiveness for the past and present sins of her sons and daughters.

POPE JOHN PAUL II

ACTION

In forming a judgment we may hesitate, but a judged action must be performed swiftly.

ST. THOMAS AQUINAS

Religious ideas have no value at all if they are not practical and positive. Religion is meant for acting more than thinking.

BLESSED FREDERIC OZANAM

We are not blessed with two separate lives — one for seeking the truth and the other for putting it into practice.

BLESSED FREDERIC OZANAM

Distinguish between fervor of sentiment and fervor of action.

CORNELIA CONNOLLY

What we are doing is just a drop in the ocean. But if that drop was not in the ocean, I think the ocean would be less because of that missing drop. I do not agree with the big way of doing things.

BLESSED MOTHER TERESA

Every action of ours must be accompanied by a reflection to orient it, to order it, to make it coherent, so that it does not lapse into a sterile and superficial activism

GUSTAVO GUTIERREZ

When we dream alone, it is only a dream. But when we dream together, it is the beginning of reality.

BRAZILIAN PROVERB

If you want to reach out to others be ready to soil your hands.

ALEX REBELLO

ADAM

Adam lay ybounden, bounden in a bond;
Four thousand winter thought he not too long;
And al was for an apple, an apple that he took,
As clerkes finden written in their book;
Ne had the apple taken been, the apple taken been,
Ne hadde never Our Lady been of heaven queen.
Blessed be the time that apple taken was!
Therefore we moun singen *Deo gratias*.

ybounden: bound; *thought he:* seemed; *moun:* must

ENGLISH CAROL (*15th century*)

O happy fault, O necessary sin of Adam,
Which gained for us so great a redeemer!
EXULTET, THE ROMAN MISSAL

ADMONITION

Admonition is naturally bitter, but when mixed with
the sugar of loving kindness, and warmed by the fire of
charity, it becomes acceptable, gracious and very cor-
dial.

JEAN PIERRE CAMUS
(*The Spirit of St. Francis de Sales*)

ADOLESCENCE

In adolescence ... there is a curious mingling of refine-
ment and brutality, stupidity and tenderness.
R. H. BENSON (*By What Authority*)

ADULTERY

The adulterer is a more grievous offender than the thief.
ST. JOHN CHRYSOSTOM (*Homilies*)

ADVENT

O come, O come, Emmanuel,
And ransom captive Israel,
That mourns in lonely exile here,
Until the Son of God appear.
Rejoice! Rejoice! Emmanuel
Shall come to thee, O Israel.

ANONYMOUS (*Veni, veni Emmanuel*;
tr. *J. Neale 13th century*)

AFFECTION

Affection, like melancholy, magnifies trifles; but the magnifying of the one is like looking through a telescope at heavenly objects; that of the other, like enlarging monsters with a microscope.

POPE PAUL VI

AGE

Growing old is like being increasingly penalized for a crime you haven't committed.
PIERRE TEILHARD DE CHARDIN, S.J.

Old age comes from God, old age leads on to God, old age will touch us only so far as He wills.
PIERRE TEILHARD DE CHARDIN, S.J.

AGGIORNAMENTO

I want to throw open the windows of the Church, so that we can see out and the people can see in.

BLESSED POPE JOHN XXIII

AIR

Wild air, world-mothering air,
Nestling me everywhere.

GERARD MANLEY HOPKINS, S.J.
(*The Blessed Virgin Compared to the Air We Breathe*)

ALMSGIVING

The giver of alms should be free from anxiety and full of joy! His gain will be greatest when he keeps back least for himself.

POPE ST. LEO THE GREAT

AMBITION

The Church is full of ambitious men ... we think no more of it than a robber's cave thinks of the spoils of the wayfarers.

ST. BERNARD OF CLAIRVAUX (*On Consideration*)

Ambition is the mother of hypocrisy and prefers to skulk in corners and dark places. It cannot endure the light of day. It is an unclean vice wallowing in the depths, always hidden, but with ever an eye to advancement.

ST. BERNARD OF CLAIRVAUX (*Letters*)

We are so presumptuous that we would be known by the whole world, and even by those who shall come when we shall be no more; and we are so vain that the esteem of five or six persons who surround us amuses and contents us.

BLAISE PASCAL (*Pensées*)

The cancer of careerism is terminal and incurable; even clerics contract it

ALEX REBELLO

AMEN

In Hebrew, *amen* comes from the same root as the word for "believe." This root expresses solidity, trustworthiness, faithfulness. And so we can understand why "Amen" may express God's faithfulness to us and our trust in him.

CATECHISM OF THE CATHOLIC CHURCH, 1062

AMERICA

I presume that your fellow-citizens will not forget the patriotic part which you played in the accomplishment of their Revolution, and the establishment of your government, or the important assistance which they received from a nation in which the Roman Catholic faith is professed.

GEORGE WASHINGTON
(*To the Roman Catholics of the United States*)

Americans, God has given you a great country: guard her well. He has made you a spectacle to the nations; he

has confided to you humanity's highest destiny; be not
unworthy of Heaven's confidence.

ARCHBISHOP JOHN IRELAND
(*American Citizenship*)

All intelligent men are agreed ... that America seems
destined for greater things. Now it is our wish that the
Catholic Church should not only share in, but help to
bring about, this prospective greatness. We deem it right
and proper that she should, by availing herself of the
opportunities daily presented to her, keep equal step
with the Republic in the march of improvement, at the
same time striving to the utmost by her virtue and her
institutions to aid in the rapid growth of the states.

POPE LEO XIII (*Longinque Oceani*)

Ours is the American Church, and not Irish, German,
Italian or Polish – and we will keep it American.

CARDINAL JAMES GIBBONS
(*speech to hierarchy, 1920*)

What got her into most hot water was her sharp social
criticism. She pointed out that patriotism was a more
powerful force in most people's lives than the Gospel.
While she hated every kind of tyranny and never ceased
to be thankful for America having taken in so many people fleeing poverty and repression, she was fierce in her
criticism of capitalism and consumerism. She said America had a tendency to treat people like Kleenex – use
them, and throw them away. "Our problems stem," she
said, "from our acceptance of this filthy, rotten system."

JIM FOREST
(*Dorothy Day – A Saint for Our Age?*)

We don't have to agree with one another. This is a country of diversity. But there doesn't have to be the bitterness, there doesn't have to be the hatred, there doesn't have to be the mistrust.

ROBERT F. KENNEDY

ANGELS

O God, who in a wonderful order has established the ministry of angels and of men, mercifully grant that, as thy holy angels ever do thee service in heaven, so they may at all times protect us on earth.

THE ROMAN MISSAL
(*Collect for the Feast of St. Michael*)

Non Angli, sed Angeli.

POPE ST. GREGORY THE GREAT
Legend has it that Gregory spotted some fair-haired slaves on sale and asked who they were. Told that they were "Angli" (English) he responded "Non Angli sed Angeli" (Not English but Angels).

There are nine orders of angels, namely, angels, archangels, virtues, powers, principalities, dominations, thrones, cherubim and seraphim.

POPE ST. GREGORY THE GREAT (*Homilies*)

The word angel is the name of a function, not of a nature. For they are always spirits, but are called angels when they are sent.

ST. ISIDORE (*Etymologies*)

They are intellectual natures, at the peak of creation.

ST. THOMAS AQUIN
(*Contra Ge*

Angels mean messengers and ministers. Their function is to execute the plan of divine providence, even in earthly things. . . .

ST. THOMAS AQUINAS (*Contra Gentes*)

The world of pure spirits stretches between the Divine Nature and the world of human beings; because Divine Wisdom has ordained that the higher should look after the lower, angels execute the divine plan for human salvation; they are our guardians, who free us when hindered and help to bring us home.

ST. THOMAS AQUINAS
(*Commentary on the Sentences*)

Make yourself familiar with the angels, and behold them frequently in spirit; for, without being seen, they are present with you.

ST. FRANCIS DE SALES
(*Introduction to the Devout Life*)

ANGER

The abbot Hyperichius said: "The monk that cannot master his tongue in time of anger will not master the passions of his body at some other time."

THE DESERT FATHERS

If the Holy Spirit is peace of soul, as He is said to be and as He is in reality, and if anger is disturbance of heart, as it actually is and as it is said to be, then nothing so prevents his presence in us as anger.

ST. JOHN CLIMACUS
(*The Ladder of Divine Ascent*)

The first step toward freedom from anger is to keep the lips silent when the heart is stirred; the next, to keep thoughts silent when the soul is upset; the last, to be totally calm when unclean winds are blowing.

ST. JOHN CLIMACUS

Is it any merit to abstain from wine if one is intoxicated with anger?

ST. AUGUSTINE

Anger is a kind of temporary madness.

ST. BASIL (*Against Anger*)

The angry man always thinks he can do more than he can.

ALBERTANO OF BRESCIA
(*Liber Consolationis*)

There is no wrong that gives man such a foretaste of hell in this life as anger and impatience.

ST. CATHERINE OF SIENA
(*Letter to Monna Agnese*)

Anger is quieted by a gentle word, as fire is quenched by water.

JEAN PIERRE CAMUS
(*The Spirit of St. Francis de Sales*)

There is a holy anger, excited by zeal, which moves us to reprove with warmth those whom our mildness failed to correct.

ST. JEAN BAPTISTE DE LA SALLE
(*Les devoirs du Chretien*)

Anger is like a stone thrown into a wasp's nest.

POPE PAUL VI

THE ANIMAL KINGDOM

If you have men who will exclude any of God's creatures from the shelter of compassion and pity, you will have men who deal likewise with their fellow men.

ST. FRANCIS OF ASSISI

There is something so very dreadful, so satanic in tormenting those who have never harmed us, and who cannot defend themselves, who are utterly in our power, who have weapons neither of offence nor defense, that none but very hardened persons can endure the thought of it.

VENERABLE JOHN HENRY NEWMAN

ANOINTING

You were rubbed with oil like an athlete, Christ's athlete, as though in preparation for an earthly wrestling match, and you agreed to take on your opponent.

ST. AMBROSE (*De Sacramentis*)

ANSWER TO PRAYER

Sister Thérèse is everywhere and her care passes nobody by . . . a young priest is instantaneously cured of advanced tuberculosis and henceforward has perfect health; a blind girl sees Sister Thérèse and at once recovers normal sight; the prioress of an Italian convent, unable to meet her bills, finds sufficient money in an empty desk; a Presbyterian minister in Edinburgh is led by her into the Church and goes to live in her old house at Alençon; an English industrialist, unjust to his

workmen, becomes their friend and benefactor, and
even their religious teacher, overnight; a child is saved
from fire and an automobile held back on the edge of
a cliff by people calling on Thérèse; one of the petals
from her crucifix banishes a cancer of the tongue; here,
she comes in person to give a snowdrop to a child in
pain and to save its mother from death; there, her statue
in a hut encourages a number of pagans to cast down
their idols. There is scarcely a country which has not
seen her blessings or where her name is not invoked:
her holiness is clear, her miracles undeniable. The voice
of the people is heard crying out on every hand.

HENRI GHÉON
(*The Secret of the Little Flower*)

Once we overdrew our account by $200. On the way
home from the printers, where we had been putting the
paper to bed, we stopped in Chinatown at the little
Church of the Transfiguration and said a prayer to St.
Joseph. When we got to the office a woman was waiting to visit with us. We served her tea and toast and
presently she went on her way, leaving us a check for
the exact amount of the overdraft. We had not men-
tioned our need.

DOROTHY DAY (*Loaves and Fishes*)

ANXIETY (see also TRUST IN GOD)

Anxiety is not only temptation in itself, but a source of
many others. . . .

If we seek to be delivered for the love of God, we
will do so patiently, gently, humbly and peacefully,
looking for our deliverance more from the goodness

and providence of God than from our own efforts and labor. . . .

This anxiety is the greatest evil that can befall us except sin, for just as revolt and sedition in a country cause havoc and sap its resistance to a foreign invasion, so we, when troubled or worried, are unable to preserve the virtues we have already acquired or resist the temptations of the devil who then diligently fishes, as they say in troubled waters. Anxiety arises from a desire to be delivered from the evil we experience, or to obtain some good for which we hope, yet nothing so aggravates the evil or impedes the good as this over-eagerness and anxiety. Birds remain ensnared because they flutter in their wild attempts to escape from the net, and in doing so get all the more entangled, so, when you desire to be delivered from some evil or to obtain some good, first strive, above all, for peace and tranquility.

ST. FRANCIS DE SALES
(*Introduction to the Devout Life*)

If any trouble afflicts your heart, make it known at once to some good friend, and the strength you will gain from this will enable you to bear your trouble easily.

ST. LOUIS (*to his son*)

All worry is atheistic, because it is a want of trust in God.

ARCHBISHOP FULTON J. SHEEN

APOLOGETICS

When you debate with unbelievers, be warned to begin with, against striving to demonstrate the articles of faith.

That would be to minimize their grandeur, for they surpass the minds of angels let alone of men. We believe them because God reveals them. Your intention should be to defend the faith, not to prove it up to the hilt.

ST. THOMAS AQUINAS
(*Concerning Reasons of Faith*)

A man should remind himself that an object of faith is not scientifically demonstrable, lest, presuming to demonstrate what is of faith, he should produce inconclusive reasons and offer occasion for unbelievers to scoff at a faith based on such grounds.

ST. THOMAS AQUINAS (*Summa Theologica*)

The reasoned arguments for the faith are not sufficiently strong to coerce the unwilling into faith, but they are stronger than any argument that can be brought against Christianity, and are quite sufficiently strong to reinforce and to strengthen the will to believe.

ARNOLD LUNN (*Now I See*)

A certain principle may be true and yet propounded with such outworn or feeble arguments as to make those who teach it incredible, and not only in this one matter but with respect to the whole message of faith.

BERNARD HÄRING, C.SS.R.

APOSTOLATE

Let us not be dumb watchdogs or silent spectators: let us not be hirelings that flee at the approach of the wolf. Let us be faithful shepherds, preaching to all . . . in season and out of season.

ST. BONIFACE

Christ has no body now on earth but yours, no hands but yours, no feet but yours, yours are the eyes with which he looks with compassion at the world, yours are the feet with which he is to go about doing good, and yours are the hands with which he is to bless us now.

ST. TERESA OF ÁVILA

Don't make yourself visible, but let others see you.

BLESSED FREDERIC OZANAM

Long face, coarse manners, a ridiculous appearance, a repelling air. Is that how you hope to inspire others to follow Christ?

ST. JOSEMARÍA ESCRIVÁ (*The Way*)

Jesus' light burns in this world only with the oil of our lives, in quiet particular circumstances, in which we can emanate liberating life or even dim or quench this light, so that the world disappears in the clouds.

EDWARD SCHILLEBEECKX, O.P.
(*Christ: The Experience of Jesus as Lord*)

ART

Art is the grandchild of God.

DANTE

May God forgive you, Brother John, for having painted me so very ugly!

ST. TERESA OF ÁVILA

Art is beauty made a sacrament. Art is finite human expression made intimate by love.

VINCENT MCNABB, O.P. (*Thoughts Twice-dyed*)

"A man can be a very good Catholic in a factory." How true! But the fact remains that the factory-made art of the Catholic repository is a very bad thing for making Catholics.

ERIC GILL
(*Beauty Looks after Herself*)

The function of all art lies in fact in breaking through the narrow and tortuous enclosure of the finite, in which man is immersed while living here below, and in providing a window on the infinite for his hungry soul.

POPE PIUS XII (*April 8, 1952*)

Wherever art – English, Greek or Chinese – has known a certain degree of grandeur and purity, it is already Christian, Christian in hope, because every spiritual radiance is a promise and a symbol of the divine harmonies of the Gospel.

JACQUES MARITAIN
(*Art and Scholasticism*)

ASCETICISM

Asceticism . . . is essentially the assertion of the body, not its negation.

ABBOT ANSCAR VONIER, O.S.B.

ASH WEDNESDAY

Remember, man, that you are dust, and to dust you shall return.

THE ROMAN MISSAL (*Imposition of Ashes*)

ATHEISM

If there were no God, there would be no atheists.

G. K. CHESTERTON
(*Where All Roads Lead*)

ATTENTION

Something in our soul has a far more violent repugnance for true attention than the flesh has for bodily fatigue. This something is much more closely connected with evil than is the flesh. That is why every time we really concentrate our attention, we destroy the evil in ourselves. If we concentrate with this intention, a quarter of an hour of attention is better than a great many good works.

SIMONE WEIL
(*Waiting for God*)

A man will be effective to the degree that he is able to concentrate. Concentration is not a mode of doing, but above all a mode of being.

MICHEL QUOIST
(*The Christian Response*)

AUSTRALIA

In a way Australia is like Catholicism. The company is questionable, the landscape is grotesque. But you always come back.

THOMAS KENEALLY, AUSTRALIAN NOVELIST
(*magazine interview*)

AUTHORITY

Wherefore, all who are superiors should not regard in themselves the power of their rank, but the equality of their nature; and they should find their joy, not in ruling over men but in helping them.

POPE ST. GREGORY THE GREAT (*Pastoral Care*)

It is [the abbot's] job to serve the brothers rather than to rule over them. . . . If he has to discipline anyone, he must do it prudently and not be too severe. If he scrapes away too hard at the rust he might break the vessel! A good abbot wants to be loved rather than feared. He must not be too headstrong in his decisions, but he must not be a worrier either. He must not be extravagant or stubborn, jealous or over-suspicious. . . .

ST. BENEDICT (*The Holy Rule*)

It is much safer to be in a subordinate position than to be in authority.

THOMAS À KEMPIS (*The Imitation of Christ*)

The highest duty is to respect authority, and obediently to submit to just law.

POPE LEO XIII (*Libertas Praestantissimum*)

All worldly power proceeds from God.

POPE LEO XIII (*Immortale Dei*)

If civil authorities legislate for or allow anything that is contrary to that order and therefore contrary to the will of God, neither the laws made nor the authorization granted can be binding on the conscience of the citizen, since God has more right to be obeyed than man.

BLESSED POPE JOHN XXIII (*Pacem in Terris*)

B

BAPTISM

Since man is of a twofold nature, composed of body and soul, the purification also is twofold: the corporeal for the corporeal and the incorporeal for the incorporeal. The water cleanses the body, and the Spirit seals the soul.

ST. CYRIL OF JERUSALEM

Baptism is God's most beautiful and magnificent gift. . . . It is called *gift* because it is conferred on those who bring nothing of their own; *grace* because it is given even to the guilty; *Baptism* because sin is buried in the water; *anointing* because it is priestly and royal as are those anointed; *enlightenment* because it radiates light; *clothing* since it veils our shame; *bath* because it washes; and *seal* as it is our guard and the sign of God's lordship.

ST. GREGORY OF NAZIANZUS (Orations)

The baby doesn't understand English and the devil knows Latin.

RONALD KNOX
(refusing to conduct a baptism in English)

BEAUTY

Glory be to God for dappled things –
For skies of couple-color as a brinded cow
For rose-moles all in stipple upon trout that swim

Fresh-firecoal chestnut-falls; finches' wings;
Landscape plotted and pieced – fold, fallow and plough;
And all trades, their gear and tackle and trim.

All things counter, original, spare, strange;
Whatever is fickle, freckled (who knows how?)
With swift, slow, sweet, sour, adazzle, dim;
He fathers-forth whose beauty is past change:
Praise him.

GERARD MANLEY HOPKINS, S.J. (Pied Beauty)

The beauty of the world is Christ's tender smile for us coming through matter.

SIMONE WEIL

Beauty and chastity are always quarreling.

SPANISH PROVERB

BELIEF

For I do not seek to understand that I may believe, but I believe in order to understand (*credo ut intelligam*). For this I also believe – that unless I believe, I should not understand.

ST. ANSELM (Prosologion)

There are few so confirmed in atheism that a pressing danger or the neighborhood of death will not force them to a recognition of the divine power.

MICHEL DE MONTAIGNE (Essays)

We can believe what we choose. We are answerable for what we choose to believe.

VENERABLE JOHN HENRY NEWMAN
(Letter to Mrs. William Froude)

When men stop believing in God they don't believe in nothing; they believe in anything.

G. K. CHESTERTON
(*attributed, but not found in his writings*)

The point of having an open mind, like having an open mouth, is to close it on something solid.

G. K. CHESTERTON

We have only to believe. And the more threatening and irreducible reality appears, the more firmly and desperately must we believe. Then, little by little, we shall see the universal horror unbend, and then smile upon us, and then take us into its more human arms.

PIERRE TEILHARD DE CHARDIN, S.J.

He that will believe only what he can fully comprehend must have a long head or a very short creed.

PIERRE TEILHARD DE CHARDIN, S.J.

Many people today live in a suburb of reality. Now, there's nothing wrong with living in a suburb, so long as you don't think that your suburb is the whole metropolis.

FRANK SHEED

BELLOC, HILAIRE

A wonderful personality . . . so rich and various that his opponents could not cope with him: but you felt he could not always cope with himself. . . . All this went into his battle for the Faith. The devotion, the learning, the gaiety, the grandeur, the courage, but something of the wilfulness too. The total effect was magnificent, and we are all so deeply in his debt that our best thanks are feeble in comparison.

FRANK SHEED

BIRTH CONTROL

Each and every marriage act must remain open to the transmission of life.

POPE PAUL VI (*Humanae Vitae*)

BIRTH AND DEATH

Any day is a good day to be born; any day is a good day to die.

BLESSED POPE JOHN XXIII

BISHOPS

Wherever the bishop appears there let the people be; as wherever Jesus Christ is, there is the Catholic Church.

ST. IGNATIUS OF ANTIOCH
(*Letter to the Smyrnaeans*)

[Bishops] are not to be looked upon as vicars of the Roman pontiffs, because they exercise a power really their own, and are most truly called the ordinary pastors of the peoples over whom they rule.

POPE LEO XIII (*Satis Cognitum*)

As books vary from one to the other, so too do bishops. Some bishops, in fact, resemble eagles, who sail loftily with solemn documents. Others are nightingales who marvelously sing the praise of the Lord. Others, instead, are poor wrens, who only twitter as humble subjects. I, Mark Twain, belong to the last category.

ALBINO LUCIANI, LATER POPE JOHN PAUL I
(*Illustrissimi*)

BITTERNESS

One must neither write nor commit any act from which bitterness might arise.

ST. IGNATIUS LOYOLA

Bitterness has sharpened your tongue. Be silent!

ST. JOSEMARÍA ESCRIVÁ (*The Way*)

THE BLESSED SACRAMENT

When you are close to the tabernacle in which love incarnate dwells, there is no distance.

BLESSED ELIZABETH OF THE TRINITY

Do you realize that Jesus is there in the tabernacle for you, for you alone? He burns with the desire to come into your heart.

ST. THÉRÈSE OF LISIEUX

. . .When the pilgrim, when the guest, when the
    traveller
Has trailed for hours through the muddy highways,
Before crossing the threshold of the church he
    carefully wipes his feet,
Before going in,
Because he is very tidy,
And the mud from the roads must not soil the
    flagstones in the church.

But once it is done, once he has wiped his feet before
    entering,
Once he has gone in he no longer thinks of his feet,
He is not always looking to see if his feet are properly
    wiped,
He has no heart, he has no eyes, he has no voice any
    more
Except for the altar where the Body of Jesus
And the memory and the expectation of the Body of
    Jesus
Shine eternally.

CHARLES PÉGUY
(*The Mystery of the Holy Innocents*)

O Holy angels, make me see God on the altar as you see
Him in heaven.

BLESSED BROTHER ANDRÉ

When you look at the Crucifix, you understand how
much Jesus loved you then. When you look at the Sacred
Host you understand how much Jesus loves you now.

BLESSED MOTHER TERESA

THE BLESSED TRINITY

Now the Catholic faith is this: that we worship one God
in Trinity, and Trinity in Unity, neither confounding the
Persons, nor dividing the substance, for there is one Person of the Father; another of the Son, and another of the
Holy Spirit; but the godhead of Father, of the Son, and
of the Holy Spirit is one, the glory equal, the majesty co-
eternal. . . .

ATHANASIAN CREED

Think of the Father as a spring of life begetting the Son like a river and the Holy Spirit like a sea, for the spring and the river and the sea are all one nature. Think of the Father as a root, of the Son as a branch, and of the Spirit as a fruit, for the substance in these three is one. The Father is a sun with the Son as rays and the Holy Spirit as heat. The Holy Spirit transcends by far every similitude and figure. So, when you hear of an off-spring of the Father, do not think of a corporeal off-spring. And when you hear that there is a Word, do not suppose him to be a corporeal word. And when you hear of the spirit of God, do not think of wind and breath. Rather, hold your persuasion with a simple faith alone. For the concept of the Creator is arrived at by analogy from his creatures.

ST. JOHN OF DAMASCUS
(*Exposition of the Orthodox Faith*)

How can plurality consist with unity, or unity with plurality? To examine the fact closely is rashness, to believe it is piety, to know it is life, and life eternal.

ST. BERNARD OF CLAIRVAUX
(*De Consideratione*)

Firmly I believe and truly – God is Three and God is One;
and I next acknowledge duly – Manhood taken by the Son.

VENERABLE JOHN HENRY NEWMAN
(*The Dream of Gerontius*)

BLOODSHED

The Church abhors bloodshed.

THE COUNCIL OF TOURS (*1163*)

BOOKS

When I get a little money I buy books; and if any is left I buy food and clothes.

ERASMUS

The books that the world calls immoral are the books that show the world its own shame.

OSCAR WILDE

When I am dead, I hope it may be said:
"His sins were scarlet, but his books were read."

HILAIRE BELLOC (*Epigrams*)

BROTHERHOOD

I want everyone here, Christian, Muslim, Jew, pagan, to look on me as a brother, a universal brother.

VENERABLE CHARLES DE FOUCAULD
(*Letter to Marie de Bondy*)

BURIAL

Let there be no heavy charge for burying people in the cemetery, since it is for all the poor; but let them pay a workman's wage to him who digs and the price of the tiles.

ST. HIPPOLYTUS
(*The Apostolic Tradition*)

C

CAPITALISM

Each needs the other; capital cannot do without labor, nor labor without capital.

POPE LEO XIII
(*Rerum Novarum*)

Capital has a right to a just share of the profits, but only to a just share.

CARDINAL WILLIAM HENRY O'CONNELL
(*Pastoral Letter on the Laborer's Rights*)

The mutual relations between capital and labor must be determined according to the laws of strictest justice, called commutative justice, supported however by Christian charity. Free competition and still more economic domination must be kept within just and definite limits, and brought under the effective control of the public authority.

POPE PIUS XI
(*Quadragesimo Anno*)

The Church has rejected the totalitarian and atheistic ideologies associated in modern times with "communism" or "socialism." She has likewise refused to accept, in the practice of "capitalism," individualism and the absolute primacy of the law of the marketplace over human labor. . . .

CATECHISM OF THE CATHOLIC CHURCH, 2425

CARE

Be slow and sure. Things are done quickly enough if done well.

BALTASAR GRACIÁN, S.J.
(*The Art of Worldly Wisdom*)

CATHOLIC

Christian is my name, and Catholic my surname. The former qualifies me, the latter manifests me for what I am.

ST. PACIANUS OF BARCELONA (*Letters*)

The greatest thing about every Catholic is that he is one.

JOHN AYSCOUGH (*Levia Pondera*)

Once a Catholic always a Catholic.

ANGUS WILSON (*The Wrong Set*)

THE CATHOLIC CHURCH

He cannot have God for his father who has not the Church for his mother.

ST. CYPRIAN

For all in common she prays, for all in common she works, in the temptations of all she is tried.

ST. AMBROSE

For whether they will or not, even heretics and schismatics when talking, not among themselves but with outsiders, call the Catholic Church nothing else but the

Catholic Church. For otherwise they would not be understood unless they distinguished the Church by that name which she bears throughout the world.

ST. AUGUSTINE
(*Concerning True Religion*)

The Church is called Sion, because from the distance of its sojourn it contemplates the promise of heavenly things; therefore it has received the name Sion, that is, contemplation. In view of the future peace of its home, it is called Jerusalem. For Jerusalem means the vision of peace.

ST. ISIDORE OF SEVILLE (*Etymologies*)

The Church consists principally of two parts, the one called the Church triumphant, the other the Church militant. The Church triumphant is that most glorious and happy assemblage of blessed spirits, and those souls who have triumphed over the world, the flesh, and the devil, and, now exempt from the troubles of this life, are blessed with the fruit of everlasting bliss. The Church militant is the society of all the faithful still dwelling on earth, and is called militant, because it wages eternal war with those implacable enemies, the world, the flesh and the devil. We are not, however, hence to infer that there are two Churches: they are two constituent parts of one Church.

CATECHISM OF THE COUNCIL OF TRENT

The Catholic Church is still sending forth to the farthest ends of the world missionaries as zealous as those who landed in Kent with Augustine, and still confronting hostile kings with the same spirit with which she confronted Attila. The number of her children is greater than in any former age. Her acquisitions in the New World have more than compensated for what she has lost in the Old. Her spiritual ascendancy extends over the vast countries which lie between the plains of Missouri and Cape Horn, countries which, a century hence, may not improbably contain a population as large as that which now inhabits Europe. . . . Nor do we see any sign which indicates that the term of her long dominion is approaching. She saw the commencement of all the governments and of all the ecclesiastical establishments that now exist in the world, and we see no assurance that she is not destined to see the end of them all.

THOMAS BABINGTON MACAULAY
(*Essay on Von Ranke*)

Herein is the strength of the Catholic Church; herein she differs from all Protestant mockeries of her. She professes to be built upon facts, not opinions; on objective truths, not on variable sentiments; on immemorial testimony; not on private judgment; on convictions or perceptions, not on conclusions. None else but she can make this profession.

VENERABLE JOHN HENRY NEWMAN
(*Difficulties of Anglicans*)

At once the most firm and the most flexible institution in the world, she is all things to all nations – educating each in her own spirit, without violence to its nature, and assimilating it to herself without prejudice to the originality of its native character.

LORD ACTON
(*Döllinger on the Temporal Power*)

The Roman Catholic Church was then, as it is now, a great democracy. There was no peasant so humble that he might not become a priest, and no priest so obscure that he might not become Pope of Christendom; and every chancellery in Europe, every court in Europe, was ruled by these learned, trained and accomplished men – the priesthood of that great and dominant body. What kept government alive in the Middle Ages was this constant rise of the sap from the bottom, from the rank and file of the great body of the people through the open channels of the priesthood.

THOMAS WOODROW WILSON

When Christ at a historic moment was establishing his great society, He chose for its corner-stone neither the brilliant Paul, nor the mystic John, but a shuffler, a snob, a coward – in a word, a man. And upon this rock he has built his Church, and the gates of Hell have not prevailed against it. All the empires and the kingdoms have failed because of this inherent and continual weakness, that they were founded by strong men upon strong men. But this one thing – the historic Christian Church – was founded upon a weak man, and for that reason it is indestructible. For no chain is stronger than its weakest link.

G. K. CHESTERTON (*Heretics*)

If Rome dies, other churches may order their coffins.

GEORGE TYRELL

The curious have remarked that one institution alone for now nineteen hundred years has been attacked not by one opposing principle but from every conceivable point.

It has been denounced upon all sides and for reasons successively incompatible: it has suffered the contempt, the hatred and the ephemeral triumph of enemies as diverse as the diversity of things could produce. This institution is the Catholic Church.

HILAIRE BELLOC

We derive from our apprehension of the living Christ the apprehension of a living Church; it is from that living Church that we take our guidance. Protestantism claims to take its guidance immediately from the living Christ. But what is the guidance he gives us, and where are we to find it?

RONALD KNOX (*The Belief of Catholics*)

All roads still lead to Rome and unless you place yourself there you will never be in the heart of the world or see it in its right perspective. To be a Protestant is to be cross-eyed.

GEORGE SANTAYANA (*Letters*)

Christ lives on in the Church, but Christ crucified. One might almost venture to say that the defects of the Church are his Cross.

ROMANO GUARDINI (*The Church and the Catholic*)

Not a hundred people in the United States hate the Roman Catholic Church, but millions hate what they mistakenly think the Roman Catholic Church is.

ARCHBISHOP FULTON J. SHEEN

The great achievement of the Catholic Church lay in harmonizing, civilizing the deepest impulses of ordinary, ignorant people.

KENNETH CLARK, ENGLISH HISTORIAN (*Civilization*)

There are three bodies no sensible man directly challenges: the Roman Catholic Church, the Brigade of Guards and the National Union of Mineworkers.

HAROLD MACMILLAN, FORMER
BRITISH PRIME MINISTER (*newspaper interview*)

CELIBACY

Let bishops, priests and deacons, and in general all the clergy who are employed in the service of the altar, abstain from conjugal intercourse with their wives and the begetting of children; let those who persist be degraded from the ranks of the clergy.

COUNCIL OF ELVIRA (*c. 305*)

The priest is emphatically not just a pious bachelor. He is wedded to the Savior's work in the world, and celibacy is the obvious, congenial expression of the priest's relationship to God and man.

JOHN LaFARGE, S.J. (*The Manner Is Ordinary*)

In the community of the faithful committed to his charge, the priest is Christ present. Thus, it is most fitting that in all things he should reproduce the image of Christ and follow in particular his example, both in his personal life as well as in his apostolic life.

POPE PAUL VI (*Priestly Celibacy*)

The only real motivation for celibacy is being faithful to the total imitation of Jesus Christ. . . . Celibacy is an issue of love, and love cannot be explained or reasoned.

CARDINAL GODFRIED DANEELS

The objection to the Catholic priest's celibacy is that it is very difficult to maintain. The spiritual resolve has to descend again and again into the rebellious body and become incarnate. Day by day, year by year, the decision to follow the virginal Christ, to cling to the equally virginal (and hence maternal) Church, must show itself stronger than the most plausible objections of sensual man. This is truly a following of Christ in the act of incarnation, and hence also a following of the "lowly handmaid" who, right down to her least spiritual faculties, is at God's disposal and is rendered fruitful by him. And as for celibacy's aspect of "rule," it is this: a person is *privileged* to make an irrevocable decision to follow Christ, just as the Son's choosing to become incarnate remains irrevocable.

CARDINAL HANS URS VON BALTHASAR

The celibate has to make space in his heart for many and not just for one. It is natural for us to want the space in our hearts to be filled by one other person. But the priest and religious must make space for all. We have to love everyone. That is the heart of the effectiveness of our ministry. With prayer goes discipline whereby we say "no" to ourselves, not in a negative and inhuman way, but in order to say "yes" to other people.

CARDINAL BASIL HUME O.S.B. (*Light in the Lord*)

If the church everywhere or in certain areas is unable to find enough clergy unless she abandons celibacy, then she must abandon it; for the obligation to provide enough pastors for the Christian people takes precedence.

KARL RAHNER, S.J.
(*Open Letter to a Brother Priest*)

CENSORSHIP

One Galileo in 2000 years is enough.

> POPE PIUS XII (*when asked to condemn the works of Teilhard de Chardin*)

CERTAINTY

What we do for ourselves in life is more certain than all the good we expect others to do for us after death.

> POPE ST. GREGORY THE GREAT

CHANGE

In a higher world it is otherwise; but here below to live is to change, and to be perfect is to have changed often.

> VENERABLE JOHN HENRY NEWMAN (*Development of Christian Doctrine*)

We can change, slowly and steadily, if we set our will to it.

> R. H. BENSON (*The Coward*)

CHARACTER

In attempts to improve your character, know what is in your power and what is beyond it.

> FRANCIS THOMPSON

Don't say, "That's the way I am – it's my character." It's your *lack* of character.

> ST. JOSEMARÍA ESCRIVÁ (*The Way*)

CHARITY

There is no stronger virtue than to scorn no man.

> THE SAYINGS OF THE FATHERS

Let the mouth also fast from disgraceful speeches and railings. For what does it profit if we abstain from fish and fowl and yet bite and devour our brothers and sisters? The evil speaker eats the flesh of his brother and bites the body of his neighbor.

ST. JOHN CHRYSOSTOM

We should love others truly, for their own sakes rather than our own.

ST. THOMAS AQUINAS
(*Concerning the True Precepts of Charity*)

Help thy kin, Christ biddeth, for there beginneth charity.

WILLIAM LANGLAND (*Piers Plowman*)

When it seems that God is showing you the faults of others, play safe. Maybe your judgment is mistaken. Let your lips remain silent.

ST. CATHERINE OF SIENA (*Letter to Sister Daniella*)

Never listen to tales of others' faults; and if anyone complains to you about someone else, ask him humbly not to speak about that person at all.

ST. JOHN OF THE CROSS
(*The Living Flame of Love*)

Every good Christian ought to be more ready to give a favorable interpretation to another's statement than to condemn it. But if he cannot do so, let him ask how the other understands it. And if the latter understands it badly, let the former correct him with love. If that does not suffice, let the Christian try all suitable ways to bring the other to a correct interpretation so that he may be saved.

ST. IGNATIUS LOYOLA (*Spiritual Exercises*)

47

If we wish to keep peace with our neighbor, we should never remind him of his natural defects.

St. Philip Neri

Charity is above all rules.

St. Vincent de Paul

All the things in the world are not worth one human thought, and all the efforts of human thought are not worth one act of charity.

Blaise Pascal (*Pensées*)

Let us learn to stand up for our convictions without hating our adversaries, and to love those who think differently from us.

Blessed Frederic Ozanam

It has been said that charity is the pardoning of the unpardonable and the loving of the unlovable.

R. H. Benson (*Lord of the World*)

The Bible tells us to love our neighbors, and also to love our enemies; probably because they are generally the same people.

G. K. Chesterton

CHASTITY

Give me chastity and continence, but not yet!

St. Augustine (*Confessions*)

Chastity without charity shall be chained in hell.

William Langland
(*The Vision of Piers Plowman*)

CHESTERTON, G. K.

His mind indeed was oceanic, subject indeed to a certain restriction of repeated phrase and manner, but in no way restricted as to the action of his mind. He swooped on an idea like an eagle, tore it with active beak into its constituent parts and brought out the heart of it. If ever a man analysed finally and conclusively, Chesterton did so.

HILAIRE BELLOC
(*Gilbert Chesterton in English Letters*)

CHILDHOOD

I have seen the greatest saints, says God. But I tell
    you
I have never seen anything so funny and I therefore
    know of nothing so beautiful in the world
As that child going to sleep while he says his prayers
(As that little creature going to sleep in all
    confidence)
And getting his Our Father mixed up with his Hail
    Mary.
Nothing is so beautiful. . . .

CHARLES PEGUY (*Basic Verities*)

There is always a moment in childhood when the door opens and lets the future in.

GRAHAM GREENE (*The Power and the Glory*)

So often people say that we should look to the elderly, learn from their wisdom, their many years. I disagree, I say we should look to the young: untarnished, without stereotypes implanted in their minds, no poison, no hatred in their hearts. When we learn to see life through the eyes of a child, that is when we become truly wise.

BLESSED MOTHER TERESA

God says: I like youngsters. I want people to be like them. I don't like old people unless they are still children. I want only children in my Kingdom; this has been decreed from the beginning of time. Youngsters — twisted, humped, wrinkled, white-bearded — all kinds of youngsters, but youngsters. There is no changing it; it has been decided. There is room for no one else.

MICHEL QUOIST (*Prayers*)

CHRIST

We confess that one and the same Christ, Lord, and only-begotten Son, is to be acknowledged in two natures without confusion, change, division or separation. The distinction between the natures was never abolished by their union, but rather the character proper to each of the two natures was preserved as they came together in one person and one hypostasis.

COUNCIL OF CHALCEDON (*451*)

No earthly pleasures, no kingdoms of this world can benefit me in any way. I prefer death in Christ Jesus to power over the farthest limits of the earth. He who died in place of us is the one object of my quest. He who rose for our sakes is my one desire. Do not talk about Jesus Christ as long as you love this world.

ST. IGNATIUS OF ANTIOCH

If He did not rise, but is still dead, how is it that He routs and persecutes and overthrows the false gods, whom unbelievers think to be alive, and the evil spirits whom they worship? For where Christ is named, idolatry is destroyed and the fraud of evil spirits is exposed; indeed, no such spirit can endure that Name, but takes to flight on sound of it. This is the work of One Who lives, not of one dead; and, more than that, it is the work of God.

ST. ATHANASIUS (*On the Incarnation*)

The river of time sweeps on, but there, like a tree planted in the water, is Our Lord Jesus Christ. He became man, willing to plant himself beside the river of time.

If you feel yourself drifting down to the rapids, lay hold of the tree; if you are caught up in the love of the world, hold on to Christ. He for you also entered into time, but he did not cease to be eternal.

ST. AUGUSTINE

Jesus Christ is not valued at all until He is valued above all.

ST. AUGUSTINE

Life extends over all beings and fills them with unlimited light, the Orient of orients pervades the universe, and he who was "before the daystar" and before the heavenly bodies, immortal and vast, the great Christ, shines over all beings more brightly than the sun. Therefore a day of long, eternal light is ushered in for us who believe in him, a day which is never blotted out: the mystical Passover

PSEUDO-HYPPOLYTUS (*De Paschate*)

Little is the Lord, and greatly to be loved. Mighty is the Lord, and greatly to be feared.

ST. BERNARD OF CLAIRVAUX

I am Eternal Truth, incapable of any lie. I am faithful to my promises.

JESUS TO ST. MARGARET MARY ALACOQUE

Jesus is living next to you, in the brothers and sisters with whom you share your daily existence.

POPE JOHN PAUL II

CHRISTIANITY

Christians are not born but made.

TERTULLIAN

In the lives of Christians we look not to the beginnings but to the endings.

ST. JEROME (*Letters*)

It seems to me, sir, that this life of ours is like the swift flight of a sparrow through the hall where you sit at dinner with us on a winter night. Outside there is rain and snow, but we have a good fire, and while he is with us the sparrow is safe from the storm. Yet in no time he flies out again into the cold and the darkness, and we see him no more.

Our life is like the sparrow's journey, pathetically brief. Of what comes before it, or what follows afterwards, we know nothing at all. If this new doctrine can teach us, then surely it deserves to be followed.

THE VENERABLE BEDE
(*Ecclesiastical History of the English People*)

Christianity is not about ideas but about deeds inspired by love.

BLESSED FREDERIC OZANAM

Christianity, considered as a moral system, is made up of two elements, beauty and severity; whenever either is indulged to the loss or disparagement of the other, evil ensues.

VENERABLE JOHN HENRY NEWMAN
(*Sermons on Subjects of the Day*)

Christianity has died many times and risen again; for it had a God who knew his way out of the grave.

G. K. CHESTERTON (*The Everlasting Man*)

The Christian ideal has not been tried and found wanting. It has been found difficult and left untried.

G. K. CHESTERTON
(*What's Wrong with the World*)

There is no such thing as a religion called "Christianity" — there never has been such a religion. There is and always has been the Church, and various heresies proceeding from a rejection of some of the Church's doctrines by men who still desire to retain the rest of her teaching and morals. But there never has been and never can be or will be a general Christian religion professed by men who all accept some central important doctrines, while agreeing to differ about others. There has always been, from the beginning, and will always be, the Church, and sundry heresies either doomed to decay, or, like Mohammedanism, to grow into a separate religion. Of a common Christianity there has never been and never can be a definition, for it has never existed.

HILAIRE BELLOC (*The Great Heresies*)

Christianity is not an object that we can hold in our hand: it is a mystery before which we are always ignorant and uninitiated.

HENRI DE LUBAC (*Paradoxes*)

Jesus Christ did not say, "If you follow me you will be praised, treated nicely and regarded with honor." He did not say, "If you follow me you will have a positive profile and your values will be admired." He said, "Take up your cross and follow me. . . ."

To be disliked, excluded and subjected to a stream of bad publicity is therefore the special vocation of the true Christian and far from feeling despondent about their collective self-image, Catholics should rejoice that the world hates the faith. For this is the proper path as spelled out by Jesus Christ.

MARY KENNY
(*Catholic Herald, January 31, 2003*)

CHRISTMAS

Hark! a herald voice is calling;
"Christ is nigh," it seems to say;
"Cast away the dreams of darkness,
O ye children of the day!"
Startled at the solemn warning,
Let the earth-bound soul arise;
Christ, her Sun, all sloth dispelling,
Shines upon the morning skies.

THE ROMAN BREVIARY
(*Lauds, Vigil of Christmas*)

Our Savior, dearly beloved, is born today, let us rejoice. It is not right to be sad today, the birthday of Life – he who has dispelled the fear of mortality and brought us to the joy of promised eternity. Let no man be cut off from a share of this rejoicing.... Let the holy exult, he draws near his palm; let the sinner rejoice, he is invited to pardon; let the Gentile be quickened, he is called to life.

POPE ST. LEO THE GREAT
(*Sermon 1 on the Nativity of the Lord*)

The Virgin today brings into the world the Eternal
And the earth offers a cave to the Inaccessible.
The angels and shepherds praise him
And the magi advance with the star,
For you are born for us,
Little Child, God Eternal!

ROMANOS THE MELODIST (*Kontakion*)

Now three years before his death it befell that he was minded, at the town of Greccio, to celebrate the memory of the Birth of the Child Jesus, with all the added solemnity that he might, for the kindling of devotion. That this might not seem an innovation, he sought and obtained license from the Supreme Pontiff, and then made ready a manger, and bade hay, together with an ox and an ass, be brought unto the place.

The brethren were called together, the folk assembled, the wood echoed with their voices, and that august night was made radiant and solemn with many bright lights, and with tuneful and sonorous praises. The man of God, filled with tender love, stood before the manger, bathed in tears, and overflowing with joy.

Solemn Masses were celebrated over the manger, Francis, the Levite of Christ, chanting the holy gospel.

Then he preached to the folk standing around the birth of the King in poverty, calling him, when he wished to name him, the Child of Bethlehem, by reason of his tender love for him.

ST. BONAVENTURE (*Life of St. Francis of Assisi*)

Celebrate the feast of Christmas every day, even every moment, in the interior temple of your spirit, remaining like a baby in the bosom of the heavenly Father, where you will be reborn each moment in the Divine Word, Jesus Christ.

ST. PAUL OF THE CROSS

As I in hoary winter's night stood shivering in the
   snow,
Surprised I was with sudden heat which made my
   heart to glow;
And lifting up a fearful eye to view what fire was near,
A pretty Babe all burning bright did in the air appear;
Who, scorchèd with excessive heat, such floods of
   tears did shed,
As though his floods could quench his flames with
   which his tears were fed.
"Alas!" quoth he, "but newly born in fiery heats I fry,
Yet none approach to warm their hearts or feel my
   fire but I.
Love is the fire, and sighs the smoke, the ashes shame
   and scorns;
The fuel justice layeth on, and mercy blows the coals;
The metals in this furnace wrought are men's defilèd
   souls;

For which, as now on fire I am to work them to their
    good,
So will I melt into a bath to wash them in my blood."
With this he vanished out of sight and swiftly shrunk
    away,
And straight I callèd unto mind that it was Christmas
    day.

    St. Robert Southwell, S.J. (*The Burning Babe*)

CHURCH POLITICS

If you wish to sail comfortably in the barque of Peter,
stay away from the engine room.

    Ronald Knox

CHURCH AND STATE

Do not interfere in ecclesiastical affairs, and do not
seek to give us orders concerning them, but rather learn
from us what is to be done. God has granted you the
empire; to us he has entrusted the affairs of the Church.
Just as anyone revolting against your rule would be
resisting the command of God, so you should fear that
by taking control of ecclesiastical affairs you will be
responsible for a great wrong.

    Hosius, Bishop of Cordova
    (*Letter to the Emperor Constantius*)

Christian emperors should defer to the rulers of the
Church in their ordinances, not presume to give orders
to them.

    Pope Gelasius I (*Letters*)

Two guides have been appointed for man to lead him to his twofold goal; there is the supreme pontiff who is to lead mankind to eternal life in accordance with revelation; and there is the emperor, who, in accordance with philosophical teaching, is to lead mankind to temporal happiness.

DANTE (*Monarchy*)

It would be very erroneous to draw the conclusion that in America is to be sought the most desirable status of the Church, or that it would be universally lawful or expedient for state and church to be, as in America, dissevered and divorced.

POPE LEO XIII (*Longinque Oceani*)

American Catholics rejoice in our separation of Church and state, and I can conceive of no combination of circumstances likely to arise which would make a union desirable for either Church or state.

CARDINAL JAMES GIBBONS
(*North American Review, March 1909*)

CIVILIZATION

Modern civilization is a worn-out garment. One cannot sew new pieces on it. It requires a total and, may I say, substantial recasting . . . a primacy of quality over quantity, of work over money, of the human race over the technological, of wisdom over science, of the common service of human persons over the individual covetousness of unlimited enrichment, of the state's covetousness of unlimited power.

JACQUES MARITAIN (*Integral Humanism*)

CLONING

The Catholic Church encourages efforts to find new ways to reduce human suffering and treat life-threatening illness. However, human cloning violates fundamental ethical and moral norms, and is to be condemned unequivocally. Human cloning does not treat any disease but turns human reproduction into a manufacturing process, by which human beings are mass-produced to preset specifications. The cloning procedure is so dehumanizing that some scientists want to treat the resulting human beings as subhuman, creating them solely so they can destroy them for their cells and tissues.

The fact that U.S. scientists have now created human embryos by cloning should serve as a wake-up call to Congress, and to all of us. Once again, a technical ability to manipulate and exploit human life is outdistancing society's ability to understand and respond to its frightening implications.

While cloning may never produce any clinical benefit, its attack on human dignity has already begun. The House of Representatives, anticipating this threat, has already overwhelmingly voted to ban human cloning. We urge the U.S. Senate to do the same without delay.

BISHOP WILTON R. GREGORY, PRESIDENT,
UNITED STATESCONFERENCE
OF CATHOLIC BISHOPS (*June 3, 2003*)

"Therapeutic cloning." This term is already being discarded by researchers, since the idea that anything "therapeutic" may come from this procedure is speculative at best. This is another euphemism for experimental cloning in which embryos are created to be destroyed.

There is, of course, nothing "therapeutic" in the cloning process itself, or in the lethal harm that will be done to the cloned embryo.

SECRETARIAT FOR PRO-LIFE ACTIVITIES,
June 3, 2003

COMMANDMENTS

God's precepts are light to the loving, heavy to the fearful.

ST. THOMAS AQUINAS
(Disputations Concerning Truth)

COMMITMENT

Avoid everything half-done.

EDEL QUINN (Spiritual Notes)

COMMUNISM

So we, who are united in mind and soul, have no hesitation about sharing property. All is common among us – except our wives.

TERTULLIAN (Apology)

Communism is by its nature anti-religious. It considers religion as "the opiate of the people" because the principles of religion which speak of a life beyond the grave dissuade the proletariat from the dream of a Soviet paradise which is of this world. . . . Those who permit themselves to be deceived into lending their aid towards the triumph of communism will be the first to fall victims of their terror.

POPE PIUS XI (Divini Redemptoris)

... If professing Christians had always been ready to live up to the Gospel, there would have been no room for the appearance of Marxian communism. The lesson of our deficiency is being dearly bought.

DOM AELRED GRAHAM, O.S.B.
(*Catholicism and the World Today*)

It would be simplistic to say that divine providence caused the fall of Communism. It fell by itself as a consequence of its own mistakes and abuses. It fell by itself because of its own inherent weaknesses.

POPE JOHN PAUL II

COMMUNITY

There is no such thing as a person alone. There are only people bound to each other to the limits of humanity and time.

MICHEL QUOIST (*With Open Heart*)

Men are called to meet the Lord insofar as they constitute a community, a people. It is a question not so much of a vocation to salvation as of a convocation.

GUSTAVO GUTIERREZ (*A Theology of Liberation*)

COMPASSION

What is a charitable heart? It is the heart of him who burns with pity for all creation – for every human being, every bird, every animal, every demon. He looks at the creatures, or remembers them, and his eyes are filled with tears. His heart is also filled with deep compassion and limitless patience; it overflows with tenderness, and cannot bear to see or hear any evil or the least grief endured by the creature.

Therefore he offers his prayers constantly for the dumb creatures and for the enemies of truth and for those who do him harm, that they may be preserved and pardoned. And for the reptiles also he prays, with great compassion, which rises without measure from the depths of his heart till he shines again and is glorious like God.

ST. ISAAK OF SYRIA

We should strive to keep our hearts open to the sufferings and wretchedness of other people, and pray continually that God may grant us that spirit of compassion which is truly the gift of God.

ST. VINCENT DE PAUL

God tempers the wind to the shorn lamb.

FRENCH PROVERB

Christianity taught us to care. Caring is the greatest thing, caring matters most.

BARON FRIEDRICH VON HÜGEL

The capacity to give one's attention to a sufferer is a very rare and difficult thing; it is almost a miracle; it is a miracle. Nearly all those who think they have this capacity do not possess it. Warmth of heart, impulsiveness, pity, are not enough.

SIMONE WEIL

Strength without compassion is violence. Compassion without justice is mere sentiment. Justice without love is Marxism. And love without justice is baloney.

CARDINAL JAIME SIN

COMPETITION

Working men are surrendered, isolated and helpless, to the hard-heartedness of employers and the greed of unchecked competition.

POPE PIUS XI (*Quadragesimo Anno*)

CONFESSION

While he is in the flesh, a man cannot help at least having some light sins. But do not despise these sins which we call "light": if you call them light when you weigh them, tremble when you count them. A number of light objects makes a great mass; a number of drops fills a river; a number of grains makes a heap. What, then, is our hope? Above all, confession. . . .

ST. AUGUSTINE (*Sermons*)

Confession heals, confession justifies, confession grants pardon of sin. All hope consists in confession. In confession there is a chance for mercy. Believe it firmly. Do not doubt, do not hesitate, never despair of the mercy of God. Hope and have confidence in confession.

ST. ISIDORE OF SEVILLE

From your confessor, your doctor and your lawyer, hide nothing.

ITALIAN PROVERB

Full sweetly heard he confession
And pleasant was his absolution.

GEOFFREY CHAUCER
(*The Canterbury Tales: Prologue*)

Though he who confesses every year is not bound to make a general confession, yet by making one there is secured greater profit and merit on account of the penitent's greater sorrow for all the sins and wickedness of his whole life.

ST. IGNATIUS LOYOLA (*Spiritual Exercises*)

It is an abuse to confess any kind of sin, whether mortal or venial, without a will to be delivered from it, since confession was instituted for no other end.

ST. FRANCIS DE SALES
(*Introduction to the Devout Life*)

Even before he was actually spoken to, the curé knew what kind of soul he was dealing with. From the moment men came into his presence, it was impossible to keep anything hidden. It was as though he had taken his stand in the very conscience of his penitents with clearer vision and better memory than themselves: almost he seemed to see and remember for them. If you tried to hide in the crowd, he came straight through the crowd. If with very little time to spare one were afraid of missing him, he seemed to hear the appeal which the penitent dared not utter aloud and would invite him to come ahead of his turn. It was exactly as though he held in his hands a thousand unseen threads linking him with everyone present, so that he had only to pull on the one he wanted, when he wanted it. It was enough for him to raise his arm; the person he had in mind felt himself pointed at and obeyed the sign.

HENRI GHÉON
(*The Secret of the Curé of Ars*)

"Father," I said, feeling that I might as well get it over while I had him in good humor, "I had it all arranged to kill my grandmother."

He seemed a bit shaken by that all right, because he said nothing for quite a while.

"My goodness," he said at last, "that'd be a shocking thing to do. What put that into your head?"

"Father," I said, feeling sorry for myself, "she's an awful woman...."

"And what would you do with the body?" he asked with great interest.

"I was thinking I could chop that up and carry it away in a barrow I have," I said.

"Begorra! Jackie," he said, "do you know you're a terrible child?"

"I know, Father," I said, "for I was just thinking the same thing myself. . . ."

"You must have great courage. Between ourselves, there's a lot of people I'd like to do the same to but I'd never have the nerve. Hanging is an awful death."

"Is it, Father?" I asked with the deepest interest – I was always very keen on hanging. "Did you ever see a fellow hanged?"

"Dozens of them," he said solemnly. "And they all died roaring."

"Jay!" I said.

"Oh, a horrible death," he said with great satisfaction. "Lots of the fellows I saw killed their grandmothers too, but they all said 'twas never worth it."

FRANK O'CONNOR (*First Confession*)

Hearing nuns' confessions is like being nibbled to death by ducks.

VINCENT MCNABB, O.P.

Hearing nuns' confessions is like being stoned to death with popcorn.

ARCHBISHOP FULTON J. SHEEN

CONSCIENCE

A guilty conscience needs no accuser.

14TH-CENTURY PROVERB

By following a right conscience you not only do not incur sin but are also immune from sin, whatever superiors may say to the contrary.

ST. THOMAS AQUINAS
(*Disputations Concerning Truth*)

Conscience warns us as a friend before it punishes us as a judge.

KING STANISLAS I OF POLAND

Let us beware of trifling with conscience. It is often said that second thoughts are best; so they are in matters of judgment, but not in matters of conscience. In matters of duty first thoughts are commonly best – they have more in them of the voice of God.

VENERABLE JOHN HENRY NEWMAN
(*Historical Studies*)

If I am obliged to bring religion into after-dinner toasts (which indeed does not seem quite the thing), I shall drink – to the Pope, if you please – still, to conscience first, and to the Pope afterwards.

VENERABLE JOHN HENRY NEWMAN
(*Letter to the Duke of Norfolk*)

Conscience has rights because it has duties.

VENERABLE JOHN HENRY NEWMAN
(*Difficulties of Anglicans*)

There is nothing commoner than for people to try and kill their own conscience.

R. H. BENSON (*The Conventionalists*)

All too often a clear conscience is simply the result of a bad memory.

ANONYMOUS

CONTEMPLATION

The higher part of contemplation is wholly caught up in this cloud of unknowing, with an intensity of love and a blind groping for the naked being of God, himself and him alone.

THE CLOUD OF UNKNOWING

Contemplative prayer in my opinion is nothing else than a close sharing between friends; it means taking time frequently to be alone with him who we know loves us.

ST. TERESA OF ÁVILA (*The Book of Her Life*)

Contemplation is a sudden gift of awareness, an awakening to the Real within all that is real. A vivid awareness of infinite Being at the roots of our own limited being. An awareness of our contingent reality as received, as a present from God, as a free gift of love.

THOMAS MERTON

The true contemplative is not one who prepares his mind for a particular message that he wants or expects to hear, but is one who remains empty because he knows that he can never expect to anticipate the words that will transform his darkness into light.

THOMAS MERTON (*Dialogs with Silence*)

CONTROVERSY

Mr. Kingsley begins then by exclaiming, "O the chi-canery, the wholesale fraud, the vile hypocrisy, the con-science-killing tyranny of Rome! We have not far to seek for an evidence of it. There's Father Newman to wit: one living specimen is worth a hundred dead ones. He, a Priest writing of Priests, tells us that lying is never any harm."

I interpose, "You are taking a most extraordinary liberty with my name. If I have said this, tell me when and where."

Mr. Kingsley replies: "You said it, Reverend Sir, in a Ser-mon which you preached, when a Protestant, as Vicar of St. Mary's, and published in 1844; and I could read you a very salutary lecture on the effects which that Sermon had at the time on my own opinion of you."

I make answer: "Oh . . . *not,* it seems, as a Priest speaking of Priests; but let us have the passage."

Mr. Kingsley relaxes: "Do you know, I like your *tone.* From your *tone I* rejoice, greatly rejoice, to be able to believe that you did not mean what you said."

I rejoin: "*Mean it!* I maintain I never *said* it, whether as a Protestant or as a Catholic."

Mr. Kingsley replies: "I waive that point."

I object: "Is it possible! What? Waive the main question! I either said it or I didn't. You have made a monstrous charge against me; direct, distinct, public. You are bound to prove it as directly, as distinctly, as publicly; or to own you can't."

"Well," says Mr. Kingsley, "if you are quite sure you did not say it, I'll take your word for it; I really will."

My word! I am dumb. Somehow I thought that it was my *word* that happened to be on trial.

VENERABLE JOHN HENRY NEWMAN
(*Apologia Pro Vita Sua*)

It is as absurd to try to argue men, as to torture them into believing.

VENERABLE JOHN HENRY NEWMAN
(*University Sermons*)

When men understand what each other mean, they see, for the most part, that controversy is either superfluous or useless.

VENERABLE JOHN HENRY NEWMAN
(*University Sermons*)

Controversy, for the most part, disfigures the question it seeks to elucidate.

F. W. FABER

As a fact – a mere fact of history – nearly everything we hold to be truth, save what comes immediately from the evidence of our senses, has been established by controversy.

HILAIRE BELLOC (*The Silence of the Sea*)

Remote and ineffectual Don
That dared attack my Chesterton
With that poor weapon, half-impelled,
Unlearnt, unsteady, hardly held,
Unworthy for a tilt with men –
Your quavering and corroded pen . . .

HILAIRE BELLOC (*Lines to a Don*)

CONVERSATION

Remain at peace regarding whatever is said or done in conversations. If it is good, you have something for which to praise God. If it is bad, you have something in which to serve God by turning your heart away from it.

ST. FRANCIS DE SALES

CONVERSION

A man who is converted from Protestantism to Popery may be sincere: he parts with nothing: he is only [super-adding] to what he already had. But a convert from Popery to Protestantism gives up so much of what he held as sacred as anything he retains; there is so much *laceration of mind* in such a conversion, that it can hardly be sincere and lasting.

DR. SAMUEL JOHNSON (*Quoted in Boswell's "Life"*)

I am a mother, and must answer for my children at the judgment seat, whatever faith I lead them to. That being so, I will go peaceably and firmly to the Catholic Church. For if faith is so important to our salvation, I will seek it where true faith first began.... The controversies on it I am quite incapable of deciding, and as the strictest Protestant allows salvation to a good Catholic, to the Catholics I will go, and try to be a good one.

ST. ELIZABETH SETON

And this is certainly remarkable, that in every one who has embraced the Catholic religion, whatever was his difficulty in first receiving it, whatever may have been the first obstacles to his complete conviction, when once he has embraced and received it, it takes as strong a hold upon his affections, and thoughts, as it could have done, if he had been educated in it from infancy.

CARDINAL NICHOLAS WISEMAN (*Letters*)

I have been in perfect peace and contentment; I never had one doubt. I was not conscious to myself, on my conversion, of any change, intellectual or moral, wrought in my mind. I was not conscious of firmer faith in the fundamental truths of revelation, or of more self-command; I had not more fervor; but it was like coming into port after a rough sea; and my happiness on that score remains to this day without interruption.

VENERABLE JOHN HENRY NEWMAN
(*Apologia pro Vita Sua*)

A convert is undeniably in favor with no party; he is looked at with distrust, contempt and aversion by all. His former friends think him a good riddance, and his new friends are cold and strange; and as to the impartial public, their very first impression is to impute the change to some eccentricity of character, or fickleness of mind, or tender attachment, or private interest. Their utmost praise is the reluctant confession that "doubtless he is very sincere."

VENERABLE JOHN HENRY NEWMAN
(*Essays Critical and Historical*)

TO THE REV. DR. JOHN H. NEWMAN
Oak Hill, Hampstead, N.W.
Aug. 28, 1866

Reverend Sir,

I address you with great hesitation knowing that you are in the midst of [your] own engagements and because you must be much exposed to applications from all sides. I am anxious to become a Catholic, and I thought that you might possibly be able to see me for a short time when I pass through Birmingham in a few days, I believe on Friday. But I feel most strongly the injustice of intruding on [your] engagements or convenience and therefore, if that is the case, I shall think it a favor if you will kindly let me know that you are unable to see me. I do not want to be helped to any conclusions of belief, for I am thankful to say my mind is made up, but the necessity of becoming a Catholic (although I had long foreseen where the only consistent position [would] lie) coming upon me suddenly has put me in a painful confusion of mind about my immediate duty in my circumstances. . . .

18 New Inn Hall Street, Oxford
St. Theresa (15 Oct.) 1866.

Very Reverend Father,

I have been up at Oxford just long enough to have heard [from] my father and mother in return for my letter announcing my conversion. Their answers are terrible: I cannot read them twice. If you will pray for them and me just now, I shall be deeply thankful. But what I am writing for is this – they urge me with the utmost entreaties to wait until I have taken my degree – more than half a year. Of course it is impossible, and since it is impossible to wait as long as they wish it seems to me useless to wait at all. [Would] you therefore wish me to come to Birmingham at once, on Thursday, Friday, or Saturday? You will understand why I have any hesitation at all, namely because if immediately after their letters urging a long delay I am received without any, it will be another blow and look like intentional cruelty. . . .

GERARD MANLEY HOPKINS, S.J. (Letters)

To become a Catholic is not to leave off thinking, but to learn how to think.

G. K. CHESTERTON
(The Catholic Church and Conversion)

I have been overwhelmed with the feeling of liberty – the "glorious liberty of the Sons of God;" it [is] a freedom from the uncertainty of mind; it was not until I became a Catholic that I became conscious of my former homelessness, my exile from the place that was my own.

RONALD KNOX

I do not contend that everybody can be converted by reason, but I do contend that some people can be converted by reason. I do not regard Christianity purely as a system of thought; I regard Christianity as a way of life *and* a system of thought.

ARNOLD LUNN (Now I See)

Most cradle Catholics have gone through, or need to go through, a second conversion which binds them with a more mature love and obedience to the Church.

DOROTHY DAY

If you're going to do a thing, you should do it thoroughly. If you're going to be a Christian, you might as well be a Catholic.

MURIEL SPARK, BRITISH NOVELIST
(newspaper interview)

COURAGE

The principal act of courage is to endure and withstand dangers doggedly rather than to attack them.

ST. THOMAS AQUINAS (*Summa Theologica*)

A man should focus his will and all his activities on God, and with only God in view, go forward unafraid, not thinking "Am I right or am I wrong?" Someone who worked out all the possible chances before starting his first fight, would never fight at all. And if, going some place, we stop to decide which foot to put down first, we'll never get there. It is our duty to do the next thing: go straight on, that is the right way.

MEISTER ECKHART

Nothing emboldens the wicked so greatly as the lack of courage on the part of the good.

POPE LEO XIII

One of the things we absolutely owe to Our Lord is never to be afraid.

VENERABLE CHARLES DE FOUCAULD

Courage is almost a contradiction in terms. It means a strong desire to live taking the form of a readiness to die.

G. K. CHESTERTON (*Orthodoxy*)

Courage is sustained . . . by calling up anew the vision of the goal.

A.G. SERTILLANGES, O.P.

Do not be held back by doubts or fears. . . . Say "yes" with courage and without reserve.

POPE JOHN PAUL II
(*World Youth Day, Rome 2000*)

COURTESY

He who sows courtesy reaps friendship, and he who plants kindness gathers love.

ST. BASIL

We may be excused for not always being bright, but we are not excused for not being always gracious, yielding and considerate.

ST. FRANCIS DE SALES
(*Treatise on the Love of God*)

It is almost a definition of a gentleman to say that he is one who never inflicts pain.

VENERABLE JOHN HENRY NEWMAN
(*The Idea of a University*)

In other countries they speak of nobility and courtesy, in London they practice it. In one shop where we were unable to get a trunk, the manager made one of his clerks accompany us and gave him instructions to help us get what we wanted.

ST. FRANCES XAVIER CABRINI
(*to her nuns in Liverpool, 1898*)

Of courtesy, it is much less, than courage of heart or
        holiness,
Yet in my walks it seems to me
That the grace of God is in courtesy.

HILAIRE BELLOC (*Courtesy*)

CREATION

If God had drawn the world from pre-existent matter, what would be so extraordinary in that? A human artisan makes from a given material whatever he wishes, while God shows his power by starting from nothing to make whatever he wishes.

ST. THEOPHILUS OF ANTIOCH (*Ad Autolycum*)

The compass of the whole earth compared to the scope of heaven is no bigger than a pin's point, which is to say that, if it be compared with the greatness of the celestial sphere, it has no size at all.

BOETHIUS (*Consolations of Philosophy*)

It is well for us to worship the Guardian of Heaven
The might of the Creator and the power of his mind.
When Eternal God began his work
He first made Heaven as a roof for Earth's children
Then the World-warden made Earth itself,
Land for men to live on, Almighty Lord!

CAEDMON

Most High, all-powerful, all-good Lord,
All praise is Yours, all glory, all honor and all
    blessings.
To you alone, Most High, do they belong,
And no mortal lips are worthy to pronounce Your
    Name.

Praised be You my Lord with all Your creatures,
Especially Sir Brother Sun,
Who is the day through whom You give us light.
And he is beautiful and radiant with great splendor,
Of You Most High, he bears the likeness.

Praised be You, my Lord, through Sister Moon and
    the stars,

In the heavens you have made them bright, precious
   and fair.

Praised be You, my Lord, through Brothers Wind and
   Air,
And fair and stormy, all weather's moods,
By which You cherish all that You have made.

Praised be You, my Lord, through Sister Water,
So useful, humble, precious and pure.

Praised be You, my Lord, through Brother Fire,
Through whom You light the night
And he is beautiful and playful and robust and
   strong.

Praised be You, my Lord, through our Sister,
Mother Earth
Who sustains and governs us,
Producing varied fruits with colored flowers and
   herbs.

Praised be You, my Lord, through those who grant
   pardon
For love of You and bear sickness and trial.
Blessed are those who endure in peace,
By You Most High, they will be crowned.

Praised be You, my Lord, through Sister Death,
From whom no-one living can escape.
Woe to those who die in mortal sin!
Blessed are they She finds doing Your Will.
No second death can do them harm.
Praise and bless my Lord and give Him thanks,

And serve Him with great humility.

ST. FRANCIS OF ASSISI
(*Canticle of Brother Sun and Sister Moon*)

Any flea as it is in God is nobler than the highest of angels in himself.

MEISTER ECKHART

The world is charged with the grandeur of God.
It will flame out, like shining from shook foil;
It gathers to a greatness, like the ooze of oil,
Crushed. Why do men then now not reck his rod?
Generations have trod, have trod, have trod;
And all is seared with trade; bleared, smeared with
     toil;
And wears man's smudge and shares man's smell: the
     soil
Is bare now, nor can foot feel, being shod.

And for all this, nature is never spent;
There lives the dearest freshness deep down things;
And though the black lights off the black West went
Oh, morning at the brown brink eastward, springs –
Because the Holy Ghost over the bent
World broods with warm breast and with ah! bright
     wings.

GERARD MANLEY HOPKINS, S.J. (*God's Grandeur*)

It is absurd for the Evolutionist to complain that it is unthinkable for an admittedly unthinkable God to make everything out of nothing, and then pretend it is *more* thinkable that nothing should turn itself into any-thing.

G. K. CHESTERTON (*St. Thomas Aquinas*)

The history of the living world can be summarized as the elaboration of ever more perfect eyes within a cosmos in which there is always something more to be seen.

PIERRE TEILHARD DE CHARDIN, S.J.
(*The Phenomenon of Man*)

Our duty, as men and women, is to proceed as if limits to our ability did not exist. We are collaborators in creation.

PIERRE TEILHARD DE CHARDIN, S.J.

CRISIS

Ours is, I believe, the period of the greatest crisis the Church has ever faced, a period in which the anathema has become unpopular and is unfortunately considered as incompatible with charity, in which authority is discredited and many prelates do not use their authority to discipline priests who are teaching heresies. In such a period, every faithful Catholic who is fully devoted to Christ, to the teaching of the Church, to the deposit of the Catholic faith, to the dogmas, is called to raise his voice in defense of orthodoxy.

DIETRICH VON HILDEBRAND

CRITICISM

Nothing would be done at all, if a man waited till he could do it so well that no one could find fault with it.

VENERABLE JOHN HENRY NEWMAN

Criticism is asserted superiority.
CARDINAL HENRY EDWARD MANNING
(*Pastime Papers*)

I hate being asked to criticize what I cannot praise.
GERARD MANLEY HOPKINS, S.J.

To a pioneering spirit who was discouraged by frequent criticism the Master said, "Listen to the words of the critic. He reveals what your friends hide from you." But he also said, "Do not be weighed down by what the critic says. No statue was ever erected to honor a critic. Statues are for the criticized."

ANTHONY DE MELLO, S.J.

CROSS

In hoc signo vinces. In this sign you will conquer.
(Reputedly seen in the sky
by the Emperor Constantine before battle)

Lo! I will tell the dearest of dreams
That I dreamed in the midnight when mortal men
Were sunk in slumber. Me seemed I saw
A wondrous Tree towering in air,
Most towering of crosses compassed with light.
Brightly that beacon was gilded with gold;
Jewels adorned it fair at the foot,
Five on the shoulder-beam, blazing in splendor.
Through all creation the angels of God
Beheld it shining – no cross of shame!
Holy spirits gazed on its gleaming,
Men upon earth and all this great creation.
Wondrous that Tree, that token of triumph,

And I a transgressor, soiled with my sins!
I gazed on the Rood arrayed in glory,
Shining in beauty and gilded with gold,
The Cross of the Savior beset with gems. . . .

THE DREAM OF THE ROOD
(*Anonymous, 7th century*)

Jesus now has many lovers of his heavenly kingdom, but few bearers of his cross.

THOMAS À KEMPIS (*The Imitation of Christ*)

He that seeks not the cross of Christ seeks not the glory of Christ.

ST. JOHN OF THE CROSS (*Spiritual Sentences*)

A God on the Cross! That is all my theology.

JEAN-BAPTISTE LACORDAIRE, O.P.

The world is full of mysteries; heaven is all mystery to us earthly creatures. But whoever embraces the cross with open heart finds there the explanation of a thousand mysteries.

ARCHBISHOP WILLIAM
BERNARD ULLATHORNE, O.S.B.
(*Humility and Patience*)

Cursed be the cross
that decorates the wall
of an oppressor's bank,
or that presides
behind an unfeeling throne,
with a coat-of-arms,
above an enticing cleavage,
before the eyes of fear.
Cursed be the cross

thrust by the mighty
on the poor
in the name of God perhaps.
Cursed be the cross
that the Church justifies
— in the name of Christ perhaps –
instead of burning
in the flames of prophecy.

Cursed be the cross
that cannot be the Cross.

BISHOP PEDRO CASALDÁLIGA
OF SAO FELIX DE ARGUAIA, BRAZIL
(*translated by John Medcalf*)

CROSSES (IN LIFE)

You cannot escape it, wherever you run. For wherever
you go you carry yourself with you, and will always find
yourself. Turn upwards or turn downwards, turn inwards
or turn outwards: everywhere, you will find the cross.

THOMAS À KEMPIS
(*The Imitation of Christ*)

If you can bear the cross gladly, it will bear you.

THOMAS À KEMPIS
(*The Imitation of Christ*)

You are sure to find another cross if you flee the one
you have.

MEXICAN PROVERB

The crosses that we fashion for ourselves are always
lighter than the ones laid on us.

ST. FRANCIS DE SALES

The greatest of all crosses is self – if we die in part every day, we shall have little to do on the last – those little daily deaths will destroy the power of the final dying.

ARCHBISHOP FRANÇOIS FÉNELON

Crosses and upsets prove to us how little Christ-like we are, and how quickly the thermometer of supposed heroism falls to zero when put to the test.

CORNELIA CONNOLLY

Take the cross *He sends,* as it is, and not as *you* imagine it to be.

CORNELIA CONNOLLY

By our suffering and our failures, by our acceptance of the cross, we unleash forces that help us to overcome the evil in the world.

DOROTHY DAY

The cross doesn't overwhelm; if its weight makes one stagger, its power gives relief.

ST. PADRE PIO

The cross is a condition of every holy work.

CARDINAL YVES CONGAR, O.P.

CRUCIFIX

Let the crucifix be not only in my eyes and on my breast, but in my heart.

ST. BERNADETTE

The secret of my ministry is in that crucifix you see beside my bed. It is there so that I can see it in my first waking moments and before going to sleep. It's there also so that I can talk to it in the long night hours. Look at it, see it as I see it. Those open arms have been the program of my pontificate: they say Christ died for all, for all. No one is excluded from his love, from his forgiveness.

BLESSED POPE JOHN XXII, *at his last anointing*

CULTURE

The Church, truly, to our great benefit has carefully preserved the monuments of ancient wisdom, has opened everywhere homes of science, and has urged on intellectual progress by fostering most diligently the arts by which the culture of our age is so much advanced.

POPE LEO XIII (*Libertas Praestantissimum*)

The Church, from the beginning down to our own time, has always followed this wise practice: let not the Gospel on being introduced into any new land destroy or extinguish whatever its people possess that is naturally good, true or beautiful. For the Church, when she calls people to a higher culture and a better way of life, under the inspiration of the Christian religion, does not act like one who recklessly cuts down and uproots a thriving forest. No, she grafts a good scion upon the wild stock that it may bear a stock of more delicious fruit.

POPE PIUS XII (*Evangelii Praecones*)

CUNNING

Use, but do not abuse, cunning.

BALTASAR GRACIÁN, S.J. (*The Art of Worldly Wisdom*)

CURIOSITY

Free curiosity is of more value in learning than harsh discipline.

ST. AUGUSTINE (*Confessions*)

Do not be curious about matters that do not concern you; never speak of them and do not ask about them.

ST. TERESA OF ÁVILA (*Maxims*)

CURSES

Curses, like chickens, come home to roost.

14TH-CENTURY PROVERB

CUSTOM

When I am at Rome, I fast on a Saturday: when I am at Milan, I do not. Do the same. Follow the custom of the church where you are.

ST. AMBROSE

CYNICISM

The habit of thinking ill of everything and everyone is tiresome to ourselves and to all around us.

BLESSED POPE JOHN XXIII

D

DEACONS

As ministers of the mysteries of Jesus Christ, the deacons should please all in every way they can; for they are not merely ministers of food and drink, but the servants of the Church of God. They must avoid all reproach as they would beware of fire.

ST. IGNATIUS OF ANTIOCH (*Letter to the Trallians*)

And a deacon when he is appointed shall be chosen according to what has been said before, the bishop alone laying hands on him in the same manner. . . . He is not ordained for the priesthood, but for the service of the bishop that he may do only the things commanded by him. . . . He does not receive the Spirit which is common to all the presbyterate . . . but that which is entrusted to him under the bishop's authority.

ST. HIPPOLYTUS (*The Apostolic Tradition*)

DEATH

Our brethren who have been freed from the world by the summons of the Lord should not be mourned, since we know they are not lost but sent before.

ST. CYPRIAN

To the good man to die is to gain.

ST. AMBROSE

The foolish fear death as the greatest of evils, and the wise desire it as a rest after labors and the end of all ills.

St. Ambrose

For what else is sleep but a daily death which does not completely remove man hence nor detain him too long? And what else is death, but a very long and very deep sleep, from which God arouses man?

St. Augustine

What, I pray you, is dying? Just what is it to put off a garment? For the body is about the soul as a garment; and after laying this aside for a short time by means of death, we shall resume it again with more splendor.

St. John Chrysostom (*Homilies*)

Blessed be God for our Sister, the death of the body.

St. Francis of Assisi

Do now, do now, what you will wish to have done when your moment comes to die.

St. Angela Merici

Happy is the man who keeps the hour of death always in mind, and daily prepares for it.

Thomas à Kempis (*The Imitation of Christ*)

We never ought to look toward death as a thing far off, considering that although he make no haste towards us, yet we never cease to make haste toward him.

St. Thomas More
(*A Dialog of Comfort Against Tribulation*)

The best way to prepare for death is to spend every day of life as though it were the last. Think of the end of worldly honor, wealth and pleasure and ask yourself: And then? And then?

ST. PHILIP NERI

Sudden death is the only thing to dread, and that is why confessors dwell with the great.

BLAISE PASCAL (Pensées)

After my death I will send a shower of roses.

ST. THÉRÈSE OF LISIEUX

At death, if at any time, we see ourselves as we are, and display our true characters.

R. H. BENSON (Infallibility and Tradition)

Those who die in grace go no further than God – and God is very near.

PIERRE TEILHARD DE CHARDIN, S.J.

The fear of death keeps us from living, not from dying.

PAUL C. ROUD

Death is the last enemy; once we've got past that I think everything will be all right.

ALICE THOMAS ELLIS, BRITISH NOVELIST
(radio interview)

DEATH PENALTY

It is in no way contrary to the fifth commandment for the representatives of the State to put criminals to death according to the law or the rule of rational justice.

ST. AUGUSTINE

If a man be dangerous and infectious to the community because of some sin, it is praiseworthy and advantageous that he be killed in order to safeguard the common good.

ST. THOMAS AQUINAS

If bloodless means are sufficient to defend human lives against an aggressor and to protect public order and the safety of persons, the public authority must limit itself to such means.

POPE JOHN PAUL II (*Evangelium Vitae*)

We believe that in the conditions of contemporary American society, the legitimate purposes of punishment do not justify the imposition of the death penalty.

STATEMENT BY U.S. BISHOPS, 1980

DECISIONS

My basic principle is that you don't make decisions because they are easy; you don't make them because they are cheap; you don't make them because they're popular; you make them because they're right.

THEODORE HESBURGH, C.S.C.

DEFENSE

Legitimate defense can be not only a right but a grave duty for someone responsible for another's life, the common good of the family or of the State. Unfortunately, it happens that the need to render the aggressor incapable of causing harm sometimes involves taking his life. In this case, the fatal outcome is attributable to the aggressor whose actions brought it about, even though he may not be morally responsible because of a lack of the use of reason.

POPE JOHN PAUL II (*Evangelium Vitae*)

DEMOCRACY

The Church's teaching now fully embraces two fundamental features of modern society about which it once had some difficulties: democracy and human rights. In the case of democracy, the Church has been able to make its own contribution to political theory by exploring the limitations of the democratic process, for instance by warning that democracy can never be a self-fulfilling justification for policies that are intrinsically immoral. Democracy is not a self- sufficient moral system. Democracy, if it is to be healthy, requires more than universal suffrage: it requires the presence of a system of common values.

CATHOLIC BISHOPS OF ENGLAND AND WALES
(*The Modern World and Catholic Social Teaching*)

DESCENT INTO HELL

Today a great silence reigns on earth, a great silence and a great stillness. A great silence because the King is asleep. The earth trembled and is still because God has fallen asleep in the flesh and has raised up all who have slept since the world began. . . . "I order you, O sleeper, to awake. I did not create you to be a prisoner in hell. Rise from the dead, for I am the life of the dead."

LITURGY OF THE HOURS, HOLY SATURDAY
(*Office of Readings*)

DESIRE

Remove every evil desire and clothe yourself with good and holy desire. For if you are clothed with good desire you will hate evil desire and bridle it as you please.

ANONYMOUS (*Shepherd of Hermas*)

Do not desire not to be what you are, but desire to be very well what you are.

ST. FRANCIS DE SALES
(*Letters to Persons in the World*)

To desire anything for any reason other than for God is to desire God less.

JEAN PIERRE CAMUS
(*The Spirit of St. Francis de Sales*)

DESPAIR

Despair is the price one pays for setting oneself an impossible aim. It is, one is told, the unforgivable sin, but it is a sin the corrupt or evil man never practices. He always has hope. He never reaches the freezing-point of knowing absolute failure. Only the man of good will carries always in his heart this capacity for damnation.

GRAHAM GREENE (*The Heart of the Matter*)

DEVELOPMENT OF DOCTRINE

Is then religion in the church of Christ incapable of progress? But surely there must be progress and that not a little! Who would be so much man's enemy and God's to try to prevent it? We must make this reservation, however, that the progress shall be a genuine progress and not an alteration of the faith. We have progress when a thing grows and yet remains itself; we have alteration when a thing becomes something else.

ST. VINCENT OF LERINS (*Commonitorium*)

The life of doctrines may be said to consist in the law or principles which they embody. Principles are abstract and general, doctrines relate to facts; doctrines develop, and principles at first sight do not; doctrines grow and are enlarged; principles are permanent; doctrines are intellectual and principles are more immediately ethical and practical.... Doctrines stand to principles, as the definitions to the axioms and postulates of mathematics.

VENERABLE JOHN HENRY NEWMAN
(*Development of Christian Doctrine*)

DEVIL

The devil comes and tempts all the servants of God. Those who are strong in the faith resist him and he goes away from them, because he cannot find entrance. So then he goes to the empty and, finding an entrance, he goes into them. In this way he does in them whatever he pleases, and makes them his slaves.

ANONYMOUS (*Shepherd of Hermas*)

The devil's snare does not catch you unless you are first caught by the devil's bait.

ST. AMBROSE
(*Explanation of Psalm 118*)

He [the devil] does not dare look at you directly because he sees the light blazing from your head and blinding his eyes.

ST. JOHN CHRYSOSTOM
(*Baptismal Homily*)

When the devil is called the god of this world, it is not because he made it, but because we serve him with our worldliness.

ST. THOMAS AQUINAS

A liar and the father of lies.

DANTE (*Inferno*)

I do not know a description of a devil in literature which does not leave one with some sense of sympathy. Milton's devils are admirable; Dante's devils stir our pity; Goethe's devils make us feel what a good thing has been wasted. Human nature seems incapable of imagining that which is wholly bad, just because it is not wholly bad itself.

ALBAN GOODIER, S.J.
(*The School of Love*)

The Devil, having nothing else to do,
Went off to tempt My Lady Poltagrue.
My Lady, tempted by a private whim,
To his extreme annoyance tempted him.

HILAIRE BELLOC (*Cautionary Verses*)

It is stupid of modern civilization to have given up believing in the devil, when he is the only explanation of it.

RONALD KNOX (*Let Dons Delight*)

DEVOTION

Devotion is a certain act of the will by which man gives himself promptly to divine service.

ST. THOMAS AQUINAS
(*Summa Theologica*)

I prefer English habits of belief and devotion to foreign, from the same causes and by the same right, which justifies foreigners in preferring their own. In following those of my people, I show less singularity, and create less disturbance than if I made a flourish with what is novel and exotic.

VENERABLE JOHN HENRY NEWMAN
(*Letter to the Rev. E. B. Pusey*)

No soul can be lost by following the simple and well-beaten path of ordinary devotion and prayer.

R. H. BENSON
(*The Light Invisible*)

We have continually to test our practical devotion to Him by our practical devotion to one another.

R. H. BENSON
(*The Friendship of Christ*)

DISCOURAGEMENT

When we yield to discouragement or despair it is usually because we give too much thought to the past and to the future.

ST. THÉRÈSE OF LISIEUX

Thou art indeed just, Lord, if I contend
With Thee; but, sir, so what I plead is just.
Why do sinners' ways prosper? and why must
Disappointment all I endeavor end?

GERARD MANLEY HOPKINS, S.J.
(*Thou Art Indeed Just, Lord*)

DISCRETION

There are some who wear out their bodies with abstinence: but because they have no discretion, they are a great way from God.

ST. ANTONY OF EGYPT
(*The Sayings of the Fathers*)

Without discretion virtue becomes vice and the natural impulses serve only to upset and wreck the personality.

ST. BERNARD
(*Sermons on the Canticle of Canticles*)

Adam, while he spake no, had paradise at will.

WILLIAM LANGLAND
(*The Vision of Piers Plowman*)

Better one word less than one word too many.

MALTESE PROVERB

It is not a secret if it is known by three people.

IRISH PROVERB

DISCRIMINATION

Discriminations and segregations in civil or political matters on grounds of religion, of race, of language, of color, are wrong and un-American.

ARCHBISHOP JOHN IRELAND (*Discourse on Patriotism*)

Any Catholic who reviles or wrongs a brother because of the color of his skin, because of race or religion, or who condemns any racial or religious group, ceases in that condemnation to be a Catholic and an American. He becomes a disobedient son of Mother Church and a disloyal citizen of the United States

CARDINAL RICHARD J. CUSHING
(*Address to Lowell Hebrew Community*)

DIVINE MERCY

My daughter, tell the whole world about My Inconceivable mercy. I desire that the Feast of Mercy be a refuge and shelter for all souls, and especially for poor sinners. On that day [the first Sunday after Easter] the very depths of My tender mercy are open. I pour out a whole ocean of graces upon those souls who approach the fount of My mercy. The soul that will go to Confession and receive Holy Communion shall obtain complete forgiveness of sins and punishment. On that day all the divine floodgates through which grace flow are opened. Let no soul fear to draw near to Me, even though its sins be as scarlet.

CHRIST, TO ST. MARIA FAUSTINA KOWALSKA

DIVINE OFFICE

The work of God *(Opus Dei).*

ST. BENEDICT
(*The Holy Rule*)

The framing of the ritual may have been the work of human hands; but the materials of which it is composed are the words of the Spirit of God.

CARDINAL HENRY EDWARD MANNING
(*The Eternal Priesthood*)

The divine office is the prayer of the Mystical Body of Jesus Christ, offered to God in the name and on behalf of all Christians, when recited by priests and other ministers of the Church and by religious, who are deputed by the Church for this.

POPE PIUS XII (*Mediator Dei*)

The Liturgy of the Hours is intended to become the prayer of the whole People of God. In it Christ himself continues his priestly work through the Church. His members participate according to their own place in the Church and the circumstances of their lives: priests devoted to the pastoral ministry, because they are called upon to remain diligent in prayer and in the service of the word; religious, by the charism of their consecrated lives; all the faithful as much as possible: Pastors of souls should see to it that the principal hours, especially Vespers, are celebrated in common on Sundays and on the more solemn feasts. The laity, too, are encouraged to recite the divine office, either with the priests, or among themselves, or even individually.

SECOND VATICAN COUNCIL (*On the Sacred Liturgy*)

DIVORCE

Divorce by now is prayed for, as if it were the proper sequel of marriage.

TERTULLIAN (*Excuse*)

Divorce is born of perverted morals, and leads, as experience shows, to vicious habits in public and private life.

POPE LEO XIII (*On Christian Marriage*)

Truly, it is hardly possible to describe how great are the evils that flow from divorce. Matrimonial contracts are by it made variable; mutual kindness is weakened; deplorable inducements to unfaithfulness are supplied; harm is done to the education and training of children; occasion is afforded for the break-up of homes; the seeds of dissension are sown among families; the dignity of womanhood is lessened and brought low, and women run the risk of being deserted after having ministered to the pleasures of men.

POPE LEO XIII (*On Christian Marriage*)

DOGMA

If you go into a shop in the Eastern Empire, the cashier will start talking about the Begotten and the Unbegotten instead of giving you your change. The baker, instead of telling you how much his loaves cost, argues that the Father is greater than the Son. And if you want a bath, the attendant assures you that the Son most certainly proceeds from nothing.

ST. GREGORY OF NYSSA

From the age of fifteen, dogma has been the fundamental principle of my religion; I know no other religion; I cannot enter into the idea of any other sort of religion; religion, as a mere sentiment, is to me a dream and a mockery.

VENERABLE JOHN HENRY NEWMAN
(*Apologia Pro Vita Sua*)

The Catholic Church alone teaches as matters of faith those things which the thoroughly sincere person of every sect discovers, more or less obscurely for himself, but dares not believe for want of external sanction.

COVENTRY PATMORE

Truths turn into dogmas the moment they are disputed.

G. K. CHESTERTON (*Heretics*)

. . . It is only the reasonable dogma that lives long enough to be called antiquated.

G. K. CHESTERTON

To say we want no dogma in religion is to assert a dogma.

ARCHBISHOP FULTON J. SHEEN (*Religion Without God*)

DOUBT

When unhappy, one doubts everything; when happy, one doubts nothing.

JOSEPH ROUX
(*Meditations of a Parish Priest*)

Ten thousand difficulties do not make one doubt.

VENERABLE JOHN HENRY NEWMAN
(*Apologia Pro Vita Sua*)

The believer will fight another believer over a shade of difference. The doubter fights only with himself.

GRAHAM GREENE (*Monsignor Quixote*)

DRINK

The drunken man is a living corpse.

ST. JOHN CHRYSOSTOM (*Homilies*)

Drunkenness is the ruin of reason. It is premature old age. It is temporary death.

ST. BASIL (*Homilies*)

Dread the delight of drink and you will do the better.
Though you long for more, measure is medicine.
What the belly asks is not all good for the soul,
What the soul loves is not all food for the body.

WILLIAM LANGLAND (*Piers Plowman*)

When the drink is in, the wit is out.

JOHN GOWER (*Confessio Amantis*)

Show me an Irish priest without this vice and he is assuredly a saint.

ST. OLIVER PLUNKETT

Drink moderately, for drunkeness neither keeps a secret, nor observes a promise.

MIGUEL DE CERVANTES

Saint Patrick was a gentleman
Who through strategy and stealth
Drove all the snakes from Ireland
Here's a drink to his health!
But not too many drinkees

Lest we lose ourselves and then
Forget the good Saint Patrick
And see them snakes again!

ANONYMOUS

The dipsomaniac and the abstainer both make the same mistake. They both regard wine as a drug and not as a drink.

G. K. CHESTERTON (*George Bernard Shaw*)

DUTY

Do you really want to be a saint? Carry out the little duty of each moment, do what you ought and put yourself into what you are doing.

ST. JOSEMARÍA ESCRIVÁ (*The Way*)

DYING WORDS

Promise to bury me secretly, so that no one shall know the place, save you alone, for I shall receive my body incorruptible from my Savior at the resurrection of the dead. And distributed my garments thus: To Athanasius, the bishop, give one of my sheepskins, and the cloak under me, which was new when he gave it to me and has grown old by me; and to Serapion, the bishop, give the other sheepskin; and do you have the haircloth garment. And for the rest, children, farewell, for Antony is going and will be with you no more.

ST. ANTONY OF EGYPT

Lay this body wherever it may be. Let no care of it disturb you: this only I ask of you, that you should remember me at the altar of the Lord wherever you may be.

St. Monica (*quoted in St. Augustine's Confessions*)

Put your pen in the ink and write quickly.

The Venerable Bede

I have loved justice and hated iniquity; therefore I die in exile.

Pope Gregory VII

In death at last let me rest with Abelard.

Héloïse

I know not to which I ought to yield – to the love of my children, which urges me to stay here, or to the love of God, which draws me to him.

St. Bernard of Clairvaux

I must confess that I have enjoyed talking to young women more than to old ones.

St. Dominic

Welcome, Sister Death.

St. Francis of Assisi

I receive you, redeeming the price of my soul. Out of love for you have I studied, watched through many nights and exerted myself. You did I preach and teach. I have never said anything against you. Nor do I persist stubbornly in my views. If I ever expressed myself erroneously on this sacrament, I submit to the judgment of the Holy Roman Church, in obedience to which I now pass from this world.

St. Thomas Aquinas
(*receiving Holy Communion for the last time*)

No, I have not sought vainglory, but only the glory and praise of God.

ST. CATHERINE OF SIENA

Oh, Gabriele, how much better it would have been for you, and how much more it would have furthered your soul's welfare, if you had never been raised to the papacy, but had been content to live a quiet and religious life in the monastery.

POPE EUGENIUS IV (*Gabriele Condolmero*)

Into thy hands, O Lord, I commend my spirit.

CHRISTOPHER COLUMBUS

Do not weep for me, nor waste your time in vain prayers for my recovery, but pray rather for the salvation of my soul.

QUEEN ISABELLA OF SPAIN

I have offended God and mankind because my work did not reach the standard it should have done.

LEONARDO DA VINCI

My soul I leave to God, my body to the earth, my worldly goods to my next of kin.

MICHAELANGELO

Had I but served God as diligently as I have served the King, he would not have abandoned me in my gray hairs.

CARDINAL THOMAS WOLSEY,
LORD CHANCELLOR TO KING HENRY VIII

Monks! Monks! Monks!

KING HENRY VIII OF ENGLAND

I have denied with Peter, I have gone out with Peter, but not yet have I wept with Peter.

> STEPHEN GARDINER, BISHOP OF WINCHESTER
> (*apostatized under Henry VIII*)

O God! O God! O God!

> ST. IGNATIUS LOYOLA

Surely they will spare me a little earth here!

> ST. TERESA OF ÁVILA
> (*dying away from her own convent*)

I'm on my way.

> ST. PHILIP NERI

I have had no enemies save those of the state.

> CARDINAL ARMAND-JEAN RICHELIEU

Ah, I would willingly give all the applause I have received for one good action more.

> LOPE DE VEGA, SPANISH PLAYWRIGHT

I would never have believed it is so sweet to die.

> FRANCISCO SUAREZ, S.J.

Adore. Be silent. Rejoice!

> ANTONIO ROSMINI

All this is good for heaven! Blessed Mary, Mother of God, pray for me – a poor sinner, a poor sinner.

> ST. BERNADETTE

Well! God's will be done. He knows best. My work with all its faults and failures is in his hands, and before Easter I shall see my Savior.

> BLESSED DAMIEN OF MOLOKAI

I am so happy! I am so happy! I am so happy!
GERARD MANLEY HOPKINS, S.J.

I have never done a crime. Maybe, oh yes, sometimes I have done some sin, but not a crime. . . . I am an innocent man. I wish to forgive some people for what they are doing to me.
BARTOLOMEO VANZETTI (*executed, 1927*)

The issue is now clear. It is between light and darkness, and everyone must choose his side.
G. K. CHESTERTON

God bless you, Sister. May all your sons be bishops.
BRENDAN BEHAN, IRISH PLAYWRIGHT
(*to a nun who nursed him*)

My bags are packed and I am ready to go.
BLESSED POPE JOHN XXIII

Above all, no fuss.
CARDINAL BASIL HUME, O.S.B.
(*announcing that he had terminal cancer*)

E

EASTER

Let the angelic choirs of Heaven now rejoice; let the divine Mysteries rejoice; and let the trumpet of salvation sound forth the victory of so great a King. Let the earth also rejoice, made radiant by such splendor; and, enlightened with the brightness of the eternal King, let it know that the darkness of the whole world is scattered. Let our mother the Church also rejoice, adorned with the brightness of so great a light; and let this temple resound with the loud acclamations of the people.

THE ROMAN MISSAL (*Exultet*)

O God, who makes this most sacred night bright with the glory of the resurrection of Our Lord; preserve in the new offspring of your family the spirit of adoption which you have given them; that, renewed in body and spirit, they may render you an exemplary service.

ROMAN MISSAL
(*Collect for the Easter Vigil*)

Christ is risen! And you, o death, are annihilated!
Christ is risen! And the evil ones are cast down!
Christ is risen! And the angels rejoice!
Christ is risen! And life is liberated!
Christ is risen! And the tomb is emptied of its dead;
for Christ having risen from the dead,
is become the first-fruits of those who have fallen
    asleep.

To Him be Glory and Power, now and forever, and
    from all ages to all ages.
Amen!

ST. JOHN CHRYSOSTOM (*Easter Sermon*)

On the third day the friends of Christ coming at day-
break to the place found the grave empty and the stone
rolled away. In varying ways they realized the new wonder; but even they hardly realized that the world had
died in the night. What they were looking at was the
first day of a new creation, with a new heaven and a
new earth; and in a semblance of the gardener God
walked again in the garden, in the cool not of the
evening but of the dawn.

G. K. CHESTERTON (*The Everlasting Man*)

EASTERN CHURCHES

I also recall the icon of the Virgin of the Cenacle, praying with the Apostles as they awaited the Holy Spirit:
could she not become the sign of hope for all those
who, in fraternal dialogue, wish to deepen their obedience of faith?

Such a wealth of praise, built up by the different
forms of the Church's great Tradition, could help hasten the day when the Church can begin once more to
breathe fully with her "two lungs," the East and the
West. As I have often said, this is more than ever necessary today.

POPE JOHN PAUL II (*Redemptoris Mater, 33,34*)

It has been stressed several times that the full union of
the Catholic Eastern Churches with the Church of

Rome which has already been achieved must not imply a diminished awareness of their own authenticity and originality. Wherever this occurred, the Second Vatican Council has urged them to rediscover their full identity, because they have "the right and the duty to govern themselves according to their own special disciplines. For these are guaranteed by ancient tradition, and seem to be better suited to the customs of their faithful and to the good of their souls." These Churches carry a tragic wound, for they are still kept from full communion with the Eastern Orthodox Churches despite sharing in the heritage of their fathers. A constant, shared conversion is indispensable for them to advance resolutely and energetically towards mutual understanding. And conversion is also required of the Latin Church, that she may respect and fully appreciate the dignity of Eastern Christians and accept gratefully the spiritual treasures of which the Eastern Catholic Churches are the bearers, to the benefit of the entire catholic communion; that she may show concretely, far more than in the past, how much she esteems and admires the Christian East and how essential she considers its contribution to the full realization of the Church's universality.

POPE JOHN PAUL II (*Orientale Lumen*)

EATING

It is a greater virtue to eat without choice what is set before you, than always to choose the worst.

ST. FRANCIS DE SALES
(*Introduction to the Devout Life*)

ECUMENISM

[Christians] are brothers and sisters in the same invisible monastery. Here we unite to praise God and to pray for each other and the world together: the walls of separation do not rise as high as heaven.

PAUL COUTURIER

The brethren divided from us also carry out many of the sacred actions of the Christian religion. Undoubtedly, in ways that vary according to the constitution of each Church or community, these actions can engender a life of grace, and can be rightly described as capable of providing access to the community of salvation.

SECOND VATICAN COUNCIL
(*Decree on Ecumenism*)

[Karl] Rahner thinks that in terms of dogma union is possible between the Protestants of the great churches and Rome. I would not disagree.

CARDINAL YVES CONGAR, O.P.
(*Diversity and Union*)

The plurality of religions is a consequence of the richness of creation itself and of the manifold grace of God. Though all coming from the same source, peoples have perceived the universe and articulated their awareness of the Divine Mystery in manifold ways, and God has surely been present in these historical undertakings of his children. Such pluralism therefore is in no way to be deplored but rather acknowledged as itself a divine gift.

CATHOLIC BISHOPS OF INDIA
(*Guidelines for Religious Dialogue*)

It has long been my belief that there is an ecumenism of the heart. Without the heart being involved we risk just speaking to each other as institutions and that is not enough.

CARDINAL BASIL HUME, O.S.B.
(*Letter to Patriarch Alexis of Moscow*)

EDUCATION

Why do we educate, unless to prepare for the world . . . ? Will it much matter in the world to come whether our bodily health or whether our intellectual strength was more or less, except of course as this world is in all its circumstances a trial for the next?

VENERABLE JOHN HENRY NEWMAN
(*The Idea of a University*)

No amount of pious training or pious culture will protect the faithful, or preserve them from the contamination of the age, if they are left inferior to non-Catholics in secular learning and intellectual development. The faithful must be guarded and protected by being trained and disciplined to grapple with the false systems of the age. . . . They must be better armed than their opponents – surpass them in the strength and vigor of their minds, and in the extent and variety of their knowledge. They must, on all occasions and against all adversaries, be ready to give a reason for the hope that is in them.

ORESTES BROWNSON (*Catholic Polemics*)

Every method of education founded wholly or in part on the denial or forgetfulness of original sin and of grace, and relying on the sole powers of human nature, is unsound.

POPE PIUS XI (*Divini Illius Magistri*)

To train a citizen is to train a critic. The whole point of education is that it should give a man abstract and eternal standards, by which he can judge material and fugitive conditions.

G. K. CHESTERTON (*All is Grist*)

If we accept the religious view of man's nature, we are compelled to take a very different, a radically different view of education. No longer can we think merely of *getting on* in the commercial and materialistic sense. We must now think of getting on in the sense of getting heavenwards. And in everything we learn and in everything we teach to our children or our pupils, we must bear this fact in mind.

ERIC GILL (*It All Goes Together*)

EFFORT

If a thing is worth doing, it is worth doing badly.

G. K. CHESTERTON
(*What's Wrong with the World*)

EMBRYO

The mere probability that a human person is involved would suffice to justify an absolutely clear prohibition of any intervention aimed at killing a human embryo.

POPE JOHN PAUL II (*Evangelium Vitae*)

ENEMIES

To pray for one's enemies in the love of Christ; to make peace with one's adversary before sundown.

ST. BENEDICT (*The Holy Rule*)

ENGLAND

The great work is complete. Catholic England has been restored to its orbit in the ecclesiastical firmament.... Truly this is a day of joy and exultation.

CARDINAL NICHOLAS WISEMAN
(*From Out the Flaminian Gate,
announcing the restoration of
the English hierarchy in 1850*)

ENGLISH, THE

It is not easy (humanly speaking) to wind up an Englishman to a dogmatic level.

VENERABLE JOHN HENRY NEWMAN
(*Apologia pro Vita Sua*)

CAUCHON:... The thick air of your country does not breed theologians.

WARWICK: You would not say so if you heard us quarreling about religion, my Lord!

GEORGE BERNARD SHAW (ST. JOAN)

Most Englishmen today are only Protestants insofar as they are not Catholics.

ARNOLD LUNN (*Now I See*)

ENVY

We fight one another and envy arms us against one another. . . . If everyone strives to unsettle the Body of Christ, where shall we end up? We are engaged in making Christ's body a corpse. . . . We declare ourselves members of one and the same organism, yet we devour one another like beasts.

ST. JOHN CHRYSOSTOM
(*Homily on Corinthians*)

Would you like to see God glorified by you? Then rejoice in your brother's progress and you will immediately give glory to God. Because his servant could conquer envy by rejoicing in the merits of others, God will be praised.

ST. JOHN CHRYSOSTOM (*Homily on Romans*)

EPIPHANY

O God, who did this day reveal your only-begotten Son to the gentiles by the leading of a star; mercifully grant that we who know you now by faith, may be brought to the contemplation of your majesty.

THE ROMAN MISSAL (*Collect for the Epiphany*)

EQUALITY

Although by Christ's will some are appointed teachers, dispensers of the mysteries and pastors for the others, yet all the faithful enjoy a true equality with regard to the dignity and the activity which they share in the building-up of the body of Christ.

SECOND VATICAN COUNCIL
(*Dogmatic Constitution on the Church*)

ERROR

All aberrations are founded on, and have their life in, some truth or other.

VENERABLE JOHN HENRY NEWMAN
(*Apologia pro Vita Sua*)

There is no error so monstrous that it fails to find defenders among the ablest men.

LORD ACTON

Most mistaken people mean well, and all mistaken people mean something. There is something to be said for every error but, whatever may be said for it, the most important thing to be said about it is that it is erroneous.

G. K. CHESTERTON (*All is Grist*)

ETERNAL LIFE

For a small living men run a great way; for eternal life many will scarcely raise a single foot from the ground.

THOMAS À KEMPIS (*The Imitation of Christ*)

Looking beyond this life, my first prayer, aim and hope is that I may see God. The thought of being blest with the sight of earthly friends pales before that thought. I believe that I shall never die; this awful prospect would crush me, were it not that I trusted and prayed that it would be an eternity in God's presence. How is eternity a boon, unless he goes with it?
And for others dear to me, my one prayer is that they may see God.

VENERABLE JOHN HENRY NEWMAN
(*Letter, February 1880*)

Life is eternal, and love is immortal, and death is only a horizon, and a horizon is nothing save the limit of our sight.

BEDE JARRETT, O.P.

EUCHARIST

O Sacred Banquet, in which Christ is received; the memory of his Passion is renewed; the mind is filled with grace; and a pledge of future glory is given unto us.

THE ROMAN MISSAL
(*O Sacrum Convivium*)

On the day we call the day of the sun, all those who dwell in the city or country gather in the same place.

The memoirs of the apostles and the writings of the prophets are read, as much as time permits.

When the reader has finished, he who presides over those gathered admonishes and challenges them to imitate these beautiful things.

Then we all rise together and offer prayers for ourselves . . . and for all others, wherever they may be, so that we may be found righteous by our life and actions, and faithful to the commandments, so as to obtain eternal salvation.

When the prayers are concluded, we exchange the kiss.

Then someone brings bread and a cup of water and wine mixed together to him who presides over the brethren.

He takes them and offers praise and glory to the Father of the universe, through the name of the Son and of the Holy Spirit and for a considerable time he gives thanks that we have been judged worthy of these gifts.

When he has concluded the prayers and thanksgivings, all present give voice to an acclamation by saying "Amen."

When he who presides has given thanks and the people have responded, those whom we call deacons give to those present the eucharistic bread, wine and water, and take them to those who are absent.

ST. JUSTIN MARTYR (*Apologiae*)

Not only do the priests offer the sacrifice, but also all the faithful; for what the priest does personally by way of his ministry, the faithful do collectively by virtue of their intention.

POPE INNOCENT III
(*De Sacro Altaris Mysterio*)

How I hate this folly of not believing in the Eucharist, etc! If the Gospel be true, if Jesus Christ be God, what difficulty is there?

BLAISE PASCAL (*Pensées*)

What Christ gives us is quite explicit if his own words are interpreted according to their Aramaic meaning. The expression "This is my body" means "This is myself."

KARL RAHNER, S.J.

Pleased as she was when home Masses were allowed and the liturgy translated into English, she didn't take kindly to smudging the border between the sacred and mundane. When a priest close to the community used a coffee cup for a chalice at a Mass celebrated in the soup kitchen on First Street, she afterwards took the cup, kissed it, and buried it in the back yard. It was no longer suited for coffee – it had held the Blood of Christ. I learned more about the Eucharist that day than I had from any book or sermon. It was a learning experience for the priest as well – thereafter he used a chalice

JIM FOREST
(*Dorothy Day – A Saint For Our Age?*)

The primary significance of the Eucharist isn't mystical but physical, almost a material clinging to the being of his friends who would stay on and live. He said "This is my body" with a tenderness that first and foremost exulted in itself. Not "This is my spirit" or "This is generalized goodness or well-being" – possibly they would not have known what to do with such things. It was necessary to them that he should remain with the only thing we really know and attach our hearts and minds to – the body, and that it should be a desirable, acceptable and homely body. That's why he looked over that tablecloth for the easiest, most familiar and most concrete thing: bread. So as to quench hunger and give pleasure. Above all so as to stay. That evening Christ measured out for us all the millions of evenings before we would see him face to face; he measured out the long separation. He knew that men forget things within a few days, that distance destroys things, that it's useless for lovers to insert a lock of hair in letters that are going far away across land and sea. If Peter himself, and John and Andrew and James would forget, then in order that their children and their grandchildren's children shouldn't forget, he had to throw between himself and me that never-ending bridge of bread. *"Do this in memory of me."*

LUIGI SANTUCCI
(*Wrestling with Christ*)

I have been able to celebrate Holy Mass in chapels built along mountain paths, on lakeshores and seacoasts; I have celebrated it on altars built in stadiums and city squares.... This varied scenario of celebrations of the Eucharist has given me a powerful experience of its universal and, so to speak, cosmic character. Yes, cosmic! Because even when it is celebrated on the humble altar of a country church, the Eucharist is always in some way celebrated on the altar of the world. It unites heaven and earth. It embraces and permeates all creation.

POPE JOHN PAUL II (*Ecclesia de Eucharistia*)

EUROPE

It is the teaching of history that when the Church pervaded with her spirit the ancient and barbarous nations of Europe, little by little the many and varied differences that divided them were diminished and the quarrels extinguished; in time they formed a homogeneous society from which sprang Christian Europe which, under the guidance and auspices of the Church, whilst preserving a diversity of nations, tended to a unity that promoted its prosperity and glory.

POPE BENEDICT XV
(*Pacem Dei Munus Pulcherrimum*)

This our European structure, built upon the noble foundations of classical antiquity, was formed through, exists by, is consonant to, and will stand only in the mold of the Catholic Church. Europe will return to the faith, or she will perish. The faith is Europe. And Europe is the faith.

HILAIRE BELLOC (*Europe and the Faith*)

If Mr. Hilaire Belloc means that Europe would be nothing without the faith and that its *raison d'etre* has been and remains to dispense the faith to the world, Mr. Belloc is right in saying that Europe is the faith. But speaking absolutely, no! Europe is not the faith and the faith is not Europe: Europe is not the Church and the Church is not Europe. . . . The Church is universal because she is born of God; all citizens are at home in her, the arms of her crucified Master are stretched over all races, above all civilizations. She does not bring nations "the benefits of civilization" but the blood of Christ and supernatural beatitude.

JACQUES MARITAIN
(*The Things That Are Not Caesar's*)

We shall never have a common peace in Europe till we have a common principle in Europe. People talk of the United States of Europe; but they forget that they needed the very doctrinal Declaration of Independence to make the United States of America. You cannot agree about nothing any more than you can quarrel about nothing.

G. K. CHESTERTON (*All Things Considered*)

EUTHANASIA

It is never licit to kill another: even if he should wish it, indeed if he request it,

EVANGELIZATION

hanging between life and death . . . nor is it licit even
when a sick person is no longer able to live.

St. Augustine

Euthanasia must be called a *false mercy*, and indeed a
disturbing "perversion" of mercy. True "compassion"
leads to sharing another's pain; it does not kill the person whose suffering we cannot bear.

Pope John Paul II (*Evangelium Vitae*)

Phrases such as *mercy killing, rational suicide, physician-
assisted suicide* and the like should not be allowed to
obscure the fact that euthanasia is killing an innocent
human being and, as such, is morally wrong and should
not be condoned by any civilized society.

Oregon & Washington Catholic Bishops
(*Living & Dying Well, 1991*)

Catholic opposition to euthanasia and assisted suicide
is as old as Christianity. In fact, moral teaching against
assisting a suicide is older than Christianity, for it is
found in Jewish tradition and in the Hippocratic Oath
which laid the groundwork for modern medicine as a
healing profession.

Cardinal Bernard Law
(*Testimony before the Massachusetts
State Legislature, 1997*)

EVANGELIZATION

The Church exists to evangelize.

Pope Paul VI (*Evangelization in the Modern World*)

EVENTS

Events often cut the knots which appear insoluble to theory.

LORD ACTON
(*Döllinger on the Temporal Power*)

EVIL

There is nothing evil except that which perverts the mind and shackles the conscience.

ST. AMBROSE

For we do not easily expect evil of those we love most.

PETER ABELARD

A thing essentially evil cannot exist. The foundation of evil is always a good subject.

ST. THOMAS AQUINAS
(*Disputations Concerning Evil*)

Evil as such cannot be desired.

ST. THOMAS AQUINAS
(*Disputations Concerning Evil*)

If all evil were prevented, much good would be absent from the universe. A lion would cease to live if there were no slaying of animals; and there would be no patience of martyrs if there were no tyrannical persecution.

ST. THOMAS AQUINAS (*Summa Theologica*)

Men never do evil so completely and cheerfully as when they do it from religious conviction.

BLAISE PASCAL (*Pensées*)

Never open the door to a lesser evil, for other and greater ones will invariably slink in after it

BALTASAR GRACIÁN, S.J.
(*The Art of Worldly Wisdom*)

Evil, when we are in its power, is not felt as evil but as a necessity, even a duty.

SIMONE WEIL (*Gravity and Grace*)

Goodness has only once found a perfect incarnation in a human body and never will again, but evil can always find a home there. Human nature is not black and white but black and gray.

GRAHAM GREENE
(*The Lost Childhood and Other Essays*)

I have always been convinced that individual and collective crimes are closely linked; and in my capacity [as] journalist I have only tried to make clear that the day to day horrors of our political history are no more than the visible consequences of the invisible history unfolding in the secrecy of the human heart.

FRANÇOIS MAURIAC (*Essays*)

EVOLUTION

The faithful cannot embrace that opinion which maintains either that after Adam there existed on this earth true men who did not take their origin through natural generation from him as from the first parent of all, or that Adam represents a certain number of first parents. Now it is in no way apparent how such an opinion can be reconciled with that which the sources of revealed truth ... propose with regard to original sin, which proceeds from sin actually committed by an individual Adam and which through generation is passed on to all and is in everyone as his own.

POPE PIUS XII (*Humani Generis*)

EXAMINATION OF CONSCIENCE

It is a great grace of God to practice self-examination; but too much is as bad as too little. Believe me, by God's help we shall advance more by contemplating the Divinity than by keeping our eyes fixed on ourselves.

ST. TERESA OF ÁVILA

He told his hearers that he was there that evening for no terrifying, no extravagant purpose; but as a man of the world speaking to his fellowmen. He came to speak to businessmen and he would speak to them in a businesslike way. If he might use the metaphor, he said, he was their spiritual accountant; and he wished each and every one of his hearers to open his books, the books of his spiritual life, and see if they tallied accurately with conscience.

Jesus Christ was not a hard taskmaster. He understood our little failings, understood the weaknesses of our poor fallen nature, understood the temptations of this life. We might have had, we all had from time to time, our temptations: we might have, we all had, our failings. But one thing only, he said, he would ask of his hearers. And that was: to be straight and manly with God. If their accounts tallied in every point to say:

"Well, I have verified my accounts. I find all well."

But if, as might happen, there were some discrepancies, to admit the truth, to be frank and say like a man:

"Well, I have looked into my accounts. I find this wrong and this wrong. But, with God's grace, I will rectify this and this. I will set right my accounts."

JAMES JOYCE (*Dubliners,* "Grace")

I quite understand, God says, that one should
     examine one's conscience.
It is an excellent practice. It should not be abused.
It is even recommended. It is quite right.
Everything which is recommended is right.
And besides, it is not only recommended. It is
     prescribed.
Consequently, it is quite right.
But at last you are in bed. What do you mean by self-
     examination, examining your conscience?
If it means thinking of all the stupid things you have
     done during the day, if it means reminding
     yourself of all the stupid things you have done
     during the day,
With a feeling of repentance, though perhaps I
     should not say of contrition,
But anyway with a feeling of penitence, which you
     offer me, all right, that's quite right,
I accept your penitence. You are decent people, good
     fellows.
But if it means sifting through and ruminating at
     night over the thanklessness of the day,
All the fevers and the bitterness of the day,
And if it means you want to chew over at night the
     stale sins of the day,
Your stale fevers and your regrets and your
     repentances and your remorse which is staler still,

And if it means you want to keep an accurate register
   of your sins,
Of all those stupidities and all those idiocies,
No, let me keep the Book of Judgment myself.
Perhaps you will be the gainer into the bargain.

CHARLES PÉGUY
(*The Mystery of the Holy Innocents*)

EXAMPLE

Were I to give parents counsel, I would warn them to
be well advised as to what persons are the companions
of their children. I profited nothing by the virtue of my
sister. But, I retained all the bad example given me by
another family member, who had haunted our house.

ST. TERESA OF ÁVILA

It is easier to exemplify values than teach them.

THEODORE M. HESBURGH, C.S.C.

EXCOMMUNICATION

Although the sword of excommunication is the chief
weapon of ecclesiastical discipline, and very useful for
keeping the people to their duties, it is to be used only
with sobriety and circumspection, for experience
teaches that if it be used rashly and for small reason it
will be more despised than feared, and will work more
evil than good.

COUNCIL OF TRENT

EXCUSES

We often do ill and do worse in excusing it.

THOMAS À KEMPIS
(*Introduction to the Devout Life*)

EXISTENCE OF GOD

God's first effect is existence. All other effects presuppose and are based on that. He is pure existence. The existence of all other things partakes of His.

ST. THOMAS AQUINAS (*Summa Theologica*)

God's existence can be proved in five ways.

ST. THOMAS AQUINAS (*Summa Theologica*)

Therefore it is necessary to arrive at a prime mover, put in motion by no other; and this everyone understands to be God.

ST. THOMAS AQUINAS (*Summa Theologica*)

"God is or he is not." But to which side shall we incline? ... Let us weigh the gain and loss in wagering that God is. Let us estimate the two chances. If you gain, you gain all; if you lose, you lose nothing. Wager, then, without hesitation, that he is.

BLAISE PASCAL (*Pensées*)

EXPERIENCE

The language of God is the experience that God writes into our lives.

ST. JOHN OF THE CROSS

Experience comprises illusions lost, rather than wisdom gained.

JOSEPH ROUX (Meditations of a Parish Priest)

EXPLOITATION

If through necessity or fear of a worse evil the workman accepts harder conditions because an employer or contractor will afford him no better, he is made the victim of force and injustice.

POPE LEO XIII (Rerum Novarum)

EYES

Do not say that you have chaste minds, if you have unchaste eyes; because an unchaste eye is the messenger of an unchaste heart.

ST. AUGUSTINE (Letter 211)

F

FAITH

Faith is the firm foundation of all the virtues.
ST. AMBROSE (*On Psalm 40*)

No one who believes, whatever may have been his condition, however great may have been his fall, need fear that he will perish. When anyone believes, the wrath of God departs and life comes.
ST. AMBROSE (*On Penitence*)

What is faith, save to believe what you do not see?
ST. AUGUSTINE (*Sermons*)

Faith is a habit of mind, which begins eternal life in us, and induces a reasonable assent to things unseen.
ST. THOMAS AQUINAS
(*Disputations Concerning Truth*)

Faith is the substance of things hoped,
and proof
Of things invisible to mortal sight.
DANTE (*Paradiso*)

Human reason is weak and can be misled; but true faith cannot be deceived.
THOMAS Á KEMPIS
(*The Imitation of Christ*)

Believe that you have it, and you have it.
ERASMUS (*Letter to St. Thomas More*)

If anyone shall say that faith cannot be made credible by outward signs, and that therefore men ought to be moved to faith solely by the internal experience of each, or by private inspiration; let him be anathema.

COUNCIL OF TRENT

It is love makes faith, not faith love.

VENERABLE JOHN HENRY NEWMAN
(*Parochial and Plain Sermons*)

It is nearly always faith which Our Lord praises and rewards. Sometimes he praises love, sometimes humility, but this is rare.... Faith, though not the supreme virtue – charity holds that place – is nevertheless the most important because it is the basis of all the others, charity included. Also it is the rarest.... Real faith, faith which inspires all one's actions, faith in the supernatural which strips the world of its mask and reveals God in everything, which makes meaningless the words "impossible," "anxiety," "danger" and "fear" . . . how rare that is!

VENERABLE CHARLES DE FOUCAULD

If we believe, everything can be transformed into Our Lord.

PIERRE TEILHARD DE CHARDIN, S.J.

The most beautiful act of faith is the one made in darkness, in sacrifice, and with extreme effort.

ST. PADRE PIO

Ultimately faith is the only key to the universe. The final meaning of human existence, and the answers to the questions on which all our happiness depends cannot be found in any other way.

THOMAS MERTON
(*Seeds of Contemplation*)

We can pray after Auschwitz because people prayed in Auschwitz.

JOHANN METZ
(*The Emergent Church*)

FAMILIARITY

We must have charity for everyone, but familiarity is not necessary.

THOMAS À KEMPIS
(*The Imitation of Christ*)

FAMILY

The family, grounded on marriage freely contracted, monogamous and indissoluble, is and must be considered the first and essential cell of human society.

BLESSED POPE JOHN XXIII

The family is, so to speak, the domestic church. In it parents should, by their word and example, be the first preachers of the faith to their children; they should encourage them in the vocation which is proper to each of them, fostering with special care vocation to a sacred state.

CONSTITUTION ON THE CHURCH
(*Dogmatic Constitution on the Church*)

This mission — to be the first and vital cell of society — the family has received from God. It will fulfill this mission if it appears as the domestic sanctuary of the Church by reason of the mutual affection of its members and the prayer that they offer to God in common, if the whole family makes itself a part of the liturgical worship of the Church, and if it provides active hospitality and promotes justice and other good works for the service of all the brethren in need.

DECREE ON THE APOSTOLATE OF THE LAITY
(*Apostolicam Actuositatem*)

A man and a woman united in marriage, together with their children, form a family.

CATECHISM OF THE CATHOLIC CHURCH (*2202*)

Through God's mysterious design, it was in that family [the Holy Family] that the Son of God spent long years of a hidden life. It is therefore the prototype and example for all Christian families. It was unique in the world. Its life was passed in anonymity and silence in a little town in Palestine. It underwent trials of poverty, persecution and exile. It glorified God in an incomparably exalted and pure way. And it will not fail to help Christian families — indeed, all the families in the world — to be faithful to their day-to-day duties, to bear the cares and tribulations of life, to be open and generous to the needs of others, and to fulfill with joy the plan of God in their regard.

POPE JOHN PAUL II (*Familiaris Consortio, 86*)

FAMILY PRAYER

The family that prays together stays together.

FATHER PATRICK PEYTON, C.S.C.

FASTING

Here is the fast you must keep for God: do not commit any wicked deed in your life and serve the Lord with a pure heart; keep his commandments by walking according to his directions and do not let any evil desire enter your heart; have faith in God.

ANONYMOUS (*Shepherd of Hermas*)

Fasting is better than prayer.

ST. CLEMENT (*Second Letter to the Corinthians*)

Devils take great delight in fullness, and drunkenness, and bodily comfort. Fasting possesses great power and it works glorious things. . . . To fast is to banquet with angels.

ST. ATHANASIUS

When the stomach is full it is easy to talk of fasting.

ST. JEROME

Whoso would pray, he must fast and be clean,
Fatten his soul and keep his body lean.

GEOFFREY CHAUCER
(*Canterbury Tales: The Summoner's Tale*)

As for the repugnance felt by Catholics of today for fasting, it is interesting to note that it occurs at the very time when the disciples of Gandhi have demonstrated the power of fasting on the level of natural mystique and non-violent resistance.

JACQUES MARITAIN

A fast is better than a bad meal.

IRISH PROVERB

He who fasts but does nothing else saves his bread but goes to hell.

ITALIAN PROVERB

FATHERHOOD

They are supported by the Church's teaching and pastoral concern for the family and also by the example of St. Joseph. The bible shows him engaged in the tasks of fatherhood, such as taking Jesus and Mary out of danger, seeing that religious and civic duties are carried out, providing a home. He is an actively involved husband and father. Were it not for him the Holy Family might have had an even tougher time than it did. The same can be said of today's fathers and their families.

H. RICHARD MCCORD *(United States Bishops' Secretariat for Family, Laity, Women and Youth)*

FEAR

Fear the Lord, then, and you will do everything well.

ANONYMOUS *(The Shepherd of Hermas)*

To fear God is never to pass over any good thing that ought to be done.

POPE ST. GREGORY THE GREAT

If fear were not a good thing, fathers would not have set schoolmasters over their children, nor lawgivers magistrates for cities.

ST. JOHN CHRYSOSTOM (*Homilies*)

If you have a fearful thought, do not share it with a weakling, whisper it to your saddle-bow and ride forth singing.

KING ALFRED THE GREAT

We must not fear fear.

ST. FRANCIS DE SALES
(*Letters to Persons in the World*)

We must fear God through love, not love him through fear.

JEAN PIERRE CAMUS
(*The Spirit of St. Francis de Sales*)

Those who love to be feared, fear to be loved; they themselves are of all people the most abject; some fear them, but they fear everyone.

JEAN PIERRE CAMUS
(*The Spirit of St. Francis de Sales*)

Short is the road that leads from fear to hate.

ITALIAN PROVERB

FEELING

Seeing's believing, but feeling is God's own truth.

IRISH PROVERB

FEMINISM

Thus the feminism that we envision is one that is able constantly to build an integral vision of a new humanizing culture beyond patriarchy without becoming closed or sectarian toward any living cultural option or human community. It remains open to authentic spirit wherever it is found, and it extends to all the invitation to join a new dance of life without which life itself may not survive.

ROSEMARY RUETHER (*Women-Church*)

One of the errors of feminists' claims was to place woman's liberation strictly in her relation to man, and offering as the only alternative either submission to him or domination of him. The only way not to engage in this relation of strength is to posit the right manner of relating to man, that is, by establishing the relation of woman with God.

JO CROISSANT
(*Wife of the Founder of Community of the Beatitudes*)

In the description found in Genesis 2:18-25, the woman is created by God "from the rib" of the man and is placed at his side as another "I", as the companion of the man, who is alone in the surrounding world of living creatures and who finds in none of them a "helper" suitable for himself. Called into existence in this way, the woman is immediately recognized by the man as "flesh of his flesh and bone of his bones" and for this very reason she is called "woman." In biblical language this name indicates her essential identity with regard to man — 'is-'issah — something which unfortunately modern languages in general are unable to express: "She shall be called woman ('issah) because she was taken out of man ('is)": Genesis 2:23.

The biblical text provides sufficient bases for recognizing the essential equality of man and woman from the point of view of their humanity. From the very beginning, both are persons, unlike the other living beings in the world about them. The woman is another "I" in a common humanity.

POPE JOHN PAUL II (*Mulieris Dignitatem*)

FERTILITY

The use of the "infertile periods" for conjugal union can be an abuse if the couple, for unworthy reasons, seeks in this way to avoid having children, thus lowering the number of births in their family below the morally correct level. This morally correct level must be established by taking into account not only the good of one's own family, and even the state of health and the means of the couple themselves, but also the good of the society to which they belong, of the Church, and even of the whole of mankind.

POPE JOHN PAUL II
(*General Audience, September 5, 1984*)

FLATTERY

Baloney is the unvarnished lie laid on so thick you hate it. Blarney is flattery laid on so thick you love it.

ARCHBISHOP FULTON J. SHEEN

FLIRTATION

Your natural beauty suffices your husband, but if flaunted before many men like a net to catch a flock of birds, what will be the result?

You will be pleased by those whom your beauty pleases, returning glance for glance, gaze for gaze, then smiles and little words of love, guarded at first, but soon becoming familiar until you are openly behaving amorously.

Take heed, my tongue, lest I mention what follows! But I will say this: Everything such foolish lovers say or do is an incitement to evil; one thing inevitably leads to another in these wretched flirtations as one piece of iron, drawn by a magnet, draws another in its turn.

ST. GREGORY NAZIANZEN

Such relationships are evil, foolish and empty: Evil because they end up in sins of the flesh and deprive God, wife or husband, of the heart and the love which is theirs by right; foolish because groundless and unreasonable; empty because fruitless, yielding neither peace nor honor; on the contrary they are a waste of time, they compromise our good name, while their only pleasure lies in vain hopes and the eager anticipation of they know not what; for these weak and foolish people are sure that their mutual expressions of love must have some value or other, though they do not know what it is, and so are never satisfied, their heart for ever disturbed by endless suspicion, jealousy and anxiety.

ST. FRANCIS DE SALES
(*Introduction to the Devout Life*)

FOOLISHNESS

You cannot imagine how great is people's foolishness. They have no sense or discernment, having lost it by hoping in themselves and putting their trust in their own knowledge.

GOD, TO ST. CATHERINE OF SIENA

FORBEARANCE

When you feel the assaults of passion and anger, then is the time to be silent as Jesus was, silent in the midst of His ignominies and sufferings.

ST. PAUL OF THE CROSS

For one pain endured with joy, we shall love the good God more forever.

ST. THÉRÈSE OF LISIEUX

Don't say, "That person bothers me." Think: "That person sanctifies me."

ST. JOSEMARÍA ESCRIVÁ (*The Way*)

FORCE

Other nations use "force"; we Britons alone use "might."

EVELYN WAUGH (*Scoop*)

FORGIVENESS

There are many kinds of alms the giving of which helps us to obtain pardon for our sins; but none is greater than that by which we forgive from our heart a sin that someone has committed against us.

ST. AUGUSTINE

If we wish to be judged mercifully, we must ourselves be merciful towards those who have offended us. For we shall be forgiven to the degree that we have forgiven those who have injured us by wrongdoing of any kind. Some people fear this, and when [The Lord's Prayer] is recited together in church by the whole congregation, they pass over this line in silence, lest by their own words they obligate rather than excuse themselves. They do not understand that it is useless to try to quibble in this way with the Judge of all, who wished to show from the outset how he would deal with those who sought his mercy. . . . Therefore, just as we want to be judged by him, so we should judge our brothers if they have offended us in any way, because there is judgment without mercy for the individual who has not acted mercifully.

ST. JOHN CASSIAN

Forgive and forget.

ANONYMOUS (Ancrene Riwle)

A man turning from an evil life is bound to be rendered desperate by the knowledge of his sins, if he does not also know how good God is, how kind and gentle, and how ready to forgive.

ST. BERNARD OF CLAIRVAUX
(Sermons on the Song of Songs)

Praised be my Lord for all those who pardon one another for his love's sake, and who endure weakness

139

and tribulation; blessed are they who peaceably shall
endure for you, O most high, will give them a crown.

ST. FRANCIS OF ASSISI

Forgive your enemies, but never forget their names.

JOHN F. KENNEDY
(*also attributed to Robert Kennedy*)

If the Catholicism that I was raised in had a fault, and
it did, it was precisely that it did not allow for mistakes.
It demanded that you get it right the first time. If you
made a mistake, you lived with it, and, like the rich
young man, you were doomed to be sad, at least for the
rest of your life.

I have seen that mark in all kinds of people,
divorcees, ex-priests, ex-religious, people who have had
abortions, married people who have had affairs, people
who have had children outside of marriage, parents
who have made serious mistakes with their children,
and countless others, who have made serious mistakes.

There is too little around to help them. We need a
theology of brokenness. . . .

We need a theology that tells us that mistakes are
not forever, that they are not even for a life-time, that
time and grace wash clean, that nothing is irrevocable.
Finally, we need a theology which teaches us that God
loves us as sinners and that the task of Christianity is
not to teach us how to live, but how to live again, and
again, and again.

RONALD ROLHEISER, O.M.I.

If God has forgiven you your past, you have no right to
continue clinging to it.

ALEX REBELLO

FORMATION

It is only great people who form other great people.

ANTONIO ROSMINI

FORTITUDE

Yet still, over all these limitations and humiliations, I felt astonishingly and profoundly free; I felt a flame, a secret little life of liberty beating away inside me, a liberty I could never lose.

They could keep me locked up; they could take me to a concentration camp tomorrow, they could torture me and make me cry out with pain, but they could never touch the sanctuary where my soul watched, where I alone was master.

They might deceive me, abuse me, weaken me; they might get words out of me when my mind staggered from their cruelty, words which they could take as an admission; they could kill me. But they could never force my will, for it could never belong to them; it was between myself and God, and no one else could ever touch it.

HENRI PERRIN, S.J.
(*Priest-Workman in Germany*)

FRATERNAL CORRECTION

Watch my behavior carefully and warn me of my faults, for four eyes can see better than two.

ST. THOMAS À BECKET

Fraternal correction, including that of prelates by their subjects, is a precept of charity. If the Faith were in danger, a subject ought to rebuke his prelate – even publicly.

ST. THOMAS AQUINAS
(*Summa Theologica 11[ii] Q.33*)

FREEDOM

I wish the intellect to range with the utmost freedom, and religion to enjoy an equal freedom, but what I am stipulating for is, that they should be found in one and the same place, and exemplified in the same persons.... I want the intellectual layman to be religious, and the devout ecclesiastic to be intellectual.

VENERABLE JOHN HENRY NEWMAN (*Letters*)

FREE TRADE

It would appear that, on the level of individual nations and of international relations, the *free market* is the most efficient instrument for utilizing resources and effectively responding to needs. But this is true only for those needs which are "solvent," insofar as they are endowed with purchasing power, and for those resources which are "marketable," insofar as they are capable of obtaining a satisfactory price. But there are many human needs which find no place on the market. It is a strict duty of justice and truth not to allow fundamental human needs to remain unsatisfied, and not to allow those burdened by such needs to perish. It is also necessary to help these needy people to acquire expertise, to enter the circle of exchange, and to develop their skills in order to make the best use of their capacities and resources.

POPE JOHN PAUL II (*Centesimus Annus, 1991*)

FREE WILL

God, it is true, foresaw the evil that man would do (foreseeing it, of course, he did not force man to do it) but at the same time he knew the good that he would himself one day make come out of it.

ST. AUGUSTINE (*De Correptione et Gratia*)

God therefore neither wills evil to be done, nor wills it not to be done, but wills to permit evil to be done, and this is good.

ST. THOMAS AQUINAS (*Summa Theologica*)

As the Catholic Church declares in the strongest terms the simplicity, spirituality, and immortality of the soul, so with unequalled constancy and publicity she ever asserts its freedom also.

POPE LEO XIII (*Libertas Praestantissimum*)

There is a tendency among many shallow thinkers of our day to teach that every human act is a reflex, over which we do not exercise human control. They would rate a generous deed as no more praiseworthy than a wink, a crime as no more voluntary than a sneeze . . . such a philosophy undercuts all human dignity . . . all of us have the power of choice in action at every moment of our lives

ARCHBISHOP FULTON J. SHEEN

FRIENDSHIP

True friendship ought never to conceal what it thinks.

ST. JEROME

Rightly has a friend been called "the half of my soul."

ST. AUGUSTINE (*Confessions*)

Just as the flattery of a friend can pervert, so the insult of an enemy can sometimes correct.

ST. AUGUSTINE (*Confessions*)

If two friends ask you to judge a dispute, don't accept, because you will lose one friend; on the other hand, if two strangers come with the same request, accept because you will gain one friend.

ST. AUGUSTINE

Friendship is the source of the greatest pleasures, and without friends even the most agreeable pursuits become tedious.

ST. THOMAS AQUINAS

We call that person who has lost his father, an orphan; and a widower that man who has lost his wife. But that man who has known the immense unhappiness of losing a friend, by what name do we call him? Here every language is silent and holds its peace in impotence.

JOSEPH ROUX
(*Meditations of a Parish Priest*)

There's nothing worth the wear of winning,
But laughter and the love of friends.

HILAIRE BELLOC (*Verses*)

We cherish our friends, not for their ability to amuse us, but for ours to amuse them.

EVELYN WAUGH (attributed)

Reckoning up is friendship's end.

IRISH PROVERB

FUTURE

The resources at our disposal today, the powers that we have released, could not possibly be absorbed by the narrow system of individual or national units which the architects of the human earth have hitherto used. . . . The age of nations has passed. Now, unless we wish to perish we must shake off our old prejudices and build the earth. . . . The more scientifically I regard the world, the less can I see any possible biological future for it except the active consciousness of its unity.

PIERRE TEILHARD DE CHARDIN, S.J.

This is what we are about:
We plant seeds that one day will grow.
We water seeds already planted,
knowing that they hold future promise.
We lay foundations that will need further
    development.
We provide yeast that produce effects beyond our
    abilities.

We cannot do everything
and realizing that gives us a sense of liberation.
This enables us to do something and to do it very
    well.

It may be incomplete but it is a beginning, a step
    along the way,
an opportunity for God's grace to enter and do the
    rest.

. . . We may never see the end results,
but that is the difference between the master builder
    and the worker.
We are workers, not master builders,
ministers, not messiahs.
We are prophets of a future not our own.

ARCHBISHOP OSCAR ROMERO

G

GAIETY

A jovial disposition. With moderation it is an accomplishment, not a defect. A grain of gaiety seasons all.
> BALTASAR GRACIÁN, S.J.
> (*The Art of Worldly Wisdom*)

GAMBLING

Let a bishop, or priest, or deacon who indulges himself in dice, or drinking, either leave off those practices, or let him be deprived. If a sub-deacon, a reader, or a singer does the like, either let him leave off, or let him be suspended; and so for one of the laity.
> ECCLESIASTICAL CANONS OF THE HOLY APOSTLES
> (*4th century*)

The devil invented gambling.
> ST. AUGUSTINE (*The City of God*)

GENEROSITY

For it is in giving that we receive.
> ST. FRANCIS OF ASSISI

Lord, teach me to be generous,
Teach me to serve you as you deserve,
To give and not to count the cost,
To fight and not to heed the wounds,

To toil and not to seek for rest,
To labor and not to ask for any reward
Save that of knowing that I do your will.

ST. IGNATIUS LOYOLA

Generosity, generosity, generosity must be the beginning and ending of our life.

CORNELIA CONNOLLY

Do your realize the privilege of giving to God? It is yours at every moment.

CORNELIA CONNOLLY

The most satisfying thing in life is to have been able to give a large part of one's self to others.

PIERRE TEILHARD DE CHARDIN, S.J.

I ask you one thing: do not tire of giving, but do not give your leftovers. Give until it hurts, until you feel the pain.

BLESSED MOTHER TERESA

It's not always easy to distinguish between genuine people and those who are not genuine, but it is always better to err on the side of generosity rather than on the side of meanness.

CARDINAL JOHN C. HEENAN

GENTLENESS

Who has ever seen people persuaded to love God by harshness?

ST. JOHN OF THE CROSS

You can catch more flies with a spoonful of honey than with a hundred barrels of vinegar.

ST. FRANCIS DE SALES

To become gentle, first be patient with your own faults.

ST. FRANCIS DE SALES

GLUTTONY

What shall we say of the belly, the queen of passions? If you can slay it or half kill it, keep a tight hold. It has mastered me, beloved, and I serve it as a slave and a vassal. It is the colleague of the demons and the home of passions. Through it we fall, and through it we rise again, when it behaves itself.

ST. GREGORY OF SINAI

An overfed belly will not study willingly.

MEDIEVAL MAXIM

To kindle and blow the fire of lechery,
That is annexed unto gluttony.

GEOFFREY CHAUCER (*The Pardoner's Tale*)

Then goeth Glutton in, and great oaths after;
Cis the Shoemaker sat on the bench,
Wat the Warrener and his wife too,
Tim the Tinker and twain of his prentice,
Hick the Hackney-man and Hugh the Needler,
Clarice of Cock's Lane and the clerk of the church,
Davie the Ditcher and a dozen others,
Sir Piers of Pridie and Peronelle of Flanders,
A ribbour, a rat-catcher, a raker of Cheap,
A roper, a riding-man, and Rose who sold dishes,

Godfrey of Garlickhithe and Griffin the
    Welshman. . . .
There was laughing and louring and "Let go the
    cup!"
They sat so till evensong and sat for a while,
Till Glutton had guzzled a gallon and a gill.
He might neither step nor stand till he his staff had;
Then began he to go, like a gleeman's bitch,
Sometimes sideways and sometimes backwards,
As one who lays lines to catch little birds.
When he drew near the doorway his eyes grew dim;
He stumbled on the threshold and sank to the floor,
Clement the Cobbler caught him by the middle
For to lift him aloft and laid him on his knees.
With all the woe in the world his wife and his wench
Bore him home to his bed and brought him therein,
And after his excess he had a fit of sloth;
He slept Saturday and Sunday till the sun went to rest
Then woke from his winking and wiped his eyes,
And the first word he uttered was "Where is my
    breakfast?"

Hackney-man: hirer of horses. *Needler:* needle-seller. *Ribibour:*
fiddler. *Raker:* scavenger.
Roper: rope-maker. *Louring:* scowling. *Gleeman:* blind street-
singer. *Cobbler:* shoe-mender.

WILLIAM LANGLAND
(*The Vision of Piers Plowman*)

GNOSIS

"New theology?" And welcome! At times, however, it's
not a matter of a new theology, but of old Gnosis. The
presumptuous mentality of the old gnostics often re-

surfaces: "We give explanations at the highest level of science; we eat up the poor, obsolete and bygone explanations of the Magisterium!" The method of Gnosis is also coming back, that of taking the arguments and terms of the Catholic faith, but only partially, usurping the right to sift them and select them, to understand them in one's own way, to mix them with extraneous ideologies and to base adherence to the faith no longer on divine authority but on human motives; on this or that philosophical opinion, for example, on the match between a particular argument and determined political choices adopted earlier.

ALBINO LUCIANI, LATER POPE JOHN PAUL I
(*Homily on Christ the Liberator*)

GOD

What is impossible to God? Not that which is difficult to his power, but that which is contrary to his nature.

ST. AMBROSE

God is not what you imagine or what you think you understand. If you understand, you have failed.

ST. AUGUSTINE (*De Trinitate*)

You have created us for yourself, and our heart is restless until it rests in you.

ST. AUGUSTINE (*Confessions*)

You never depart from us, yet we find it difficult to return to you.

ST. AUGUSTINE (*Confessions*)

It is easy to want things from the Lord and yet not want the Lord Himself; as though the Gift could ever be preferable to the Giver.

ST. AUGUSTINE (*Commentary on the Psalms*)

How distant you are from my sight, while I am present to your sight! You are wholly present everywhere and I do not see you.

ST. ANSELM (*Proslogion*)

God and nature do nothing in vain.

AUCTORITATES ARISTOTELIS

God be in my head
And in my understanding;
God be in my eyes
And in my looking;
God be in my mouth
And in my speaking;
God be in my heart
And in my thinking;
God be at my end
And at my departing.

THE SARUM MISSAL (*11th century*)

As truly as God is our Father, so just as truly is God our Mother.

JULIAN OF NORWICH (*Revelations of Divine Love*)

God is a great underground river that no one can dam up and no one can stop.

MEISTER ECKHART

God is most happy, and therefore supremely conscious.

ST. THOMAS AQUINAS
(*Commentary on the Metaphysics*)

"Person" in God signifies a relation subsisting in the divine nature.

ST. THOMAS AQUINAS (*Summa Theologica*)

God is closer to us than water is to a fish.

ST. CATHERINE OF SIENA

God does not offer himself to our finite beings as a thing all complete and ready to be embraced. For us, he is eternal discovery and eternal growth. The more we think we understand him, the more he reveals himself as otherwise. The more we think we hold him, the further he withdraws, drawing us closer into the depths of himself.

PIERRE TEILHARD DE CHARDIN, S.J.

Not peace as such, but God, is the absolute good.

DIETRICH VON HILDEBRAND

I remember something I was told when I was a very small boy. . . . In the larder there was a stack of apples. A small boy wanted an apple. He had been told by some grown-up that he must not take things from the larder without permission. . . . Why not take one? Nobody would know. It just seemed common sense. Nobody would see him. Was that true? Nobody? One person would. That was God. He sees everything you do, and then punishes you for the wrongdoing, so I was told.

It took me many, many years to recover from that story. Deep in my subconscious was the idea of God as somebody who was always watching us just to see if we were doing anything wrong. He was an authority figure, like a teacher or a policeman or even a bishop.

Now, many years later, I have an idea that God would have said to the small boy, "Take two."

CARDINAL BASIL HUME, O.S.B.

In no way is God in man's image. He is neither man nor woman. God is pure spirit in which there is no place for the difference between the sexes. But the respective "perfections" of man and woman reflect something of the infinite perfection of God: those of a mother and those of a father and husband.

CATECHISM OF THE CATHOLIC CHURCH, 370

We cannot describe God by his positive qualities but only by what he is not. He is without end, without time, without parts, without gender; he lacks no power that it is possible to have, he lacks no knowledge of anything that can be known. He who is – the uncontingent ground of all being – cannot be grasped by the contingent mind.

QUENTIN DE LA BÉDOYÈRE

GOD'S GLORY

The glory of God is a human being fully alive

ST. IRENAEUS

To lift up the hands in prayer gives God glory, but a man with a dungfork in his hands, a woman with a slop-pail, give him glory too. He is so great that all things give him glory, if you mean that they should.

GERARD MANLEY HOPKINS, S.J.

GOD'S LOVE

And we must dare to affirm that the Creator, by reason of love, is drawn from his transcendent throne above all things, to dwell within the heart of all things, while yet he stays within himself.

DIONYSIUS THE AEREOPAGITE

God's love for us is not greater in heaven than it is now.

ST. THOMAS AQUINAS

All things in this world are created out of God's love, and they become a framework of gifts, offered to us so that we can know God more easily and make a return of love more readily.

ST. IGNATIUS LOYOLA

Every existing thing is equally upheld in its existence by God's creative love. The friends of God should love him to the point of merging their love into his with regard to all things here below.

SIMONE WEIL (*Waiting for God*)

Remember that God loves your soul, not in some aloof, impersonal way, but passionately, with the adoring, cherishing love of a parent for a child. The outpouring of his Holy Spirit is really the outpouring of his love, surrounding and penetrating your little soul with a peaceful, joyful delight in his creature: tolerant, peaceful, a love full of longsuffering and gentleness, working quietly, able to wait for results, faithful, devoted, without variableness or shadow of turning. Such is God's love.

ABBÉ HENRI DE TOURVILLE (*Letters of Direction*)

I am a little pencil in the hand of a writing God who is sending a love letter to the world.

BLESSED MOTHER TERESA

Once, while preaching in a parish, I suddenly caught sight of a young mother with her child, and you could see the love between them. I was terribly tempted to say to the congregation: "Forget what I am saying and look over there, and you will see what we mean to God!"

CARDINAL BASIL HUME, O.S.B.

God's love isn't a reward for being good, doing our duty, resisting temptation, bearing the heat of the day in fidelity, saying our prayers, remaining pure, or offering worship, good and important though these are. God loves us because God is love and God cannot not love and cannot be discriminating in love.

RONALD ROLHEISER, O.M.I.

GOD'S POWER

It is only the impossible that is possible for God. He has given over the possible to the mechanics of matter and the autonomy of his creatures.

SIMONE WEIL (*Selected Essays*)

GOD'S WILL

God often gives in one brief moment what he has for a long time denied.

THOMAS À KEMPIS

As regards the will of God, even if some take scandal, we must not let this hamper our freedom of action.

ST. BASIL (*The Morals*)

In his will is our peace.

DANTE (*Paradiso*)

Let us remember these great truths: (1) There is nothing, however small or apparently indifferent, which has not been ordained or permitted by God – even to the fall of a leaf. (2) God is sufficiently wise, good, powerful and merciful to turn those events which are apparently the most calamitous to the good and the advantage of those who know how to adore and accept with humility all that his divine and adorable will permits.

JEAN-PIERRE DE CAUSSADE, S.J.
(*Abandonment to Divine Providence*)

God's will – peacefully do at each moment what at that moment ought to be done.

ST. KATHERINE DREXEL

The weakest of sinners can frustrate or crown a hope of God.

CHARLES PEGUY

A broken heart and God's will done would be better than that God's will should be avoided.

R. H. BENSON (*Come Rack! Come Rope!*)

It needs a very pure intention, as well as great spiritual discernment, always to recognize the divine voice.

R. H. BENSON (*The Friendship of Christ*)

Loss and possession, death and life are one.
There falls no shadow where there shines no sun.

HILAIRE BELLOC

GOOD FRIDAY

Today is suspended upon the Tree he who suspends the earth upon the waters *(thrice)*. He that is the king of angels is crowned with thorns. He who covers the heavens with clouds is covered with derisive purple. He who freed Adam in the Jordan is buffeted. The Bridegroom of the Church is pierced with nails. The Son of the Virgin is wounded with a spear. We adore your passion, O Christ *(thrice)*. Let us also behold your glorious resurrection.

BYZANTINE LITURGY (Triodion)

All creation was changed by fear when it saw you, O Christ, hanging upon the cross; the sun was darkened, and the foundations of the earth were shaken. All things suffered with the Creator of all things. O Lord, who for us did willingly endure, glory to you.

BYZANTINE LITURGY (Triodion)

GOODNESS

At the bottom of the heart of every human being, from earliest infancy until the tomb, there is something that goes on indomitably expecting, in the teeth of all experience of crimes committed, suffered and witnessed, that good and not evil will be done.

SIMONE WEIL

GOOD WORKS

Let your good works be deposits, that you may receive the sum due to you.

ST. IGNATIUS OF ANTIOCH
(Letter to St. Polycarp)

How quickly are the prayers of those who do good works heard! For it is precisely in fasting, almsgiving and prayer that our righteousness in this life consists. If you would have your prayers fly to God, equip them with the two wings of fasting and almsgiving.

ST. AUGUSTINE
(*On Psalm 42*)

Start by doing what is necessary, then do what is possible, and suddenly you are doing the impossible.

ST. FRANCIS OF ASSISI

Men's chief study nowadays, seems to be how they may best do without good works. They will go hanging and idling about God's vineyard, rather than come up, and be hired into it.

ST. THOMAS MORE

A Christian should always remember that the value of his good works is not based on their number and excellence, but on the love of God which prompts him to do these things.

ST. JOHN OF THE CROSS

Love's secret is to be always doing things for God, and not to mind because they are such very little ones.

F. W. FABER

They will be hushed by a good deed who laugh at a wise speech.

FRENCH PROVERB

An act of goodness, the least act of true goodness, is the best proof of the existence of God.

JACQUES MARITAIN

Tomorrow God isn't going to ask
What did you dream?
What did you think?
What did you plan?
What did you preach?
He's going to ask, What did you do?

MICHEL QUOIST (*With Open Heart*)

GOSPEL

Lord, help me to preach the Gospel wherever I go, and if I must, even through words.

ST. FRANCIS OF ASSISI

GOSSIP

Whoever gossips to you will gossip of you.

SPANISH PROVERB

GOVERNMENT

The best form of government is in a state or kingdom, wherein one is given the power to preside over all, while under him are others having governing powers: and yet a government of this kind is shared by all, both because all are eligible to govern, and because the rulers are chosen by all. For this is the best form of polity, being partly kingdom, since there is one at the head of all; partly aristocracy, in so far as a number of persons are set in authority; partly democracy, i.e. government by the people, and the people have the right to choose their rulers.

ST. THOMAS AQUINAS
(*Summa Theologica*)

Power resides, as in its subject, immediately in the whole state, for this power is by divine law, but divine law gives this power to no particular man, therefore divine law gives this power to the collected body.

ST. ROBERT BELLARMINE
(*De Laicis*)

Every country has the government it deserves.

JOSEPH DE MAISTRE

There is no worse heresy than that the office sanctifies the holder of it. That is the point at which the negation of Catholicism and the negation of Liberalism meet and keep high festival, and the end learns to justify the means.

LORD ACTON

There is no government without mumbo-jumbo.

HILAIRE BELLOC

GRACE

It is not enough for me that God has given me grace once, but he must give it always. I ask, that I may receive; and when I have received, I ask again. I am covetous of receiving God's bounty. He is never slow in giving, nor am I ever weary of receiving. The more I drink, the more thirsty I become.

ST. JEROME

Every holy thought is the gift of God, the inspiration of God, the grace of God.

ST. AMBROSE
(*Concerning Cain*)

It is not that we keep His commandments first, and that then He loves; but that He loves us, and then we keep His commandments. This is that grace, which is revealed to the humble, but hidden from the proud.

ST. AUGUSTINE

Grace has five effects in us: first, our soul is healed; second, we will good; third, we work effectively for it; fourth, we persevere; fifth, we break through to glory.

ST. THOMAS AQUINAS
(*Summa Theologica*)

Grace should not be reputed to be in the sacraments as though they were receptacles or vessels.

ST. THOMAS AQUINAS
(*Summa Theologica*)

You do yourself no credit if you watch and fast until you give yourself a headache.

You will derive no benefit from running barefoot to Rome or Jerusalem. You will not gain anything if you make people hang on your every word as you preach. You will not achieve anything by building churches or chapels, or by feeding the poor or by building hospitals. But you will have achieved something worthwhile if you truly love your neighbor and hate his sin. It is true that all the above-mentioned deeds are good, but they are performed by good and bad people alike. Anybody could do them if he had the inclination and the means. I do not think you achieve much by doing what everybody else can do. But to love your neighbor and hate his sin is something that only good men can do. And they can only do it if they have received God's grace for this. They are unable to achieve this through their own effort. As St. Paul has said: "God has poured out his love into our hearts by the Holy Spirit, whom he has given us" (Rom 5:5). This is much more difficult to achieve. Without this gift, no matter what good deeds are performed, nobody will be able to reach heaven. Through this gift all the deeds of a good man are indeed good. All of God's other gifts are given both to the elect and to the reprobate, and to the good and to the bad. This gift of love is reserved for some specially selected souls.

WALTER HILTON (*The Ladder of Perfection*)

Few souls understand what God would accomplish in them if they were to abandon themselves unreservedly to Him and if they were to allow His grace to mold them accordingly.

ST. IGNATIUS LOYOLA

The priest was still on his way, and finally I was bound to voice my deep regret that such delay threatened to deprive my comrade of the final consolations of our Church. He did not seem to hear me. But a few moments later he put his hand over mine, and his eyes entreated me to draw closer to him. He then uttered these words almost in my ear. And I am quite sure that I have recorded them accurately, for his voice, though halting, was strangely distinct.

"Does it matter? Grace is . . . everywhere."

I think he died just then.

GEORGES BERNANOS
(*The Diary of a Country Priest*)

You have no idea how much nastier I would be if I were not a Catholic. Without supernatural aid I should hardly be a human being.

EVELYN WAUGH (*to a friend*)

GRIEF

There are wounds of the spirit which never close, and are intended in God's mercy to bring us ever nearer to him, and to prevent us leaving him, by their very perpetuity. Such wounds, then, may almost be taken as a pledge, or at least as a ground for the humble trust, that God will give us the great gift of perseverance to the end. . . . This is how I comfort myself in my own great bereavements.

VENERABLE JOHN HENRY NEWMAN

GUARDIAN ANGEL

Have confidence in your guardian angel. Treat him as a very dear friend – that's what he is — and he will do a thousand services for you in the ordinary affairs of each day.

ST. JOSEMARÍA ESCRIVÁ (*The Way*)

H

HABIT

Habit is a shirt made of iron.

CZECH PROVERB

HAPPINESS

Happiness is the practice of the virtues.

ST. CLEMENT OF ALEXANDRIA

No one is really happy because he has what he wants, but only if he has things he ought to want.

ST. AUGUSTINE (On Psalm 26)

For in every ill-turn of fortune the most unhappy sort of unfortunate man is the one who has been happy.

BOETHIUS
(The Consolations of Philosophy)

Be merry, really merry. The life of a true Christian should be a perpetual jubilee, a prelude to the festivals of eternity.

ST. THEOPHANE VENARD

Much happiness is lost because it doesn't cost anything.

OSCAR WILDE

Happiness is a mystery like religion, and should never be rationalized.

G. K. CHESTERTON (Heretics)

HATRED

Whoever entertains in his heart any trace of hatred for anyone, regardless of what the offence may have been, is a stranger to the love of God. Love of God and hatred of any man are absolutely incompatible with one another.

ST. MAXIMUS THE CONFESSOR
(*Centuries on Charity*)

A hurtful act is the transference to others of the degradation which we feel in ourselves.

SIMONE WEIL

HEART

To my God, a heart of flame; to my fellow men, a heart of love; to myself, a heart of steel.

ST. AUGUSTINE

The hairs on your head are far easier to count than your feelings and the movements of your heart.

ST. AUGUSTINE (*Confessions*)

The heart has its reasons which reason cannot know.

BLAISE PASCAL (*Pensées*)

HEAVEN

God forbid that in a higher state of existence she should cease to think of me, to long to comfort me, she who loved more than words can tell.

ST. AUGUSTINE
(*of his mother, St. Monica*)

If you love me, do not weep. If you only knew the gift of God and what heaven is! If only you could hear the angels' songs from where you are, and see me among them! If you could only see before your eyes the eternal fields with their horizons and the new paths in which I walk! If only you could contemplate for one moment the Beauty that I see, Beauty before which all others fail and fade!

Why do you who saw me and loved me in the land of shadows, why do you think you will not see me and love me again in the land of unchanging realities?

Believe me, when death breaks your chains as it has broken mine, when, on the day chosen by God, your soul reaches heaven where I have preceded you, then you will see her who loved you and still loves you. You will find her heart the same, her tenderness even purer than before.

God forbid that on entering a happier life, I should become less loving, unfaithful to the memories and joys of my other life. You will see me again transfigured in ecstasy and happiness, no longer waiting for death, but ever hand in hand with you, walking in the new paths of light and life, slaking my thirst to the full at the feet of God from a fount of which one never tires, and which you will come to share with me.

Wipe away your tears, and if you love me truly, weep no more.

ST. AUGUSTINE (*of St. Monica*)

Is not this house as nigh heaven as my own?

ST. THOMAS MORE
(*imprisoned in the Tower of London*)

Farewell, my dear child, and pray for me, and I shall for you and your friends, that we may meet merrily in heaven.

ST. THOMAS MORE
(*last letter to his daughter, Margaret*)

The world is only peopled to people heaven.

ST. FRANCIS DE SALES
(*Letters to Persons in the World*)

I will spend my heaven doing good upon earth.

ST. THÉRÈSE OF LISIEUX

HELL

An ever-burning gehenna will burn up the condemned . . . weeping will be useless and prayer ineffectual. Too late they will believe in eternal punishment who would not believe in eternal life.

ST. CYPRIAN
(*To Demetrianus the Proconsul of Africa*)

Here sighs, with lamentations and loud moans,
Resounded through the air pierced by no star,
That e'en I wept at entering. Various tongues,
Horrible languages, outcries of woe,
Accents of anger, voices deep and hoarse,
With hands together smote that swelled the sounds,
Made up a tumult that forever whirls
Round through that air with solid darkness stain'd,
Like to the sand that in the whirlwind flies.

DANTE (*The Inferno*)

Abandon all hope, ye who enter here.

DANTE (*The Inferno*)

That the saints may enjoy their beatitude and the grace of God more abundantly they are permitted to see the punishment of the damned in hell.

ST. THOMAS AQUINAS
(*Summa Theologica*)

We are each our own devils and we make this world our hell.

OSCAR WILDE
(*The Duchess of Padua*)

Now of all these spiritual pains by far the greatest is the pain of loss, so great, in fact, that it is in itself a torment greater than all the others. Saint Thomas, the greatest doctor of the church, the angelic doctor, as he is called, says that the worst damnation consists in this that the understanding of man is totally deprived of divine light and his affection obstinately turned away from the goodness of God. God, remember, is a being infinitely good and therefore the loss of such a being must be infinitely painful. In this life we have not a very clear idea of what such a loss must be, but the damned in hell, for their greater torment, have a full understanding of that which they have lost, and understand that they have lost it through their own sins and have lost it for ever.

JAMES JOYCE
(*A Portrait of the Artist as a Young Man*)

Plunged into the flames were demons and lost souls, as if they were red hot coals, transparent and black or bronze colored, in human form, which floated about in the conflagration, borne by the flames, which issued from them, with clouds of smoke falling on all sides . . .

amid shrieks and groans of sorrow and despair that horrified us and caused us to tremble with fear. The devils could be distinguished by horrible and loathsome forms of animals, frightful and unknown, but transparent like black coals that have turned red hot.

SISTER LUCIA *(describing a vision at Fátima, July 13, 1917)*

You have told me, O God, to believe in hell. But you have forbidden me to think, with any certainty, of any man as damned.

PIERRE TEILHARD DE CHARDIN, S.J.
(Le Milieu Divin)

Yes, because it is a dogma of the Church – but I don't believe anyone is in it.

ABBÉ ARTHUR MUGNIER
(when asked if he believed in hell)

Hell, madam, is to love no more.

GEORGES BERNANOS
(Diary of a Country Priest)

There is a hell. A trite enough statement, you think. I will repeat it, then: there is a hell!
Echo it, at the right moment, in the ears of one friend, and another, and another.

ST. JOSEMARÍA ESCRIVÁ
(The Way)

Hell is full of noise, and is probably full of clocks, that emphasize the time that never passes.

ARCHBISHOP FULTON J. SHEEN

HERESY

The world trembled and groaned to find itself Arian.

ST. JEROME

If forgers and malefactors are put to death by the secular power, there is much more reason for excommunicating and even putting to death one convicted of heresy.

ST. THOMAS AQUINAS
(*Summa Theologica*)

The denial of a scheme wholesale is not heresy, and has not the creative power of a heresy. It is of the essence of heresy that it leaves standing a great part of the structure it attacks. On this account it can appeal to believers and continues to affect their lives through deflecting them from their original characters. Wherefore, it is said of heresies that "they survive by the truths they retain."

HILAIRE BELLOC
(*The Great Heresies*)

HISTORY

Should the reader discover any inaccuracies in what I have written, I humbly beg that he will not impute them to me because, as the laws of history require, I have labored honestly to transmit whatever I could ascertain from common report for the instruction of posterity.

THE VENERABLE BEDE
(*The Ecclesiastical History of the English People*)

The first law of history is not to dare to utter falsehood; the second, not to fear to speak the truth.

POPE LEO XIII
(*On the Opening of the Vatican Archives*)

Truth lies in proportion. You do not tell a historical truth by merely stating a known fact; nor even by stating a number of facts in a certain and true order. You can tell it justly only by stating the known things in the order of their values.

HILAIRE BELLOC (*The Crisis of Civilization*)

Every major question in history is a religious question. [Religion] has more effect in molding life than nationalism or a common language.

HILAIRE BELLOC

We possess nothing certainly except the past.

EVELYN WAUGH (*Brideshead Revisted*)

HOLINESS

Not to go along the way to God is to go back.

ST. THOMAS AQUINAS (*Commentary on Ephesians 4*)

It is not what we do that makes us holy. We make holy what we do.

MEISTER ECKHART

God has not called his servants to a mediocre, ordinary life, but rather to the perfection of a sublime holiness.

BLESSED HENRY SUSO

God deliver me from sullen saints!

ST. TERESA OF ÁVILA

The whole sanctity and perfection of a person consists in loving Jesus Christ.

ST. ALPHONSUS LIGUORI

Sanctity is the love of God and of man, carried to a sublime extravagance.

JEAN-BAPTISTE LACORDIARE, O.P.

You cannot be half a saint. You must be a whole saint or no saint at all.

ST. THÉRÈSE OF LISIEUX

Without reserve fly from what the world loves. Seek to be despised, but not to merit it. . . . God wills me to be a saint. I will to be a saint. *Therefore I shall be a saint.* Live for Eternity, Eternity, Eternity.

CORNELIA CONNOLLY

Holiness rather than peace.

(*A motto of* VENERABLE JOHN HENRY NEWMAN)

Holiness consists not in doing uncommon things, but in doing all common things with uncommon fervor.

CARDINAL HENRY EDWARD MANNING
(*The Eternal Priesthood*)

The "stuff" of saints. That's what is said about some people – that they have the stuff of saints. But apart from the fact that saints are not made of "stuff," having "stuff" is not sufficient.

A great spirit of obedience to a director and a great readiness to correspond to grace are required.

ST. JOSEMARÍA ESCRIVÁ (*The Way*)

HOLOCAUST

We who live beneath a sky still stained with the smoke of crematoria, have paid a high price to learn that evil is really evil.

FRANÇOIS MAURIAC (*Essays*)

HOLY COMMUNION

And let all take care that no unbaptized person taste of the Eucharist nor a mouse or other animal, and that none of it at all fall and be lost. For it is the Body of Christ to be eaten by them that believe and not to be lightly thought of.

ST. HIPPOLITUS (*The Apostolic Tradition*)

As two pieces of wax fused together make one, so he who receives holy communion is so united with Christ that Christ is in him and he is in Christ.

ST. CYRIL OF ALEXANDRIA

If it is daily bread, why do you take it once a year, as the Greeks in the east are accustomed to do? Take daily what is to profit you daily. So live that you may deserve to receive it daily. He who does not deserve to receive it daily, does not deserve to receive it once a year.

ST. AMBROSE (*On The Sacraments*)

If you have received worthily, you are what you have received.

ST. AUGUSTINE

If anybody knows from experience that daily communion increases fervor without lessening reverence, then let him go every day. But if anybody finds that devotion is lessened and devotion not much increased, then let him sometime abstain, so as to draw nigh afterwards with better dispositions.

ST. THOMAS AQUINAS
(*Commentary on the Sentences*)

Every consecrated Host is made to burn itself up with love in a human heart.

ST. JOHN VIANNEY (*The Curé of Ars*)

In one day the Eucharist will make you produce more for the glory of God than a whole lifetime without it.

ST. PETER JULIAN EYMARD

Jesus has prepared not just one Host, but one for every day of our life. The Hosts for us are ready. Let us not forfeit even one of them.

ST. PETER JULIAN EYMARD

Holy Communion is the shortest and safest way to heaven.

POPE ST. PIUS X

Never lose a communion by your own fault. Communion is more than life, more than all the goods of this world, more than the entire universe. It is God Himself, it is Jesus. Can you prefer anything else? If you love Jesus sincerely, can you willfully lose the grace of his coming within you? Jesus asks you to love him with all the energy and the simplicity of your heart.

VENERABLE CHARLES DE FOUCAULD

The culmination of the Mass is not the consecration, but communion.

ST. MAXIMILIAN KOLBE

If angels could be jealous of men, they would be so for one reason: Holy Communion.

ST. MAXIMILIAN KOLBE

The day's food for the day's march . . . that is what holy communion is meant to be.

RONALD KNOX

You are worried and sad because your communions are cold and barren. Tell me, when you approach the sacrament, do you seek yourself or do you seek Jesus? If you seek yourself, there is reason indeed to be sad. But if you seek Christ – as you ought – can you want a surer sign than the Cross than to know you've found him?

ST. JOSEMARÍA ESCRIVÁ (*The Way*)

When Catholics are asked, "Do you have a personal relationship with Jesus Christ?" they should answer a resounding YES! There is no closer union with Jesus than when you receive him in the Eucharist. You too can say with St. Paul, " . . . and the life I now live is not my own CHRIST IS LIVING IN ME." (Gal 2:20)

RICHARD L. CARROLL

It is in keeping with the very meaning of the Eucharist that the faithful, if they have the required dispositions, *receive communion each time* they participate in the Mass.

CATECHISM OF THE CATHOLIC CHURCH, 1388

HOLY SOULS

It cannot be denied that the souls of the dead obtain relief through the piety of their living friends, when they have the Sacrifice of the Mediator offered for them, or when alms are given in the church on their behalf. But these things benefit only those who during their lives merited that these services should one day help them.

ST. AUGUSTINE (Enchiridion)

O God, the Creator and Redeemer of all the faithful, grant to the souls of thy servants departed the remission of all their sins, that, by our devout prayers, they may obtain that pardon for their sins which they have always desired.

THE ROMAN MISSAL
(Collect for First Mass of All Souls)

HOLY SPIRIT

Those who are led by the Holy Spirit have true ideas; that is why so many ignorant people are wiser than the learned. The Holy Spirit is light and strength.

ST. JOHN VIANNEY,
(The Curé of Ars)

Now I wish you all the seven gifts of the Holy Ghost and that his Holy Spirit may whisper in your ear all that he wishes you to do.

CORNELIA CONNOLLY

I am a man of hope, not for human reasons, nor from any natural optimism, but because I believe the Holy Spirit is at work in the Church and in the world, even when his name remains unheard.

CARDINAL LEO SUENENS

The depths in us are not stagnant pools of bitterness but the waters of infinity springing up into eternal life. It is easy to stir up the slime, but it needs faith to see behind and through all these dark forces a much more powerful force – the power of the presence of the Holy Spirit.

KARL RAHNER, S.J. (*On Prayer*)

There is a gentle breeze if we can but catch it, which blows all the time to help us on our journey through life to our final destination. That breeze is the Holy Spirit. But the wind cannot be caught or used unless the sail is hoisted, and the hoisting is our task. We must be on the watch, ready to recognize it and play our part. God does hold us, and will lead us, if we want it; but we must want it.

CARDINAL BASIL HUME, O.S.B.

Today I realize what it is that I have been noticing since yesterday: everyone is kind. I have not met one person who is not friendly, solicitous and generous. The police officers and soldiers are patient and polite at the barricaded checkpoints. On the way into the site, Salvation Army volunteers cheerfully offer me sodas, bottled water, and candy bars. The firefighters who work during their grief and shock ask me how I am doing. One is surrounded by the physical signs of charity as well: food, clothing, tents, trucks, blankets and, most touching of all, hundreds of handwritten notes from elementary school children.

Here it feels as if everyone is working together for a common good. It is an experience of love and community unlike any I have ever known. And to me it signals the presence of the Holy Spirit. For it is the Spirit that brings unity and concord, that causes peace and harmony, that banishes division and strife.

JAMES MARTIN, S.J.
(*Searching for God at Ground Zero*)

HOMELESS

I am my brother's keeper, and he's sleeping pretty rough these days.

ARCHBISHOP DEREK WORLOCK

HOMOSEXUALITY

The number of men and women who have deep-seated homosexual tendencies is not negligible. They do not choose their homosexual condition; for most of them it is a trial. They must be accepted with respect, compassion and sensitivity. Every sign of unjust discrimination in their regard must be avoided. These persons are called to fulfill God's will in their lives and, if they are Christians, to unite to the sacrifice of the Lord's Cross the difficulties they may encounter from their condition.

CATECHISM OF THE CATHOLIC CHURCH, 2358

For those who really want it, reparative growth is a possibility and happens regularly. Men and women leave behind not only the homosexual lifestyle but also the very feelings of same-sex attraction. While all can investigate this option, teens and young adults are especially invited to consult competent therapists.

FATHER JOHN HARVEY,
Founder of *Courage*

HOPE

If you do not hope, you will not find what is beyond your hope.

ST. CLEMENT OF ALEXANDRIA (*Stromateis*)

May he support us all the day long, till the shades lengthen, and the evening comes, and the busy world is hushed, and the fever of life is over, and our work is done! Then in his mercy may he give us a safe lodging, and a holy rest, and peace at last.

VENERABLE JOHN HENRY NEWMAN
(*Sermons Bearing on Subjects of the Day*)

I'm not very conscious of his presence, but I hope he's dogging my footsteps.

GRAHAM GREENE
(*newspaper interview*)

Each time a man stands up for an ideal, or acts to improve the lot of others, or strikes out against injustice, he sends forth a tiny ripple of hope. And crossing each other from a million different centers of energy and daring, those ripples build a current which can sweep down the mightiest walls of oppression

ROBERT F. KENNEDY

HOSPITALITY

A brother came to a certain solitary, and when he was going away from him he said: "Forgive me, Father, for I have made you break your rule." He answered: "My rule is to receive you with hospitality and send you away in peace."

THE DESERT FATHERS

Every guest who comes to the monastery shall be received as if he were Christ himself.

ST. BENEDICT (*The Holy Rule*)

The doorkeeper should always have a cell near the gate, so that anyone arriving is always sure of finding someone on hand to give him a welcome. As soon as anyone knocks, the doorkeeper must answer *Deo Gratias,* or give him a blessing, and open the gate quickly.

ST. BENEDICT (*The Holy Rule*)

Every parish should have its Works of Mercy Center, where the poor are fed daily, without question, in the name of Jesus Christ who himself was hungry and homeless at times on this earth.

DOROTHY DAY
(*The Catholic Worker, March 1938*)

A day never passed without Dorothy speaking of the works of mercy. . . . She helped us to understand that a merciful life has so many levels: there is a hunger not only for food but for faith, not only for a place at the table but for a real welcome, not only for assistance but also for listening, not only for kind words but also for truthful words. There is not only hospitality of the door but also of the face and heart.

JIM FOREST
(*Dorothy Day – A Saint for Our Age?*)

HUMAN RACE

The human race, to which so many of my readers belong. . . .

G. K. CHESTERTON
(*The Napoleon of Notting Hill*)

The Big Lie tells us that we are strangers and sojourners on this planet, that our flesh, our blood, our instincts for survival are our enemies. Originally we lived as discarnate orbs of light in the heavenly light. We have fallen to this earth and into this clay through accident or sin. We must spend our lives suppressing our hungers and thirsts and shunning our fellow-beings, so that we can dematerialize and fly away to our stars.

ROSEMARY RUETHER
(*Sexism and God-Talk*)

HUMAN RIGHTS

By our Apostolic authority we define and proclaim that Indians, or any peoples who may hereafter be discovered by Catholics, although they be not Christian, must in no way be deprived of their liberty or their possessions.

POPE PAUL III (*Sublimis Deus*)

In times past, cruel practices were commonly used by legitimate governments to maintain law and order, often without protest from the Pastors of the Church, who themselves adopted in their own tribunals the prescriptions of Roman law concerning torture. Regrettable as these facts are, the Church always taught the duty of clemency and mercy. She forbade clerics to shed blood. In recent times it has become evident that these cruel practices were neither necessary for public order, nor in conformity with the legitimate rights of the human person. On the contrary, these practices led to ones even more degrading. It is necessary to work for their abolition. We must pray for the victims and their tormentors.

THE CATECHISM OF THE CATHOLIC CHURCH, 2298

HUMILITY

Humility is the garment of God. The incarnate Word was clothed in it, and through it, conversed with us in our bodies, covering the radiance of his greatness and his glory by this humility, lest the creature be scorched by the sight of him. The creature could not have looked at him, had he not taken on some part of it and so conversed with it. Therefore every man who clothes himself in garments of humility becomes clothed in Christ himself. . . .

ST. ISAAK OF SYRIA

No structure of virtue can possibly be raised in our soul unless, first, the foundations of true humility are laid in our heart.

ST. JOHN CASSIAN

There is something in humility which strangely exalts the heart.

ST. AUGUSTINE (*The City of God*)

For he is less in need who is without a garment, than he who is without humility.

POPE ST. GREGORY THE GREAT (*Morals*)

Humility, which humiliation teaches us to practice, is the foundation of the entire spiritual fabric. Thus humiliation is the way to humility, as patience to peace, as reading to knowledge. If you long for the virtue of humility, you must not flee from the way of humiliation. For if you do not allow yourself to be humiliated, you cannot attain to humility.

ST. BERNARD OF CLAIRVAUX (*Letters*)

Great graces cannot be obtained without humility. . . .
When you yourself experience humiliation, you should
take it as a sure sign that some great grace is in store.

ST. BERNARD OF CLAIRVAUX
(*Sermons on the Canticle of Canticles*)

Humility in itself is nothing other than a man's true
knowing and feeling about himself as he is.

THE CLOUD OF UNKNOWING

Never listen to or say evil of anyone except yourself, and
when that gives you pleasure you are making progress.

ST. TERESA OF ÁVILA (*Maxims*)

If someone else is well spoken of, be more pleased than
if it were yourself; this is easy enough, for if you were
really humble, it would vex you to be praised. . . . Force
your will, as far as possible, to comply in all things
with [others'] wishes, even though sometimes you may
lose your own rights by doing so. Forget your self-inter-
ests for theirs, however much nature may rebel.

ST. TERESA OF ÁVILA
(*The Interior Castle*)

Real excellence and humility are not incompatible one
with the other; on the contrary, they are twin sisters.

JEAN-BAPTISTE LACORDAIRE, O.P.

The gate of heaven is very low; only the humble can
enter it.

ST. ELIZABETH SETON

Humility is one of the most difficult virtues both to
attain and to ascertain. It lies close upon the heart itself,

and its tests are exceedingly delicate and subtle. Its counterfeits abound.

VENERABLE JOHN HENRY NEWMAN
(*The Idea of a University*)

The science of humility rests upon the knowledge of God and of oneself.

ARCHBISHOP WILLIAM BERNARD ULLATHORNE, O.S.B.
(*Humility and Patience*)

Humility does not consist in ignorance of truth. If a man is above the average height of men, he cannot help knowing it.

CARDINAL HENRY EDWARD MANNING
(*Pastime Papers*)

O Jesus, meek and humble of heart, hear me.
From the desire of being esteemed, deliver me, O Jesus.
From the desire of being loved, deliver me, O Jesus.
From the desire of being extolled, deliver me, O Jesus.
From the desire of being honored, deliver me, O Jesus.
From the desire of being praised, deliver me, O Jesus.
From the desire of being preferred to others, deliver me,
    O Jesus.
From the desire of being consulted, deliver me, O Jesus.
From the desire of being approved, deliver me, O Jesus.
From the fear of being humiliated, deliver me, O Jesus.
From the fear of being despised, deliver me, O Jesus.
From the fear of suffering rebukes, deliver me, O Jesus.
From the fear of being calumniated, deliver me,
    O Jesus.
From the fear of being forgotten, deliver me, O Jesus.
From the fear of being ridiculed, deliver me, O Jesus.
From the fear of being wronged, deliver me, O Jesus.

From the fear of being suspected, deliver me, O Jesus.

That others may be loved more than I, Jesus, grant me the grace to desire it.

That others may be esteemed more than I, Jesus, grant me the grace to desire it.

That, in the opinion of the world, others may increase and I may decrease, Jesus, grant me the grace to desire it.

That others may be chosen and I set aside, Jesus, grant me the grace to desire it.

That others may be praised and I go unnoticed, Jesus, grant me the grace to desire it.

That others may be preferred to me in everything, Jesus, grant me the grace to desire it.

That others may become holier than I, provided that I become as holy as I should, Jesus, grant me the grace to desire it.

CARDINAL RAPHAEL MERRY DEL VAL

The day you see yourself as you are, you will think it natural to be despised by others.

ST. JOSEMARÍA ESCRIVÁ (*The Way*)

You're not humble when you humble yourself, but when you are humbled by others and you bear it for Christ.

ST. JOSEMARÍA ESCRIVÁ (*The Way*)

Humility is the mother of all virtues; purity, charity and obedience. It is in being humble that our love becomes real, devoted and ardent. If you are humble nothing will touch you, neither praise nor disgrace, because you know what you are. If you are blamed you will not be discouraged. If they call you a saint you will not put yourself on a pedestal.

BLESSED MOTHER TERESA (*The Joy in Loving*)

The Lord so loves humility that at times he allows grave sins. Why? That those who have committed them, these sins, after repenting, be humbled. We would never believe we are half a saint, half an angel, when we know we are guilty of grievous sins. The Lord so urged us: be humble. Even if you have done great things, say: We are useless servants.

POPE JOHN PAUL I
(*General Audience, September 6, 1978*)

HYPOCRISY

. . . You ought to use the greatest caution, even in doing good things. For it may be that, in carrying out some good works, you are seeking only the favor and good graces of men: or the desire of praise may overtake you, and what is done for outward effect, fail of its inward reward.

POPE ST. GREGORY THE GREAT
(*Homily 12 on the Gospels*)

When Christ condemned the Pharisees, make sure he did not have you in mind.

QUENTIN DE LA BÉDOYÈRE

I

IDEALS

If we put an absurdly high ideal before us, it ceases to be an ideal at all, since we have no idea of acting upon it.

F. W. FABER
(*Spiritual Conferences*)

IDLENESS

Idleness is the enemy of the soul.

ST. BENEDICT (*The Holy Rule*)

Never be entirely idle: but be either reading, or writing, or praying, or meditating, or endeavoring something for the public good.

THOMAS À KEMPIS
(*The Imitation of Christ*)

To have too much to do is, for most men, safer than to have too little.

CARDINAL HENRY EDWARD MANNING
(*The Eternal Priesthood*)

We only deliberately waste time with those we love – it is the purest sign that we love someone if we choose to spend time idly in their presence when we could be doing something more constructive.

SHEILA CASSIDY
(*Prayer for Pilgrims*)

IDOLATRY

How guilty are people who hang on to their idols and their miserable superstitions! Idols have eyes and do not see, they have ears and do not hear, noses and do not smell, hands and do not feel, feet and do not walk. . . . Though we have tried hard to understand why you cling to your belief in these home-made gods, we remain bewildered that you should be so deceived.

POPE BONIFACE V
(*Letter to Edwin, King of Northumbria*)

Whatever a man seeks, honors or exalts more than God, that is the god of his idolatry.

ARCHBISHOP WILLIAM BERNARD ULLATHORNE, O.S.B.
(*Humility and Patience*)

IGNATIUS OF LOYOLA

He was always rather inclined toward love; moreover, he seemed all love, and because of that he was universally loved by all. There was no one in the Society who did not have much great love for him and did not consider himself much loved by him.

LUIS GONCALVES DE CAMARA, S.J.

Going abroad with his companion, he wore a sombrero and the ecclesiastical cloak yet used in Spain: his lowered eyes he lifted not to a woman when she spoke to him. The wounded leg of Pamplona, always painful to the touch, made him limp somewhat, though he tried to hide the limp; and, save when he raised his hand in salute, nothing was to be seen but his face. That was quiet and grave; but those who saw him in old age averred that it seemed to them divine in conversation. To the last he retained the extraordinary power and control of his eyes, when the downcast glance was lifted to one who spoke with him. His dress was now neat, and he especially enjoined neatness on his followers, without departing from the homeliness proper to their poverty. They were to follow the dress of the place where they lived, avoiding singularity. But, provided the garb were clean and tidy, he so inculcated poverty that Lainez and Salmeron appeared even before the Council of Trent in patched clothes.

FRANCIS THOMPSON
(*The Life of St. Ignatius Loyola*)

IMAGINATION

Keep your imagination under control. You must sometimes correct it, sometimes assist it. For it is all important for our happiness and balances reason. The imagination can tyrannize ... unless you lord over it with the most prudent self-control.

BALTASAR GRACIÁN, S.J.
(*The Art of Worldly Wisdom*)

IMMORTALITY

The world cannot reconcile itself to the silence of the grave; it is haunted and, in idle moments when it is taken off its guard, it shows itself thoroughly committed to some kind of belief in an after-life.

M.C. D'ARCY, S.J.
(*Death and Life*)

Primitive men did not philosophize; but for all that, they had their own way, an instinctive, non-conceptual way, of believing in the soul's immortality. It was a belief rooted in an obscure experience of the self, and in the natural aspirations of the spirit in us to overcome death.

JACQUES MARITAIN
(*The Range of Reason*)

The belief in immortality rests not very much on the hope of going on. Few of us want to do that, but we would very much like to begin again.

HEYWOOD BROUN (*Pieces of Hate*)

Man is sinful. Life is sad. There is something beyond.

CARDINAL RICHARD J. CUSHING

IMPRISONMENT

The first step in punitive action, the arrest, must not be done wantonly, but must respect juridical norms. It is not permissible that even the most culpable citizen should be liable to arbitrary arrest and to disappear without a word into prison. To send someone into a concentration camp and keep him there without any regular trial is a mockery of the law.

POPE PIUS XII (*Address to 6th International Congress of Penal Law, 1953*)

INCARNATION

He became what we are that he might make us what he is.

ST. ATHANASIUS

Every Christian must be Christ himself.

ANGELUS SILESIUS

Indeed I think myself that the chief reason why the unseen God willed to appear in the flesh and mix with men was that he might draw to himself in flesh the love of those who were not yet able to love save in a carnal manner, and so to lead them on gradually to spiritual love.

ST. BERNARD OF CLAIRVAUX
(Sermons on the Canticle of Canticles)

It is safer to teach that the Incarnation was ordained by God as a remedy for sin, and that if no sin had come the Incarnation would not have taken place. Nevertheless, God's power should not be circumscribed: he might have become incarnate even if sin had never entered.

ST. THOMAS AQUINAS
(Summa Theologica)

INCULTURATION

In my numerous pastoral visits I have seen, throughout the world, the great vitality with which the celebration of the Eucharist can have when marked by the forms, styles and sensibilities of different cultures. By adaptation to the changing conditions of time and place, the Eucharist offers sustenance not only to individuals but to entire peoples, and it shapes cultures inspired by Christianity.

POPE JOHN PAUL II
(Ecclesia de Eucharistia)

INDULGENCES

I can't see why Almighty God shouldn't indulgence all sorts of pious practices which aren't indulgenced by the Church; shouldn't give you or me the equivalent of a seven years' indulgence when we get up to make room for an old lady in a bus.

RONALD KNOX

INDUSTRIALISM

Dead matter leaves the factory ennobled and transformed, whereas men are corrupted and degraded.

POPE PIUS XI (*Quadragesimo Anno*)

INGRATITUDE

Ingratitude is the soul's enemy; it empties it of merit, scatters its virtues, and deprives it of graces. Like a hot, parching wind it dries up the wellspring of holiness, the dew of mercy and the streams of grace.

ST. BERNARD OF CLAIRVAUX
(*Sermons on the Canticle of Canticles*)

INQUISITION

The heretic in the hands of the Holy Office is safe from violence, is assured of a fair trial, and cannot suffer death, even when guilty, if repentance follows sin. Innumerable lives of heretics have been saved because the Holy Office has taken them out of the hands of the people, and because the people have yielded them up, knowing that the Holy Office would deal with them. Before the Holy Office existed, and even now when its officers are not within reach, the unfortunate wretch suspected of heresy, perhaps quite ignorantly and unjustly, is stoned, torn in pieces, drowned, burned in his house with all his innocent children, without a trial, unshriven, unburied save as a dog is buried: all of them deeds hateful to God and most cruel to man. Gentlemen: I am compassionate by nature as well as by my profession; and though the work I have to do may seem cruel to those who do not know how much more cruel it would be to leave it undone, I would go to the stake myself sooner than do it if I did not know its righteousness, its necessity, its essential mercy.

GEORGE BERNARD SHAW (*St. Joan*)

INSULT

A harvest of virtues should be reaped from a crop of insults and injuries.

J. P. CAMUS
(*The Spirit of St. Francis de Sales*)

INTEGRITY

You compel your subjects to know and obey your laws. With far more energy you should exact of yourself knowledge and obedience to the laws of Christ, your king! You judge it an infamous crime, for which there can be no punishment terrible enough, for one who has sworn allegiance to his king to revolt from him. On what grounds, then, do you grant yourself pardon and consider as a matter of sport and jest the countless times you have broken the laws of Christ, to whom you swore allegiance in your baptism, to whose cause you pledged yourself, by whose sacraments you are bound and pledged?

ERASMUS
(*The Education of a Christian Prince*)

INTELLECT AND IMAGINATION

The first difficulty in the way of the intellect's functioning well is that it hates to function at all, at any rate beyond the point where the functioning begins to require effort. The result is that when any matter arises which is properly the job of the intellect, then either nothing gets done at all, or the imagination leaps in and does it instead. There is nothing to be done with the intellect until imagination has been put firmly in its place. . . .

. . . Imagination acts as a censor upon what the intellect shall accept. Tell a man, for instance, that his soul has no shape or size or color or weight, and the chances are that he will retort that such a thing is inconceivable. If we reply that it is not inconceivable but only unimaginable, he will consider that we have conceded his case – and will proceed to use the word "unimaginable" with the same happy finality as the word "inconceivable." For indeed in the usage of our day, the two words have become interchangeable. That they are thus interchangeable is a measure of the decline of thinking, and to sort them out and see them as distinct is an essential first step in the mind's movement towards health.

FRANK SHEED (*Theology and Sanity*)

INTELLECTUALS

If there is one class of men whom history has proved especially and supremely capable of going quite wrong in all directions, it is the class of highly intellectual men. I would always prefer to go by the bulk of humanity; that is why I am a democrat.

G. K. CHESTERTON (*All Things Considered*)

INTERCESSION

You victorious martyrs who endured torments gladly for the sake of the God and Savior, you who have boldness of speech towards the Lord Himself, you saints, intercede for us who are timid and sinful men, full of sloth, that the grace of Christ may come upon us, and enlighten the hearts of all of us that so we may love him.

ST. EPHRAIM OF SYRIA
(*Commentary on Mark*)

INTOLERANCE

I heartily pray that religious intolerance may never take root in our favored land. May the only king to force our conscience be the King of kings; may the only prison erected among us for the sin of unbelief be the prison of a troubled conscience; and may our only motive for embracing the truth be not the fear of man, but the love of truth and of God.

CARDINAL JAMES GIBBONS
(*The Faith of Our Fathers*)

IN VITRO FERTILIZATION

Human embryos obtained in vitro are human beings and are subjects with rights; their dignity and right to life must be respected from the first moment of their existence. It is immoral to produce human embryos destined to be exploited as disposable biological material.

POPE JOHN PAUL II
(*Evangelium Vitae*, 1995)

Stepping away from God's law always introduces chaos into our lives. Nowhere is this truer than in the case of in vitro fertilization. The reproductive revolution has had the ability to separate genetic parenting from gestational parenting and from social parenting; and the agent who brings it all about, a biotechnician, will be still another person.

In other words, we can arrange from the outset that one or more of the genetic parents are different from the woman who will carry the child, or the couple who will bring the child up. One or both of the donors might be deceased, for even the eggs might be extracted from aborted fetuses or a recently deceased woman.

Sperm and eggs are being bought and sold and wombs are being rented. Typical prices for ova are $6,500, sperm $1,800 and surrogate motherhood $45,000. In California there is a Nobel Prize Winners' sperm bank where someone can purchase "genius sperm" in the first step towards the "designer baby." Anyone who has enough money can contract for the production of human beings according to the desired specifications.

BISHOP SEAN P. O'MALLEY, O.F.M., CAP. *(In Vitro Fertilization: Ethical Implications & Alternatives: A Pastoral Letter)*

IRISH, THE

The land of saints and scholars.

ANONYMOUS

The Irish are Christian in name but pagan in fact.

ST. BERNARD OF CLAIRVAUX

IRISH BLESSINGS

May the road rise to meet you,
May the wind be always at your back,
May the sun shine warm upon your face,
The rains fall soft upon your fields,
And, until we meet again,
May God hold you in the hollow of his hand.

Deep peace of the Running Wave to you.
Deep peace of the Flowing Air to you.
Deep peace of the Quiet Earth to you.
Deep peace of the Shining Stars to you.
Deep peace of the Son of Peace to you.

May God be with you and bless you,
May you see your children's children,
May you be poor in misfortune, rich in blessings,

May you know nothing but happiness
From this day forward.

ANONYMOUS (Wedding Blessing)

Grant me a sense of humor, Lord,
the saving grace to see a joke,
To win some happiness from life,
And pass it on to other folk.

May you have the hindsight to know where you've been
the foresight to know where you're going
and the insight to know when you're going too far.

May you live to be a hundred years, with one extra
year to repent!

May you be in heaven half an hour before the devil
knows you're dead.

God save all here, barrin' the cat.

TRADITIONAL

ISLAM

Islam shook me deeply. Seeing such faith, seeing people living in the continual presence of God, I came to glimpse something worthy and more real than worldly occupations.

VENERABLE CHARLES DE FOUCAULD

The Church regards with esteem also the Muslims.... Though they do not acknowledge Jesus as God, they revere him as a prophet. They also honor Mary, His Virgin Mother, at times even calling on her with devotion....

Since in the course of centuries not a few quarrels and hostilities have arisen between Christians and Muslims, this sacred synod urges all to forget the past and to work sincerely for mutual understanding, and also to preserve and promote together for the benefit of all mankind social justice, moral welfare, peace and freedom

SECOND VATICAN COUNCIL
(*Non-Christian Religions*)

J

JESUS PRAYER

The more rain falls on the earth, the softer it makes it; similarly, Christ's holy name gladdens the earth of our heart the more we call upon it.

St. Hesychois the Priest
(*from the Philokalia*)

In the days when Russia was Christian there lived a man who longed to obey the precept "Pray without ceasing." A holy old priest advised him to repeat over and over again the words: "Lord Jesus Christ, have mercy upon me." This he called the Prayer of Jesus, and from 1,500 he passed to 3,000 and presently 6,000 repetitions a day. He went on increasing the number until at last, verbally or mentally, he spoke the words with every breath he drew.

Changed slightly, in the spirit of the Our Father, to "Lord Jesus Christ, have mercy upon *us,*" they become the perfect words with which to calm the fret and fill the empty, idle business of modern life. We can say them as we queue for fish or for a bus. We can repeat them upon each bead of our rosaries – praying for our fellow guildsmen, for all our friends, for all Christians, for all the world.... We can, too, from time to time, vary the words by saying, "Lord Jesus Christ, have mercy upon the souls in Purgatory."

Catholic Evidence Guild Prayer Book

JEWS

The race of the Hebrews is not new, but is honored among all men for its antiquity and is itself well known to all.

> EUSEBIUS OF CAESARIA
> (*Ecclesiastical History*)

For us the Jews are Scripture's living words, because they remind us of what Our Lord suffered. They are not to be persecuted, killed, or even put to flight.

> ST. BERNARD OF CLAIRVAUX

God holds the Jews most dear for the sake of their Fathers . . . . Since the spiritual patrimony common to Christians and Jews is thus so great . . . the Jews should not be presented as rejected or accursed by God . . . the Church decries . . . displays of anti-Semitism, directed against Jews at any time and by anyone.

> SECOND VATICAN COUNCIL
> (*Non-Christian Religions*)

The Jews are our elder brothers in faith.

> POPE JOHN PAUL II

JOHN PAUL II, POPE

The pontiff's beliefs and actions are driven by a passionate desire to improve the spiritual, moral and material world of each person. . . . I wish from the bottom of my heart that heaven allows him to serve mankind under God's guidance for as long as possible.

> MIKHAIL GORBACHEV

JOY

We may always rejoice, if we will only keep our head a little raised above the flood of human things.

ST. JOHN CHRYSOSTOM

I should like a great lake of ale
For the King of Kings.
I should like the family of heaven
To be drinking it through time eternal . . .
I should like cheerfulness
To be in their drinking;
I should like Jesus,
Too, to be there among them.
I should like the three
Marys of illustrious renown;
I should like the people
Of heaven there from all parts . . .

ST. BRIGID (*attributed*)

Let the brothers ever avoid appearing gloomy, sad, and clouded, like the hypocrites; but let one ever be found joyous in the Lord, gay, amiable, joyous, as is meet.

ST. FRANCIS OF ASSISI

If there is joy in the world, surely the man of pure heart possesses it.

THOMAS À KEMPIS (*The Imitation of Christ*)

The most profound joy has more of gravity than gaiety in it.

MICHEL DE MONTAIGNE (ESSAYS)

Joy is the echo of God's life in us.

BLESSED COLUMBA MARMION, O.S.B.

Joy is the gigantic secret of the Christian.

G. K. CHESTERTON

Joy is the infallible sign of the presence of God.

LÉON BLOY

It is wrong to be sad.
Christians cannot be pessimists.
Christians must always nourish in their hearts the
    fullness of joy.
Try it, brothers and sisters;
I have tried it many times and in the darkest
    moments,
when slander and persecution were at their worst;
to unite myself intimately with Christ, my friend
and to feel a comfort
that all the joys of the earth do not give –
the joy of feeling oneself close to God,
even when humans do not understand one.
It is the deepest joy the heart can have.

ARCHBISHOP OSCAR ROMERO
(*The Violence of Love*)

By believing in Christ we are believing in joy, by embracing the crucified Christ we are embracing joy without knowing it, and the Cross expands within us our capacity for the happiness to come.

RENÉ VOILLAUME

One filled with joy preaches without preaching.

BLESSED MOTHER TERESA

JUDGING OTHERS

A certain brother had sinned, and the priest commanded him to go out from the church. But Bessarion rose up and went out with him, saying, "I too am a sinful man."

THE SAYINGS OF THE FATHERS

Those who look well after their own consciences rarely fall into the sin of judging others.

JEAN PIERRE CAMUS
(*The Spirit of St. Francis de Sales*)

We cannot judge a man's virtues, since we do not know his starting point. And the best we can do with our own is to make a crude judgment about whether we are progressing or regressing.

QUENTIN DE LA BÉDOYÈRE

JUSTICE

Audi alteram partem.
Hear the other side.

ST. AUGUSTINE
(*De Duabus Animabus*)

Fiat jus et pereat mundus.
Let justice be done, though the world perish.

ST. AUGUSTINE (*On St. John the Evangelist*)

You, too, must take up your cross, or Christ will have none of you. "What," you ask, "is my cross?" I will tell you: Follow the right, do violence to no one, plunder no one, sell no public office, be corrupted by no bribes.... But while you are conducting yourself in this fashion, which befits a true Christian prince, there will be plenty to call you a dolt, and no prince at all. Hold fast to your cause. It is better to be a just man than an unjust prince.

ERASMUS
(*The Education of a Christian Prince*)

Make yourself a seller when you are buying and a buyer when you are selling. That way you will sell and buy justly.

ST. FRANCIS DE SALES

Justice without force is powerless; force without justice is tyrannical.

BLAISE PASCAL (*Pensées*)

We ought to speak, shout out against injustices, with confidence and without fear. We proclaim the principles of the Church, the reign of love, without forgetting that it is also a reign of justice.

BLESSED MIGUEL PRO, S.J.

Justice: to be ever ready to admit that another person is someone quite different from what we read when he is there, or what we think about him. Or rather, to read in him that he is certainly something different; perhaps something completely different, from what we read in him. Every being cries out to be read differently.

SIMONE WEIL

No injury is greater than not being looked upon as a human being. The deepest kind of hurt is when you find you are not welcome, when even by the tone of voice you are addressed you know that you are not considered to be anyone. We are interested in justice and in not confusing justice with charity.

CESAR E. CHAVEZ

There is no peace without justice, and no justice without forgiveness.

POPE JOHN PAUL II (*February 8, 2003*)

K

KICKING

It is contrary to decency and to Christian mildness to kick anyone, no matter who it may be.

ST. JEAN BAPTISTE DE LA SALLE
(*The Rules of Christian Manners and Civility*)

KINDNESS

... A kindly word is of greater value than a gift, however precious.

ST. BENEDICT (*The Holy Rule*)

Be kind to all and severe to yourself.

ST. TERESA OF ÁVILA (*Maxims*)

Kindness has converted more sinners than zeal, eloquence or learning.

F. W. FABER

Kind words are the music of the world.

F. W. FABER

Kind words can be short and easy to speak, but their echoes can be endless.

BLESSED MOTHER TERESA

KINGDOM OF GOD

To want all that God wants, always to want it, for all occasions and without reservations, this is the kingdom of God which is all within.

ARCHBISHOP FRANÇOIS FÉNELON

O World invisible, we view thee,
O World intangible, we touch thee,
O world unknowable, we know thee,
Inapprehensible, we clutch thee!

Does the fish soar to find the ocean,
The eagle plunge to find the air —
That we ask of the stars in motion
If they have rumor of thee there?

Not where the wheeling systems darken
And our benumbed conceiving soars! —
The drift of pinions, would we hearken,
Beats at our own clay-shuttered doors.

The angels keep their ancient places; —
Turn but a stone, and start a wing!
'Tis ye, 'tis your estranged faces,
That miss the many-splendored thing.

FRANCIS THOMPSON
(*In No Strange Land*)

But the process of liberation will not have conquered the very roots of oppression and the exploitation of man by man without the coming of the Kingdom. Moreover we can say that the historical, political liberating event is the growth of the Kingdom and is a salvific event; but it is not the coming of the Kingdom, not all of salvation.

GUSTAVO GUTIERREZ
(*A Theology of Liberation*)

KNOWLEDGE

Nothing is more excellent than knowledge.
ST. JOHN OF DAMASCUS

Learn everything you possibly can, and you will discover later that none of it was superfluous.
HUGH OF SAINT-VICTOR

A scrap of knowledge about sublime things is worth more than any amount of trivialities.
ST. THOMAS AQUINAS
(*Summa Theologica, 1,1,5*)

All men naturally desire to know.
AUCTORITATES ARISTOTELIS

There should be no enmity among seekers after truth.
AUCTORITATES ARISTOTELIS

The more and better you know, the heavier will be your judgment, unless your life also is more holy.
THOMAS À KEMPIS (*The Imitation of Christ*)

Really know what you say you know: know what you know and what you do not know; get one thing well before you go on to a second.
VENERABLE JOHN HENRY NEWMAN
(*Idea of a University*)

That only is true enlargement of mind which is the power of viewing many things at once as one whole, of referring them severally to their true place in the universal system, of understanding their respective values, and determining their mutual dependence.

VENERABLE JOHN HENRY NEWMAN
(*Idea of a University*)

Jesus needs neither books nor Doctors of Divinity in order to instruct souls; He, the Doctor of Doctors, He teaches without noise of words.

ST. THÉRÈSE OF LISIEUX

Apart, therefore, from merely making acts of gratitude to God for giving me the faith, I have also to study, according to my ability, the truths of the Catholic religion; for the deeper my knowledge of him, the more I must be drawn to love him. The more clearly I can grasp his revelation of himself, the more surely shall I be attracted by him. He is so perfect, so infinite in his perfections, that truer knowledge of him must end in truer love.

BEDE JARRETT, O.P.
(*Meditations for Layfolk*)

All knowledge is sterile which does not lead to action and end in charity.

CARDINAL DÉSIRÉ JOSEPH MERCIER

... To neglect the intellect costs dearly. A reign of the heart which would not presuppose in the heart an absolute will to truth, a Christian renewal which would think it could do without wisdom and theology, would be suicide in the disguise of love. The age is swarming with fools who disparage reason.

JACQUES MARITAIN
(*Art and Scholasticism*)

L

LABOR UNIONS

The denial of the right of workers to form unions for protection against oppression by the employing class is criminal injustice.

POPE PIUS XI
(*Quadragesimo Anno*)

[Labor priests] made the unions their parishes. . . . They became known as labor priests because, in season and out, they supported the God-given right of workers to organize and bargain collectively. Moreover, they vigorously supported the exercise of this right.

MONSIGNOR GEORGE HIGGINS
(*The Labor Priest*)

Effective labor unions are still by far the most powerful force in society for the protection of the laborer's rights and the improvement of his or her condition. No amount of employer benevolence, no diffusion of a sympathetic attitude on the part of the public, no increase of beneficial legislation, can adequately supply for the lack of organization among the workers themselves.

MONSIGNOR JOHN A. RYAN

LAITY

I want a laity, not arrogant, not rash in speech, not disputatious, but men who know their religion, who enter into it, who know just where they stand, who know what they hold, and what they do not, who know their creed so well that they can give an account of it, who know so much of history that they can defend it. I want an intelligent, well-instructed laity.

VENERABLE JOHN HENRY NEWMAN
(*Present Position of Catholics in England*)

What is the province of the laity? To hunt, to shoot, to entertain? These matters they understand, but to meddle with ecclesiastical matters they have no right at all.... Dr. Newman is the most dangerous man in England, and you will see that he will make use of the laity against your Grace. You must not be afraid of him. It will require much prudence, but you must be firm. The Holy Father still places his confidence in you; but if you yield and do not fight the battle of the Holy See against the detestable spirit growing up in England, he will begin to regret Cardinal Wiseman, who knew how to keep the laity in order.

MONSIGNOR WILLIAM TALBOT,
CHAMBERLAIN TO POPE PIUS IX
(*to Archbishop [later Cardinal] Manning of Westminster*)

In accord with the knowledge, competence and pre-eminence which they possess, [lay people] have the right and even at times a duty to manifest to the sacred pastors their opinion on matters which pertain to the good of the Church, and they have a right to make known

213

their opinion to the other Christian faithful, with due regard to the integrity of faith and morals and reverence towards their pastors, and with consideration for the common good and the dignity of persons.

CODE OF CANON LAW, 212.3

Hence the laity, dedicated as they are to Christ and anointed by the Holy Spirit, are marvelously called and prepared so that the richer fruits of the Spirit may be produced in them. For all their works, prayers and apostolic undertakings, family and married life, daily work, relaxation of mind and body, if they are accomplished in the Spirit – indeed even the hardships of life, if patiently borne – all these become spiritual sacrifices acceptable to God through Jesus Christ. In the celebration of the Eucharist these may most fittingly be offered to the Father along with the body of the Lord. And so, worshipping everywhere by their holy actions, the laity consecrate the world itself to God, everywhere offering worship by the holiness of their lives.

SECOND VATICAN COUNCIL
(*Dogmatic Constitution on the Church*)

The laity can also feel called, or be in fact called, to cooperate with their pastors in the service of the ecclesial community, for the sake of its growth and life. This can be done through the exercise of different kinds of ministries according to the grace and charisms which the Lord has been pleased to bestow on them.

POPE PAUL VI
(*On Evangelization in the Modern World*)

What have I done with my baptism and confirmation? Is Christ really at the center of my life?

Do I have time for prayer in my life?
Do I live my life as a vocation and mission?

POPE JOHN PAUL II
(*Message to World Congress of Catholic Laity, 2000*)

LANGUAGE

In 1215, the Church defined dogmatically that all our language and concepts about God are more inaccurate than accurate, more inadequate than adequate, and speak more about how God is different from us than similar. . . . All talk of the sacred is limited by our imaginations and our language. We are finite creatures trying to picture and talk about the infinite, an impossible task by definition. . . .

[Language] lays out some boundaries within which I should stay if I don't want to stray from the truth, and it stretches my intellect and my heart beyond their normal resting-places. . . . It's inadequate, but it's all that we have.

RONALD ROLHEISER, O.M.I.

Boundaried by space and time, none of us can know God save by metaphor and analogy.

QUENTIN DE LA BÉDOYÈRE

LAST JUDGMENT

Whether I eat or drink, whatever else I do, the dreadful trumpet of the last day seems always sounding in my ears: "Arise, ye dead, and come to judgment."

ST. JEROME

LAW

This is the beginning of our law, that we shall bow to the east and ask Holy Christ for peace and good years, that our land may have many people and that we may be loyal to our king. May he be a friend to us and we to him and may God be a friend to us all.

ST. OLAF (*Code of Law, Norway*)

The highest test of a people's fitness for free institutions is their willingness to obey law.

ARCHBISHOP JOHN IRELAND
(*American Citizenship*)

LEARNING

From that time on [age 7] I have spent the whole of my life in the monastery. I devoted all my time to the study of scripture; except, of course, when I was singing the divine office in church and carrying out all my other monastic duties. Learning, teaching and writing were always my delight.

THE VENERABLE BEDE
(*Ecclesiastical History of the English People*)

It is easy enough to say that the cultured man should be the crowd's guide, philosopher and friend. Unfortunately, he has nearly always been a misguiding guide, a false friend and a very shallow philosopher. And the actual catastrophe we have suffered, including those we are now suffering, have not in historical fact been due to prosaic practical people who are supposed to know nothing, but almost invariably to the highly theoretical people who knew that they knew everything. The world may learn by its mistakes; but they are mostly the mistakes of the learned.

G. K. CHESTERTON
(*The Common Man*)

Pray always for all the learned, the oblique, the delicate. Let them not be quite forgotten at the throne of God when the simple come into their kingdom.

EVELYN WAUGH

A little learning leads men away from the truth; a large learning confirms the truth.

HILAIRE BELLOC
(*Essays of a Catholic*)

LECTURING

First I tell them what I am going to tell them, then I tell them, then I tell them that I have told them.

HILAIRE BELLOC

LEISURE

All too often modern man becomes the plaything of his circumstances because he no longer has any leisure time; he doesn't know how to provide himself with the leisure he needs to stop and take a good look at himself.

MICHEL QUOIST
(*The Christian Response*)

LENT

For Lent. No puddings on Sundays. No tea except if to keep me awake and then without sugar. Meat only once a day. No verses in Passion Week or on Fridays. Not to sit in armchair except can work in no other way. Ash Wednesday and Good Friday, bread and water.

GERARD MANLEY HOPKINS, S.J. (*Journal, 1866*)

LIBERATION THEOLOGY

The theology of Liberation attempts to reflect on the experience and meaning of the (Christian) faith based on the commitment to abolish injustice and to build a new society; this theology must be verified by the practice of that commitment, by active, effective participation in the struggle which the exploited social classes have undertaken against their oppressors. Liberation from every form of exploitation, the possibility of a more human and dignified life, the creation of a new humankind — all pass through this struggle.

GUSTAVO GUTIERREZ

LIBERTY

Christianity is the companion of liberty in all its conflicts, the cradle of its infancy, and the divine source of its claims.

ALEXIS DE TOCQUEVILLE

Liberty is not a means to a higher political end. It is itself the highest political end.

LORD ACTON

LIES

The unjust word of a just man can do endless damage. It is like a poison dispensed by a doctor: the more reputable its source, the more it will be spread about and the more people it will kill.

CARDINAL FRANÇOIS XAVIER NGUYEN VAN THÛAN
(*The Road of Hope*)

LIFE

Blessed is he that has a short life.

POPE ST. CLEMENT I
(*Letter to the Corinthians*)

Life is only for love, and time is only that we may find God.

ST. BERNARD OF CLAIRVAUX

To live without faith, without a patrimony to defend, without a steady struggle for truth, that is not living, but existing.

BLESSED PIER GIORGIO FRASSATI

The law of life is sacrifice and discipline.

CHRISTOPHER DAWSON
(*Gifford Lectures, 1947*)

God, the Lord of life, has entrusted to men the noble mission of safeguarding life, and men must carry it out in a manner worthy of themselves. Life must be protected with the utmost care from the moment of conception: abortion and infanticide are abominable crimes.

SECOND VATICAN COUNCIL
(*Gaudium et Spes*)

A person has a moral obligation to use ordinary or proportionate means of preserving his or her life. Proportionate means are those that in the judgment of the patient offer a reasonable hope of benefit and do not entail an excessive burden or impose excessive expense on the family or community.

UNITED STATES CATHOLIC BISHOPS
(*Ethical & Religious Directives for Catholic Health Care Services, 1994*)

LISTENING TO GOD

Of all human activities, man's listening to God is the supreme act of his reasoning and will.

POPE PAUL VI

LITERATURE

If literature is to be made a study of human nature, you cannot have a Christian literature. It is a contradiction in terms to attempt a sinless literature of sinful man.

VENERABLE JOHN HENRY NEWMAN
(*Idea of a University*)

I wouldn't give up writing about God at this stage, if I were you. It would be like P.G. Wodehouse dropping Jeeves half-way thro' the Wooster series.

EVELYN WAUGH (*Letter to Graham Greene*)

LITURGY

The sacred liturgy, as a matter of fact, includes divine as well as human elements. The former, instituted as they have been by God, cannot be changed in any way by men. But the human components admit of various modifications, as the needs of the age and the good of souls may require, and as the ecclesiastical hierarchy, under the guidance of the Holy Spirit, may have authorized.

POPE PIUS XII (*Mediator Dei*)

In the earthly liturgy we share in a foretaste of that heavenly liturgy which is celebrated in the Holy City of Jerusalem towards which we journey as pilgrims, where Christ is sitting at the right hand of God, Minister of the sanctuary and of the true tabernacle. With all the warriors of the heavenly army we sing a hymn of glory to the Lord; venerating the memory of the saints, we hope for some part and fellowship with them; we eagerly await the Savior, our Lord Jesus Christ, until he, our life, shall appear and we too will appear with him in glory.

SECOND VATICAN COUNCIL
(*On the Sacred Liturgy*)

Liturgy is like a strong tree whose beauty is derived from the continuous renewal of its leaves, but whose strength comes from the old trunk, with solid roots in the ground.

POPE PAUL VI

It must be lamented that, especially in the years following the post-conciliar liturgical reform, as a result of a misguided sense of creativity and adaptation there have been a number of abuses which have been a source of suffering for many. A certain reaction against "formalism" has led some, especially in certain regions, to

consider the "forms" chosen by the Church's great liturgical tradition and her magisterium as non-binding and
to introduce unauthorized innovations which are often
completely inappropriate.

POPE JOHN PAUL II
(*Ecclesia de Eucharistia*)

LIVING IN GOD'S PRESENCE

I have a capacity in my soul for taking in God entirely.
I am as sure as I live that nothing is so near to me as
God. God is nearer to me than I am to myself; my exis-
tence depends on the nearness and the presence of God.

MEISTER ECKHART

Having found in many books different methods of
going to God, and divers practices of the spiritual life, I
thought this would serve rather to puzzle me, than facil-
itate what I sought after, which was nothing but how to
become wholly God's.... I renounced for the love of
Him everything that was not He; and I began to live as
though there was none but He and I in the world.... I
worshipped Him as often as I could, keeping my mind
in His holy Presence, and recalling it as often as I found
it wandered from Him. I found no small pain in this
exercise, and yet I continued it notwithstanding all the
difficulties that occurred.... When we faithfully keep
ourselves in His holy Presence, and set Him always
before us; this not only hinders our offending Him, at
least willfully, but it also begets holy freedom and, if I
may so speak, a familiarity with God....

BROTHER LAWRENCE
(*The Practice of the Presence of God*)

Brother Lawrence had found such an advantage in walking in the presence of God, it was natural for him to recommend it earnestly to others; but his example was a stronger inducement than any argument he could propose. His very countenance was edifying, such a sweet and calm devotion appearing in it, as could not but affect the beholders. And it was observed that, in the greatest hurry of business in the kitchen, he still preserved his recollection and heavenly mindedness. He was never hasty or loitering, but did each thing in season, with an even uninterrupted composure and tranquility of spirit. "The time of business," he said, "does not with me differ from the time of prayer; and in the noise and clatter of my kitchen, while several people are at the same time calling for different things, I possess God in as great tranquility as if I were upon my knees before the Blessed Sacrament."

(The Practice of the Presence of God:
Letters and Conversations of Brother Lawrence)

There is never a moment when God does not come forward in the guise of some suffering or some duty, and all that takes place within us, around us and through us both includes and hides his activity.

JEAN-PIERRE DE CAUSSADE, S.J.
(Abandonment to Divine Providence)

To live in the presence of God should be as natural for a Christian as to breathe the air which surrounds him. Furthermore, to live consciously and worthily in this presence should never have for him even the appearance of a duty which he is bound to perform in obedience to some external law. No, for him to live in the presence of the Almighty is a birthright; it is the deepest aspiration of his nature, it is the spontaneous expression of his love for the Lord when he knows he is a child of God.

ABHISHIKTANANDA (HENRI LE SAUX, O.P.)

LONELINESS

Essentially loneliness is the knowledge that one's fellow human beings are incapable of understanding one's condition and therefore are incapable of bringing the help most needed. It is not a question of companionship – many are ready to offer this and companionship is certainly not to be despised – but rather one of strictly sharing, of identifying. No two human beings can manage this, so to a varying extent loneliness at times is the lot of all.

HUBERT VAN ZELLER, O.S.B. (*Considerations*)

The biggest disease today is not leprosy or tuberculosis, but rather the feeling of being unwanted, uncared for and deserted by everybody.

BLESSED MOTHER TERESA

LORD'S PRAYER

If we are praying properly, we are saying nothing that does not already have a place in the Our Father.

ST. AUGUSTINE

The Lord's prayer is the most perfect of prayers. . . . In it, we ask not only for all the things that we can rightly desire, but also in the sequence that they should be desired. This prayer teaches us not only to ask for things, but in what order we should desire them.

ST. THOMAS AQUINAS
(*Summa Theologica II*)

While the Spanish civil war was raging, the chaplain of one of Franco's troops arranged a Requiem Mass for those fallen in battle. He was announcing the intention of the Mass as "for our fallen" when one of the men interrupted him: "Just a minute, Father. We want it for our fallen and for their fallen." Here was a man who had learned the meaning of the "our" in "Our Father." He was sane.

CARROLL E. SIMCOX

Don't say *Father*
If each day you don't behave like a son.
Don't say *Our*
if you live shut off in yourself.
Don't say *Who art in Heaven*
if you think only of worldly things.
Don't say *hallowed be Thy Name*
unless you really honor it.
Don't say *Thy Kingdom come*
if you have a material outcome in mind.
Don't say *Thy Will be done*
unless you're ready to accept it when it hurts.
Don't say *our daily bread*
unless you care about the hungry.
Don't say *forgive us our trespasses*
if you bear a grudge against someone.
Don't say *deliver us from evil*
unless you're prepared to make a stand against it.

Let the words of the Our Father sink in.
Don't say *Amen* unless you really mean it.
> *(Found on the wall of a church in Uruguay)*

LOVE OF GOD

Love and do what you will.
St. Augustine

To fall in love with God is the greatest of all romances;
To seek Him, the greatest adventure;
To find him, the greatest human achievement.
St. Augustine

Would you understand your Lord's meaning in this thing? Understand it well: Love is his meaning. Who showed it to you? Love. What did He show you? Love. Wherefore did he show it to you? For Love. . . . Thus did I learn that Love is Our Lord's meaning.
Julian of Norwich
(Revelations of Divine Love)

Love God, serve God: everything is in that.
St. Clare of Assisi

For I who am infinite God want you to serve me with what is infinite, and you have nothing infinite except your soul's love and desire.
God, to St. Catherine of Siena (Dialog)

Let us make God the beginning and end of our love, for he is the fountain from which all good things flow and into him alone they flow back.
Richard Rolle of Hampole

By love can God be got and held, by thought and knowledge never.

THE CLOUD OF UNKNOWING

For silence is not God, nor speaking; fasting is not God, nor eating; solitude is not God, nor company; nor any other pair of opposites. He is hidden between them and cannot be found by anything your soul does, but only by the love of your heart.

THE CLOUD OF UNKNOWING

All love is lost, but upon God alone.

WILLIAM DUNBAR

Someone whose actions are done for the pure love of God, not only acts so as not to be seen by men, he does not even act to be seen by God. Even if he thought it possible that God would not see what he does, he would still act with the same joy and the same purity of love.

ST. JOHN OF THE CROSS
(*The Living Flame of Love*)

Nothing is obtained from God, except by love.

ST. JOHN OF THE CROSS

Make many acts of love, for they set the soul on fire and make it gentle.

ST. TERESA OF ÁVILA (*Maxims*)

God does not need us to say many words to him, nor to think many thoughts. He sees our hearts, and that is enough for him. He sees very well our suffering and our submission. We have only to repeat continuously to a person we love: "I love you with all my heart." It even often happens that we go a long time without thinking that we love him, and we love no less during this period than in those in which we make the most tender protestations. True love rests in the depths of the heart.

ARCHBISHOP FRANÇOIS FÉNELON

You want to compete with his affection before you have understood it; that is your mistake.... Come, then! Show a little more deference to our Lord and let him go first. Let him love you now a great deal before you have succeeded in loving him even a little as you would wish to love him. That is all our Lord asks of you.

ABBÉ HENRI DE TOURVILLE (*Letters of Direction*)

To give heart and mind to God, so that they are ours no longer — to do good without being conscious of it, to pray ceaselessly and without effort as we breathe — to love without stopping to reflect upon our feelings — such is the perfect forgetfulness of self, which casts us upon God, as a babe rests upon its mother's breast.

JEAN NICOLAS GROU, S.J.
(*Being Devoted to God*)

It is always springtime in the heart that loves God.

ST. JOHN VIANNEY, THE CURÉ OF ARS

We are born to love, we live to love, and we will die to love still more.

ST. JOSEPH CAFASSO

Love consumes us only in the measure of our self-surrender.

ST. THÉRÈSE OF LISIEUX

Why would I fear Him? I love Him so much.

BLESSED FREDERIC OZANAM

Oh my friend! May the law of love be our law, and then, trampling all vainglory underfoot, our heart will no longer burn for anything else but for God, for men and for true happiness.

BLESSED FREDERIC OZANAM

To know God is to love him.

MIGUEL DE UNAMUNO

We have only this life, and perhaps a short one, in which to prove our love.

EDEL QUINN

All the good that you will do will come not from you but from the fact that you have allowed yourself to be used by God's love. Think of this more and gradually you will be free from the need to prove yourself and you can be more open to the power that will work through you without your knowing it.

THOMAS MERTON

The first step in personhood is to allow ourselves to be loved. To know ourselves loved is to have the depths of our own capacity to love opened up.

JOHN MAIN, O.S.B.
(*The Present Choice*)

What you are in love with, what seizes your imagination, will affect everything. It will decide what will get you out of bed in the morning, what you will do with your evenings, how you spend your weekends, what you read, who you know, what breaks your heart, and what amazes you with joy and gratitude. Fall in love, stay in love and it will decide everything.

PEDRO ARRUPE, S.J.

To love as Jesus loves, that is not only the law's precept, it is our vocation. When all is said and done it is the one thing we have to learn, for it is perfection.

RENÉ VOILLAUME
(*Seeds of the Desert*)

Don't worry about what you ought to do. Worry about loving. Don't interrogate heaven repeatedly and uselessly, saying, "What course of action should I pursue?" Concentrate on loving instead.

And by loving you will find out what is for you. Loving, you will listen to the Voice. Loving, you will find peace.

CARLO CARRETTO
(*Letters from the Desert*)

LOVE OF NEIGHBOR

Happy is the man who is able to love all men alike.

ST. MAXIMUS THE CONFESSOR
(*Centuries on Charity*)

We have an obligation not only to love each other but also in our love to make ourselves as loveable as possible so that it is easy for our sisters and brothers to love us.

WILLIAM OF SAINT THIERRY

Anything done for another is done for oneself.

POPE BONIFACE VIII

We cannot be sure whether we love God, though there may be strong reasons for thinking so, but there can be no doubt about whether we love our neighbor or not.

Be sure that as far as you advance in brotherly love, you are increasing in your love of God.

ST. TERESA OF ÁVILA
(*The Interior Castle*)

He who does not love his neighbor abhors God.

ST. JOHN OF THE CROSS
(*Spiritual Sentences*)

Where there is no love, put love — and you will find love.

ST. JOHN OF THE CROSS

We can never love our neighbor too much.

ST. FRANCIS DE SALES (*Spiritual Conferences*)

Love is infinitely inventive.

ST. VINCENT DE PAUL

The earth has become a chilly place. It is up to us Catholics to rekindle the flame of human warmth which is going out. It is up to us to recommence the great work of regeneration even if it means another era of martyrs. Can we remain passive in the midst of a world which is suffering and groaning? And as for us, my dear friend, are we going to make no attempt to be like those saints whom we love? If we do not know how to love God, for it seems that we need to see in order to love and we can only see God with the eyes of faith, and our faith is so weak! But men, the poor, we see them with our eyes of flesh! They are there before us and we can place our finger and hand in their wounds and the marks of the Crown of Thorns are visible on their foreheads. Thus there is no possible room for unbelief and we should fall at their feet and say to them with the apostle: "My Lord and my God. You are our master and we will be your servants. You are for us the sacred image of the God that we cannot see." Since we know not how to love him otherwise, we will love him in your person.

BLESSED FREDERIC OZANAM

To love is to wish the other's highest good.

R. H. BENSON
(*Come Rack! Come Rope!*)

Let us love our enemies, bless those who curse us, pray for those who persecute us. For love will conquer and will endure for all eternity. And happy are those who live and die in God's love.

FRANZ JÄGERSTÄTTER

We like someone because. We love someone although.

HENRI DE MONTHERLANT

One cannot but be surprised (when one looks at it with a mind not dulled by habit) at the extraordinary care taken by Christ to urge upon men the importance of loving one another.

PIERRE TEILHARD DE CHARDIN, S.J.
(*Hymn of the Universe*)

There is no way on earth of making a person worthy of love, except by loving them.

THOMAS MERTON

At the corner of Fourth and Walnut, in the center of the shopping district, I was suddenly overwhelmed with the realization that I loved all those people . . . that we could not be alien to one another even though we were total strangers.

THOMAS MERTON

We cannot do great things in life: we can only do small things with great love.

BLESSED MOTHER TERESA

LOVE OF GOD AND NEIGHBOR

I ask you to love me with the same love with which I love you. But for me you cannot do this, for I loved you without being loved. Whatever love you have for me you owe me, so you love Love of God and Neighbor not gratuitously but out of duty, while I love you not out of duty but gratuitously. So you cannot give me the kind of love I ask of you. This is why I have put you among your neighbors: so that you can do for them what you cannot do for me — that is, love them without any concern for thanks and without looking for any profit for yourself. And whatever you do for them I will consider done for me.

GOD, TO ST. CATHERINE OF SIENA (*Dialog*)

Through love of God we conceive virtues, and through love of our neighbor, they are brought to the birth.

ST. CATHERINE OF SIENA

When men have harnessed the winds, the waves, the tides and gravity, they will harness for God the energies of love, and then for the second time in the history of this world, man will have discovered Fire.

PIERRE TEILHARD DE CHARDIN, S.J.

LUXURY

If I dare to protest against these abuses, I am told that I, as a mere monk, have no right to sit in judgment on bishops. But even if I remain silent, do you think no one else is going to cry out? The naked, the cold, the hungry – you will hear them saying: "Tell us, priests, why do you have all this gold on your horses' bridles? We are starving. The bitter weather eats into our bones. Yet you are spending on luxuries money that should keep us, your brothers, alive!"

ST. BERNARD OF CLAIRVAUX

Wooden chalice, golden priest; golden chalice, wooden priest.

ST. OLIVER PLUNKETT

[Your fiancé] is very anxious about rings for you. He wants to send me here a large share of all the precious gems of Paris, so that I may purchase whatever I prefer for you. Actually I should prefer that you had none of them, for to speak quite frankly, my dearest daughter, ladies of quality no longer wear jewelry at Court.

ST. JANE FRANCES DE CHANTAL
(*to her daughter, 1620*)

M

MAGI

These men, who have disappeared from our horizon, had royal hearts. If their real journey continued on to the invisible, eternal light – indeed, if it really began only when they returned to their own country – then such royal hearts found their definitive home. And that is why we want to call them by that joyous name of days gone by: the holy kings of the East.... Throw down your defenses! The star is shining! Whether or not you make it the lode-star of your journey, it stands in your sky, and even your defiance and your weakness do not extinguish it. Why shouldn't we, then, believe and go on the journey? Why shouldn't we look to the star in the firmament of our hearts? Why not follow the light?

KARL RAHNER, S.J. (*The Eternal Year*)

MAGISTERIUM

Our belief in the teachings of the Church *de fide* must be an absolute and unconditional one, but we should not imagine that our fidelity to the Church's theoretical authority is satisfied merely by acceptance of *ex cathedra* pronouncements. We also must adhere whole-heartedly to teachings of the Church in matters of morality, even if they are not defined *ex cathedra*. The teachings of the encyclical *Humanae Vitae*, for example, is binding because its content has always been part of the teaching of the Church; in it we are confronted with the theoretical authority of the Church embodied in the tradition of the ordinary Magisterium. It is not a mere practical commandment of the Church, like the commandment to go to church on Sunday.

DIETRICH VON HILDEBRAND

MAN

Man is nothing else than . . . a sack of dung, the food of worms.

ST. BERNARD OF CLAIRVAUX

What a man is in the sight of God, so much he is and no more.

ST. FRANCIS OF ASSISI

Man is a reed, the most thinking thing in nature, but he is a thinking reed.

BLAISE PASCAL (*Pensées*)

We cannot be sheltered as finite persons, except in an infinite Person, who alone can fully comprehend us and lift us from the state of dereliction that is inherent in our finiteness.

DIETRICH VON HILDEBRAND

Let us consider ourselves a little. We are made from nothing but we are not made for nothing and will never return into nothing. Without God we should be nothing, but we are not without him and will never be without him. He made us not only into something, but into something that is like him; and not only into something that is like him, but into something that he could himself become, something that he thought enough of to die for. Spiritual and immortal, made in the likeness of God, redeemed by Christ, we are clustered with splendors.

FRANK SHEED
(*Theology and Sanity*)

Though mankind today is struck with wonder at its own discoveries and its power, it often raises anxious questions about the current trend of the world, about the place and role of man in the universe, about the meaning of his individual and collective strivings, and about the ultimate destiny of reality and humanity.

SECOND VATICAN COUNCIL
(*The Church in the Modern World*)

MANNERS

Manners makyth man.

WILLIAM OF WYKEHAM

MARRIAGE

Young husbands should say to their wives: "I have taken you in my arms, and I love you, and I prefer you to my life itself. For the present life is nothing, and my most ardent dream is to spend it with you in such a way that we may be assured of not being separated in the life reserved for us. . . . I place your love above all things and nothing would be more bitter or painful to me than to be of a different mind than you."

ST. JOHN CHRYSOSTOM
(*Homilies on Ephesians*)

Let a woman show deference, not being a slave to her husband; let her show she is ready to be guided, not coerced. . . . Let the husband, too, manage his wife like a steersman, pay honor to her as his life partner, share with her as the co-heir of grace.

ST. AMBROSE (*Letters*)

I am asking our Lord to be as generous to you as he once was to the bridal pair at Cana. May He invariably change the water into wine! I mean, may He prolong His gift of happiness, and as far as possible sweeten the bitter trials you will meet with on your way. Trials! Fancy introducing that word into my letter—how could I?—at a moment when I realize that life for you is all sunshine.

ST. THÉRÈSE OF LISIEUX
(*to her newlywed cousin, 1894*)

Let those about to enter into wedlock pray diligently for divine help, so that they may make their choice in accordance with Christian prudence, not led by the blind and unrestrained impulse of lust, nor by any desire for riches, nor by any other base influence, but by a true and noble love and sincere affection for the future partner.

POPE PIUS XI
(*Casti Conubii*)

They are not considered as acting against nature who, in the married state, use their right in the proper manner, even though, on account of natural reasons, either of time or of defect, new life cannot be brought forth.

POPE PIUS XI
(*Casti Connubii*)

The Creator himself established that in the [generative] function, spouses should experience pleasure and enjoyment of body and spirit. Therefore, the spouses do nothing evil in seeking this pleasure and enjoyment. They accept what the Creator has intended for them. At the same time, spouses should know how to keep themselves within the limits of just moderation.

POPE PIUS XII
(*Discourse, October 29, 1951*)

. . . There is all the difference in the world between utilizing one's awareness of the periods of infertility, and arrogating to oneself the right to impose radical restrictions on fertility by the use of artificial contraception. . . . For in using the infertile days they are not setting bounds to their love. Otherwise, one would have to say that intercourse in the full Christian sense is impossible after a woman's change of life. Married persons who think as Christians set no barriers between the two objects of marriage: procreation and the expression of mutual love. They let the two stand together, the physical side with its own proper laws, and the personal side. One's awareness of the opportunities provided by nature does not mean that one is imposing calculation on the inner spirit of love.

CARDINAL HANS URS VON BALTHASAR
(*A Meditation on Ephesians 5*)

The conjugal act does not in any way lose its full meaning and value when one knows that a conception is out of the question, as when age, or an operation for the sake of health, or pregnancy excludes it. The knowledge that a conception is not possible does not in the least taint the conjugal act with irreverence. In such cases, if the act is an expression of a deep love, anchored in Christ, it will rank even higher in its quality and purity than one that leads to a conception in a marriage in which the love is less deep and not formed by Christ. And even when for good and valid reasons conception should be avoided, the marital act in no way loses its raison d'etre, because its meaning and value is the actualization of the mutual self-donation of the spouses. The intention of avoiding conception does not actively interfere in order to cut the link between the conjugal act and a possible conception.

Nor is the practice of rhythm to avoid conception in any way irreverent, because the existence of rhythm — that is to say, the fact that conception is limited to a short period — is itself a God-given institution.

DIETRICH VON HILDEBRAND
(*The Encyclical Humanae Vitae:
A Sign of Contradiction*)

Today there are numerous Catholics in many countries who have recourse to civil divorce and contract new civil unions.... Towards Christians who live in this situation, and who often keep the faith and desire to bring up their children in a Christian manner, priests and the whole community must maintain an attentive solicitude, so that they do not consider themselves separated from the Church, in whose life they can and must participate as baptized persons:

They should be encouraged to listen to the Word of God, to attend the Sacrifice of the Mass, to persevere in prayer, to contribute to works of charity and to community efforts for justice, to bring up their children in the Christian faith, to cultivate the spirit and practice of penance and thus implore, day by day, God's grace.

POPE JOHN PAUL II (*Familiaris Consortio*)

MARTYRDOM

Please let me be thrown to the wild beasts; through them I can reach God. I am God's wheat; I am going to be ground by the wild beasts so that I may become the pure bread of Christ. If anything, coax the beasts on to become my sepulchre and to leave nothing of my body undevoured so that, when I am dead, I may be no trouble to anyone.

ST. IGNATIUS OF ANTIOCH (*Letter to the Romans*)

Thanks be to God.

ST. CYPRIAN
(*when sentenced to death*)

In body I am a child but I bear a man's heart, and by the grace of my Master Jesus Christ, your threats seem as vain to me as this idol which stands before me. And as for the gods which you want me to adore, they are nothing but imposters, who sully the women of their own household and don't spare their own kin. If your slaves behaved like these gods, you would put them to death in a hurry. And I wonder that you don't blush to adore such gods.

ST. PANCRAS
(*aged 14, to the Emperor Diocletian*)

The blood of the martyrs is the seed of the Church.

TERTULLIAN (*Apology*)

I am prepared to die for Christ and his Church. I charge you in the name of the Almighty not to hurt any other person here, for none of them has been concerned in the late transactions.

ST. THOMAS À BECKET

I die the King's good servant, but God's first.

ST. THOMAS MORE

I will pray God in a language we both well understand.

ST. EDMUND CAMPION
(*rebuked on the scaffold for praying in Latin*)

Weep not for me, for I do but pay the rent before the rent-day.

ST. RICHARD GWYN

I will not pray with you and you shall not pray with me; neither will I say amen to your prayers, nor shall you to mine.

ST. MARGARET CLITHEROW (*at her execution*)

After all this long search, my lord, you have got your boast.

ST. JOHN BOSTE
(*to the Earl of Huntingdon, after his capture*)

Speak up, man, and be not afraid!

ST. JOHN RIGBY (*to the jury foreman who
ashamed, mumbled the verdict*)

That is a fleabite in comparison to what it pleased my sweet savior Jesus to suffer for my salvation. I freely forgive your lordship, and the poor jury, and all other persecutors whatever.

ST. JOHN RIGBY (*after sentence*)

Here is a numerous assembly – may the great Savior of the world save every soul of you all! I believe you are here met not only to see a fellow native die, but also to hear a fellow native speak.

My religion is the Roman Catholic; in it I have lived above these 40 years; in it I now die, and so fixedly die, that if all the good things in this world were offered me to renounce it, all should not remove me one hair's-breadth from my Roman Catholic faith.

A Roman Catholic I am; a Roman Catholic priest I am; a Roman Catholic priest of that religious order called the Society of Jesus I am; and I bless God who first called me.

Please now to observe: I was condemned for reading Mass, hearing confessions, and administering the sacraments. . . . Dying for this, I die for religion.

ST. DAVID LEWIS, S.J. (*1679*)

I have deserved a worse death, for though I have been a faithful and true subject to my king, I have been a grievous sinner against God. Thieves and robbers that rob on highways would have served God in a greater perfection than I have done, had they received so many graces and favors from him as I have. . . .

By the assistance of God I am willing to die; and I had rather die than doubt any point of faith taught by our Holy Mother, the Roman Catholic Church.

ST. JOHN PLESSINGTON (1679)

A slight sabre-cut will separate my head from my body, like the spring flower which the Master of the garden gathers for His pleasure. We are all flowers planted on

this earth, which God plucks in His own good time:
some a little sooner, some a little later. . . .

ST. THÉOPHANE VÉNARD
(*martyred in China, 1861*)

May God forgive him! I want him in heaven!

ST. MARIA GORETTI
(*stabbed by Alessandro Serenelli
while defending her virginity*)

Maria Goretti, now a Saint, was my good Angel, sent
to me through Providence to guide and save me. I still
have impressed upon my heart her words of rebuke
and of pardon. She prayed for me, she interceded for
her murderer.

ALESSANDRO SERENELLI
(*he became a Capuchin tertiary
after 27 years in jail*)

Hail, Christ the King!

BLESSED MIGUEL PRO, S.J.
(*as he faced the firing squad*)

I am bound as a pastor, by divine command, to give my
life for those whom I love, and that is all Salvadorans,
even those who are going to kill me.

ARCHBISHOP OSCAR ROMERO

If it should happen one day – and it could be today –
That I become a victim of the terrorism which now
    seems ready to engulf all the foreigners living in
    Algeria,
I would like my community, my Church, my family,
To remember that my life was given to God and to
    this country.

I ask them to remember that the Sole Master of all
    life
Was not a stranger to this brutal departure.
I ask them to pray for me –
For how could I be worthy of such an offering?
I ask them to be able to link this death with the many
    other deaths which were just as violent,
But forgotten through indifference and anonymity.
My life has no more value than any other.
Nor any less value.
In any case it has not the innocence of childhood.
I have lived long enough to know that I am an
    accomplice in the evil
Which seems, alas, to prevail in the world,
Even in that which would strike me blindly.
I should like, if the time comes, to have that moment
    of lucidity
Which would allow me to beg the forgiveness of God
And of my fellow human beings.
And at the same time forgive with all my heart the
    one who would strike me down. . . .
I certainly include you, friends of yesterday and
    today,
And you, my friends of this place,
Along with my mother and father, my sisters and
    brothers and their families,
The hundredfold granted as was promised!
And also you, the friend of my final moment, who
    would not be aware of what you were doing.
Yes, I also say this Thank you, and this A-Dieu to
    you, in whom I see the face of God.

And may we find each other, happy and good thieves
  in Paradise, if it pleases God, the Father of us
  both. Amen! In sha'Allah!

> CHRISTIAN DE CHERGÉ, O.C.S.O.
> (*Spiritual Testimony;*
> *Prior of the Trappist Abbey of Our Lady*
> *of Atlasin Tibhirine, Algeria, Dom Christian*
> *de Chergé and six of his brother monks were*
> *killed by Islamic fundamentalists in May 1996.*)

MASS

The best way to economize time is to "lose" half an
hour each day attending Holy Mass.

> BLESSED FREDERIC OZANAM

It is the Mass that matters.

> AUGUSTINE BIRRELL
> (*What, Then, Did Happen at the Reformation?*)

"The Mass is long," you say. And I reply: "Because your
love is short."

> ST. JOSEMARÍA ESCRIVÁ (*The Way*)

Since once again, O Lord, in the steppes of Asia, I
  have no bread, no wine, no altar, I will raise
  myself above those symbols to the pure majesty
  of reality, and I will offer to you, I, your
priest, upon the altar of the entire earth, the labor
  and the suffering of the world.

> PIERRE TEILHARD DE CHARDIN, S.J.
> (*Mass on the Altar of the World*)

MASTURBATION

Both the Magisterium of the Church, in the course of a constant tradition, and the moral sense of the faithful have been in no doubt and have firmly maintained that masturbation is an intrinsically and gravely disordered action. . . .

To form an equitable judgment about the subjects' moral responsibility and to guide pastoral action, one must take into account the affective immaturity, force of acquired habit, conditions of anxiety or other psychological or social factors that lessen or even extenuate moral culpability.

CATECHISM OF THE CATHOLIC CHURCH, 2352

MATERIALISM

The world would become better off if people tried to become better. And people would become better if they stopped trying to become better off.

PETER MAURIN

It is not wrong to want to live better; what is wrong is a style of life which is presumed to be better when it is directed toward "having" rather than "being."

POPE JOHN PAUL II (*Centesimus Annus*)

MATTER AND SPIRIT

In a concrete sense there is not matter and spirit. All that exists is matter becoming spirit. There is neither spirit nor matter in the world; the stuff of the universe is spirit-matter.

PIERRE TEILHARD DE CHARDIN, S.J.
(*A Sketch of a Personalistic Universe*)

MEDIA

The means of social communication (especially the mass media) can give rise to a certain passivity among users, making them less vigilant consumers of what is said or shown. Users should practice moderation and discipline in their approach to the mass media. They will want to form enlightened and correct consciences, the more easily to resist unwholesome influences.

By the very nature of their profession, journalists have an obligation to serve the truth and not offend against charity in disseminating information. They should strive to respect, with equal care, the nature of the facts and the limits of critical judgment concerning individuals. They should not stoop to defamation.

CATECHISM OF THE CATHOLIC CHURCH, 2496-7

If protesters against a film do not do their homework, they risk looking ignorant and silly. If they protest in the name of the Church, they need to have seen the film and consider their protest thoroughly so that it is not dismissed as impassioned but thoughtless, and the diaologue between the Church and the professional world of media is cut off....

PETER MALONE
("Discerning When to Use the Power of Protest"—
Catholic Herald, October 4, 2002)

MEDITATION

Where there is peace and meditation, there is neither anxiety nor doubt.

ST. FRANCIS OF ASSISI

MERCY

The mercy of God may be found between the bridge and the stream.

ST. AUGUSTINE (*Confessions*)

Teach me to feel another's woe,
To hide the fault I see;
That mercy I to others show,
That mercy show to me.

ALEXANDER POPE

It is not our perfection which is to dazzle God, Who is surrounded by myriads of angels. No, it is our misery, our wretchedness avowed which draws down his mercy.

BLESSED COLUMBA MARMION, O.S.B.

Nobody is ever lost in God's eyes, even when society has condemned him.

CARDINAL JEAN-MARIE LUSTIGER

MICHAEL THE ARCHANGEL (SAINT)

Holy Michael, archangel, defend us in the day of battle; be our safeguard against the wickedness and snares of the devil. May God rebuke him, we humbly pray, and do thou, by the power of God thrust down to hell

Satan and all wicked spirits who wander through the world for the ruin of souls. Amen.

*(Prayer formerly recited for Russia
at the end of every Low Mass)*

MIND

The mind is always at work. If it is kept busy in good things, it won't have time for bad things.

BLESSED JAMES ALBERIONE, S.S.P.

MIRACLES

Miracles are not contrary to nature, but only contrary to what we know about nature.

ST. AUGUSTINE

The saint who works no miracles has few pilgrims.

ENGLISH PROVERB

If anyone shall say that miracles are impossible, and that therefore all the accounts regarding them, even those contained in Holy Scripture, are to be dismissed as fabulous or mythical, or that miracles can never be known with certainty, and that the divine origin of Christianity is not proved by them; let him be anathema.

FIRST VATICAN COUNCIL (*1870*)

MISERY

Man alone is miserable.

BLAISE PASCAL (*Pensées*)

MISSION

Gregory . . . sent Augustine and several other God-fearing monks with him, to preach the word of God to the English nation. They . . . were on their journey seized with a sudden fear, and began to think of returning home, rather than go to meet a barbarous, fierce and unbelieving nation, to whose very language they were strangers; and this they unanimously agreed was the safest course. . . . The Pope, in reply, sent them an encouraging letter. . . .

"Since it would be better not to begin a good work, rather than abandon it once you have begun it, you really must, my beloved sons, carry out the good work which, with Our Lord's help, you have undertaken. So do not let the hardship of the journey, nor the tongues of evil-speaking men, deter you; but with all possible earnestness and zeal perform that which, by God's direction, you have undertaken, being assured that much labor is followed by an eternal reward."

THE VENERABLE BEDE
(*The Ecclesiastical History of the English Nation*)

Make yourselves liked by all, become all things to all men in humility and love, adapting yourselves to the customs of the people.

ST. IGNATIUS LOYOLA

Many innocent hands are lifted up to heaven for you daily by those English students, whose posterity shall never die, which beyond seas, gathering virtue and sufficient knowledge for the purpose, are determined never to give you over, but either to win you to heaven, or to die upon your pikes. And touching our Society, be it known to you that we have made a league – all the Jesuits in the world, whose succession and multitude must over-reach all the practices of England – cheerfully to carry the cross you shall lay upon us, and never to despair your recovery, while we have a man left to enjoy your Tyburn, or to be racked with your torments, or consumed with your prisons. The expense is reckoned, the enterprise is begun; it is of God, it cannot be withstood. So the faith was planted, so it must be restored....

ST. EDMUND CAMPION, S.J.
(*"Campion's Brag," Challenge to the Privy Council*)

When we come to the service of Christ, we come to a rough profession.

ST. ROBERT SOUTHWELL, S.J.

When you reach the Hurons . . . you will arrive at a time of the year when fleas will keep you awake almost all night. And this petty martyrdom, to say nothing of mosquitoes, sandflies, and suchlike gentry, lasts usually not less than three or four months of the summer.

ST. JOHN DE BREBEUF, S.J.
(*to his brother Jesuits in France, 1636*)

Go not to the east, but to the west.

POPE LEO XIII
(*Upon sending St. Frances Xavier
Cabrini to the United States*)

MODERNISM

The basis of these new ideas . . . may be said to be this: in order that dissidents may be brought more readily to acknowledge Catholic truth, the Church should show itself more sympathetic to the tolerant spirit of the present age, and, relaxing its former strictness, be more indulgent towards modern views and methods. Many think that this should be so not only with regard to disciplinary matters, but also with regard to doctrinal matters affecting the deposit of faith. . . .

POPE LEO XIII (*Testem Benevolentiae –*
Letter to Cardinal Gibbons)

Undoubtedly, were anyone to attempt the task of collecting together all the errors that have been broached against the faith and to concentrate into one the sap and substance of them all, he could not succeed in doing so better than the Modernists have done. Nay, they have gone further than this, for . . . their system means the destruction not of the Catholic religion alone, but of all religion.

POPE ST. PIUS X
(*Pascendi Dominici Gregis*)

There is a species of parson called a "Modern Churchman" who draws the full salary of a beneficed clergyman but need not commit himself to any religious belief.

EVELYN WAUGH (*Decline and Fall*)

MODESTY

The forms taken by modesty vary from one culture to another. Everywhere, however, modesty exists as an expression of the spiritual dignity proper to man. It is born with the awakening consciousness of being a subject. Teaching modesty to children and adolescents means awakening in them respect for the human person.

CATECHISM OF THE CATHOLIC CHURCH, 2524

I never look at them, and neither does anyone else, because they are all looking at me to see how I am reacting.

BLESSED ANGELO RONCALLI,
LATER POPE JOHN XXIII
(As papal nuncio in Paris, he was asked whether women's plunging necklines embarrassed him.)

MONARCHY

In modern times the absolute monarchy in Catholic countries has been, next to the Reformation, the greatest and most formidable enemy of the Church.

LORD ACTON
(Political Thoughts on the Church)

MONASTIC LIFE

First and foremost, the monk should own nothing in this world, but he should have as his possessions solitude of the body, modesty of bearing, a modulated tone of voice and a well-ordered manner of speech.

ST. BASIL
(A Discourse on Ascetical Discipline)

He who renounces worldly things, such as women and wealth and so on, makes the outer man a monk but not yet the inner man. But he who renounces the passionate thought of these things, makes a monk of the inner man as well, that is, the mind. Such a man is a true monk.

HESYCHIUS OF JERUSALEM *(Philokalia)*

Let the brothers fear God and love their abbot, sincere and humble in their affection. Let them prefer nothing whatever to Christ. . . .

Let them put up with one another's weaknesses, whether of body or character, as patiently as possible. . . .

Let no one follow what he thinks is good for himself, but rather what is good for his brother. . . .

Over and above everything, we must take care of the sick; they must be served as though they were Christ Himself. . . .

ST. BENEDICT (*The Holy Rule*)

God, and God alone, in solitude!

ST. BRUNO

Do not be sad about Geoffrey, or weep for him. He is going swiftly to joy, not to sorrow. I will be father, mother, brother and sister to him. I will make the crooked paths straight and the rough places smooth. I will organize things so that his soul will advance but his health will not suffer.

ST. BERNARD OF CLAIRVAUX

The cowl does not make the monk.

14TH-CENTURY PROVERB

A monastery can never be merely an escape from the world. Its very purpose is to enable us to face the problems of the world at their deepest level, that is to say, in relation to God and eternal life. Everything in the monastic life down to the deepest level has to be viewed from this angle.

BEDE GRIFFITHS, O.S.B.
(*The Golden String*)

MONEY

Nothing that is God's is obtainable by money.

TERTULLIAN
(*The Christian's Defence*)

Money is a good Catholic.

SPANISH PROVERB

The chief and most excellent rule for the right use of money is one which the Christian philosophers hinted at, but which the Church has traced out clearly, and has not only made known to men's minds, but has impressed upon their lives. It rests upon the principle that it is one thing to have a right to the possession of money and another to have the right to use money as one wills.

POPE LEO XIII
(*Rerum Novarum*)

If you have money, consider that perhaps the only reason God allowed it to fall into your hands was in order that you might find joy and perfection by throwing it away.

THOMAS MERTON
(*Seeds of Contemplation*)

MORNING PRAYER

I know that soldiers have a lot to endure, and to endure in silence. If upon rising they would only take the trouble to say to our Lord every morning this tiny phrase: "My God, I desire to do and to endure everything today for love of Thee," what glory they would heap up for eternity!

ST. BERNADETTE
(*to her brother Jean-Marie, 1876*)

MORTIFICATION

The day you leave the table without having made some small mortification, you will have eaten like a pagan.

ST. JOSEMARÍA ESCRIVÁ (*The Way*)

The inappropriate word you left unsaid; the joke you didn't tell; the cheerful smile for those who bother you; that silence when you are unjustly accused; your kind conversation with people you find boring and tactless; the daily effort to overlook one irritating detail or another in those who live with you . . . this, with perseverance, is indeed solid interior mortification.

ST. JOSEMARÍA ESCRIVÁ (*The Way*)

MOTHERHOOD

Every mother is like Moses. She does not enter the promised land. She prepares a world she will not see.

POPE PAUL VI

MOURNING

O Lord, you gave him to us to be our joy and consolation. You have taken him away from us. We give him back to you without a murmur, though our hearts are wrung with sorrow.

ST. EPHRAIM THE SYRIAN

MUSIC

It is the best of all trades, to make songs, and the second best to sing them.

HILAIRE BELLOC

I have a sweet tooth for song and music. This is my Polish vice.

POPE JOHN PAUL II

MYSTICAL BODY

Or have we not one God, and one Christ, and one Spirit of grace poured out upon us? And is there not one calling in Christ? Why do we divide and tear asunder the members of Christ, and raise up strife against our own body, and reach such a pitch of madness as to forget that we are members one of another?

POPE ST. CLEMENT I
(*Letter to the Corinthians*)

Moreover, why should you not be concerned in the Virgin's childbearing, seeing that you are the members of Christ? Mary gave birth to your Head; the Church gave birth to you.

ST. AUGUSTINE
(*Sermons*)

One difference between an organic body and the Church's mystical body is this: the members of an organism are all knit together at one given period of time, whereas the members of the mystical body are dispersed throughout the ages, for the Church's body is made up of people of every century, from the beginning to the end of the world.

ST. THOMAS AQUINAS (*Summa Theologica*)

That the mystical body of Christ and the Catholic Church in communion with Rome are one and the same thing, is a doctrine based on revealed truth.

POPE PIUS XII (*Humani Generis*)

Our own civilization will pass, as those of the past have done; there is no need to regret it. For the "schema," the outward form of this world, as St. Paul called it, is passing away; but beneath the outward form there is being built up continuously the Body of Christ, which is the unity of mankind in truth and charity. It is a hidden and mysterious process, which will only be realized in its fullness when this world of space and time has passed away altogether. Then we shall see the Church as it really is, as the fulfillment of the whole creation, the achievement of man's destiny by his participation in the life of God.

BEDE GRIFFITHS, O.S.B. (*The Golden String*)

MYSTICAL EXPERIENCE

Unto this Darkness which is beyond light we pray that we may come, and through loss of sight and knowledge may see and know that which transcends sight and knowledge, by the very fact of not seeing and knowing; for this is real sight and knowledge.

PSEUDO-DIONYSIUS (*Mystical Theology*)

Lord, if you are not here, where shall I seek you, being absent? But if you are everywhere, why do I not see you present? Truly you live in unapproachable light. But what is unapproachable light, or how shall I come to it? Or who shall lead me to that light and into it, that I may see you in it?

ST. ANSELM (*Prosologion*)

While Brother Thomas was saying his Mass one morning, in the chapel of St. Nicholas at Naples, something happened which profoundly affected and altered him. After Mass he refused to write or dictate, indeed he put away his writing materials. He was in the third part of the *Summa,* at the questions on Penance. And Brother Reginald, seeing that he was not writing, said to him: "Father, are you going to give up this great work, undertaken for the glory of God and to enlighten the world?" But Thomas replied: "Reginald, I cannot go on." ... Then he added: "All that I have written seems to me like straw compared to what has been revealed to me."

THE FIRST CANONIZATION INQUIRY ON ST. THOMAS AQUINAS (*1319*)

God in the depths of us receives God who comes to us; it is God contemplating God.

BLESSED JOHN OF RUYSBROECK

I saw an angel close by me, on my left side, in bodily form ... I saw in his hand a long spear of gold, and at the iron's point there seemed to be a little fire. He appeared to me to be thrusting it at times into my heart, and so to pierce my very entrails; when he drew it out, he seemed to draw them out also, and to leave me all on fire with a great love of God.

ST. TERESA OF ÁVILA (*Autobiography*)

One dark night,
> fired with love's urgent longings
> — ah, the sheer grace! —
> I went out unseen,
> my house being now all stilled.

In darkness, and secure,
> by the secret ladder, disguised,
> — ah, the sheer grace! —
> in darkness and concealment,
> my house being now all stilled.

On that glad night
> in secret, for no one saw me,
> nor did I look at anything
> with no other light or guide
> than the one that burned in my heart.

This guided me
> more surely than the light of noon
> to where he was awaiting me
> — him I knew so well —
> there in a place where no one appeared.

ST. JOHN OF THE CROSS (*The Dark Night*)

A dark night through which the soul passes in order to attain the Divine Light of the perfect union of the love of God.

ST. JOHN OF THE CROSS
(*The Ascent of Mount Carmel*)

But this at least can be asserted for all devout souls, that as long as they continue to think or feel in prayer, they are still outside the Spiritual Castle. They should never be satisfied with any wonderful thought or any marvelous sense of peace they may experience. God is beyond....

There are plenty of printed maps and guides for the antechambers of the Castle, for the external courtyards of the Temple. There are signboards on the gates outside. But once you have entered, the only guide is the Spirit. Those who have already entered may invite you.... But the last stages of the path, reaching to the shrine, are to be trodden by each one alone. In fact, doors will open themselves, one after another, from inside, once faith and love are strong enough.

ABHISHIKTANANDA [HENRI LE SAUX, O.P.] (*Prayer*)

The language of mystics cannot meet the language of science or reason, but nevertheless in a world that craves experiential testimony, it will always be one of the roads by which our contemporaries can find God.

RENÉ VOILLAUME
(*Contemplation in the Church in Our Time*)

I was in bed, eyes open, really suffering for the first time in my life.... It was then that a cry burst from my breast, an appeal for help. – "My God!" – and instantly, like a violent wind which passes over without anyone knowing where it comes from, the spirit of the Lord seized me by the throat. I had an impression of infinite power and kindness and, from that moment onward, I believed with an unshakeable conviction that has never left me.

JACQUES FESCH
(*In Five Hours I Shall See Jesus*)

N

NATIONALISM

"My country, right or wrong" is a thing that no patriot would think of saying, except in an extreme case. It is like saying, "My mother, drunk or sober."

G. K. CHESTERTON (*The Defendant*)

Nationalism isolates people from their true good.

POPE PAUL VI (*Populorum Progressio*)

NATURE

The trees and the stones will teach you what you will never learn from the masters.

ST. BERNARD OF CLAIRVAUX

NEED

Never see a need without trying to do something about it.

BLESSED MARY MACKILLOP

NIGHT

Father, a thousand tiny lights break through
The great gray darkness of the city night
And are as candles lit before Thy Shrine.

CARDINAL FRANCIS SPELLMAN
(*What America Means to Me
and Other Poems and Prayers*)

NON-CHRISTIAN RELIGIONS

The Catholic Church rejects nothing that is true and holy in these religions. She regards with sincere reverence those ways of conduct and of life, those precepts and teachings which, though differing in many aspects from the ones she holds and sets forth, nonetheless often reflect a ray of that Truth which enlightens all men.

SECOND VATICAN COUNCIL
(*Non-Christian Religions*)

The plurality of religions is a consequence of the richness of creation itself and of the manifold grace of God. Though all coming from the same source, peoples have perceived the universe and articulated their awareness of the Divine Mystery in manifold ways, and God has surely been present in these historical undertakings of his children. Such pluralism therefore is in no way to be deplored but rather acknowledged as itself a divine gift

CATHOLIC BISHOPS' CONFERENCE OF INDIA
(*Guidelines for Religious Dialogue*)

NOTORIETY

Wealth is one idol of the day and notoriety a second.... Notoriety, or the making of a noise in the world – it may be called "newspaper fame" – has come to be considered a great good in itself, and a ground of veneration.

VENERABLE JOHN HENRY NEWMAN
(*Discourses to Mixed Congregations*)

NUCLEAR WEAPONS

If there had been no cliff, the Gadarene swine would have had nowhere to hurl themselves. The bomb constitutes a cliff, and we should be duly grateful for it.

MALCOLM MUGGERIDGE

O

OBEDIENCE

Obedience unites us so closely to God that in a way transforms us into Him, so that we have no other will but His. If obedience is lacking, even prayer cannot be pleasing to God.

ST. THOMAS AQUINAS

I must not belong to myself at all, but to my Creator and to his vicar. I must be like a ball of wax, ready to be directed and moved about just as it allows itself to be kneaded. . . . I must be like a corpse, without will or understanding; like a tiny crucifix, which is moved about without resisting; like a staff in the hand of an old man, to be placed wherever he wishes and can use it best.

ST. IGNATIUS LOYOLA
(*Spiritual Exercises*)

We may easily suffer ourselves to be surpassed by other religious orders in fasting, watching, and other austerities of diet and clothing, which they practice according to their rule, but in true and perfect obedience and the abnegation of our will and judgment, I greatly desire, most dear brethren, that those who serve God in this society should be conspicuous.

ST. IGNATIUS LOYOLA
(*Letter to Jesuits in Portugal*)

I know the power obedience has of making things easy which seem impossible.

ST. TERESA OF ÁVILA

Man finds in obedience the annihilation of self-love, and the true liberty of the children of God.

ST. VINCENT DE PAUL

Jesus preferred obedience even in his life.

ST. VINCENT DE PAUL

A little drop of simple obedience is worth a million times more than a whole vase of the choicest contemplation.

ST. MARIA MADDALENA DE PAZZI

The Pope is the boss, and I will obey even if I disagree.

CARDINAL BASIL HUME, O.S.B.
(*in a TV interview*)

OBSTINACY

Divine Goodness does not only NOT reject penitent souls, but goes out in search of obstinate souls.

ST. PADRE PIO

ORIGINAL SIN

Certain new theologians dispute original sin, which is the only part of Christian theology which can really be proved.

G. K. CHESTERTON

OUR LADY

I am the Immaculate Conception.

OUR LADY TO ST. BERNADETTE
(*Lourdes, March 3, 1858*)

Look, my child, at my heart surrounded with thorns, which ungrateful men continuously nail into me with their blasphemies and sins. You, at least, try to console me and tell everyone that those who go to confession on the first Saturday of every month for five months, receive holy communion, say the rosary and keep me company for a quarter of an hour – these I promise to assist at the time of their death with the necessary graces for their salvation.

THE BLESSED VIRGIN MARY
(*Fátima, August 13, 1917*)

Him whom the heavens cannot contain, the womb of one woman bore. She ruled our Ruler; she carried him in whom we are; she gave milk to our bread.

ST. AUGUSTINE (*Sermons*)

I am bowed down with many temptations and evil deeds, and with soul and body I bow down to thee O pure one, and ceaselessly cry, Do thou convert me.

BYZANTINE LITURGY
(*Euchologion*)

He willed us to have all through Mary.

ST. BERNARD OF CLAIRVAUX

I sing of a maiden
That is makeles:
King of all kings
To her son she ches.

He came al so stil
There his mother was,
As dew in April
That falleth on the grass.

He came al so still
To his mother's bour,
As dew in April
That falleth on the flour.
He came al so still
There his mother lay,
As dew in April
That falleth on the spray.

Mother and maiden
Was never none but she;
Well may such a lady
Goddes mother be.

Makeless: matchless; *Ches*: chose

ENGLISH CAROL
(*15th century*)

No worship of Mary is more gracious than if you imitate Mary's humility.

ERASMUS (*Enchiridion*)

P

PALM SUNDAY

When fishes flew and forests walked
    And figs grew upon thorn,
    Some moment when the moon was blood
    Then surely I was born;

With monstrous head and sickening cry
    And ears like errant wings,
    The devil's walking parody
    On all four-footed things.

The tattered outlaw of the earth,
    Of ancient crooked will;
    Starve, scourge, deride me: I am dumb,
    I keep my secret still.

Fools! For I also had my hour;
    One far fierce hour and sweet:
    There was a shout about my ears,
    And palms before my feet.

              G. K. CHESTERTON (*The Donkey*)

PAPACY

Roma locuta, causa finita est
Rome having spoken, that decided the matter.

              ST. AUGUSTINE

I am the servant of the servants of God.

POPE ST. GREGORY THE GREAT

Nothing that happens in the world should escape the notice of the Supreme Pontiff.

POPE INNOCENT III (*1190*)

If till now you haven't been very firm in truth, I want you, I beg you, for the little time that is left, to be so — courageously and like a brave man — following Christ, whose vicar you are. . . .

Don't be afraid, for divine help is near. Just attend to spiritual affairs, to appointing good pastors and administrators in your cities, for you have experienced rebellion because of bad pastors and administrators. Do something about it! And take heart in Christ Jesus and don't be afraid.

Pursue and finish with true holy zeal what you have begun by holy intent — I mean your return [to Rome] and the sweet holy crusade. Delay no longer, for your delaying has already been the cause of a lot of trouble. . . .

Up, Father! No more irresponsibility! . . .

Forgive me Father, for talking to you like this. Out of the fullness of the heart the mouth speaks, you know. I am sure that if you are the kind of tree I want you to be, nothing will stand in your way.

ST. CATHERINE OF SIENA
(*to Pope Gregory XI, in exile at Avignon, 1326*)

Since God has given us the papacy, let us enjoy it.

POPE LEO X

We are prepared to go to the gates of Hell – but no further.

POPE PIUS VII
(*trying to achieve peace with Napoleon*)

Tell my son Joseph that he will meet my divisions in heaven.

POPE PIUS XII
(*Stalin had sneered "How many divisions has the Pope?"*)

The pope is becoming a missionary, you will say. Yes, the pope is becoming a missionary, which means a witness, a shepherd, an apostle on the move.

POPE PAUL VI

It often happens that I awake at night and begin to think about a serious problem and decide I must tell the Pope about it. Then I wake up completely and remember that I am the Pope.

BLESSED POPE JOHN XXIII

Anyone can be a Pope; the proof of this is that I have become one.

BLESSED POPE JOHN XXIII
(*to a boy who wrote asking whether to be a Pope or a policeman*)

Just think what Mom would say if she were here!

POPE JOHN PAUL I
(*to his sister, after his election*)

If someone had told me I would be Pope one day, I would have studied harder.

POPE JOHN PAUL I

I would have made a good Pope.

RICHARD M. NIXON

PAPAL AUDIENCES

Get out of my sight! Get out of my sight! Away! Away!
We grant blessing to no one who provokes the world to
war!

POPE ST. PIUS X
(*to Emperor Franz Josef of Austria, 1914*)

I expect you know my friend Evelyn Waugh, who, like
your Holiness, is a Roman Catholic.

RANDOLPH CHURCHILL, ENGLISH JOURNALIST
(*to Pope Pius XII*)

I'm sorry we're late, we misread the timetable. But there
– nobody's infallible.

GEOFFREY FISHER
ARCHBISHOP OF CANTERBURY
(*to Blessed Pope John XXIII*)

PARENTS

Don't hold your parents up to contempt. After all, you
are their son and it's just possible you may take after
them.

EVELYN WAUGH (*The Tablet, May 9, 1951*)

PATIENCE

Fly a thousand miles from saying, "I was in the *right*: it
was not *right* for me to suffer this, they had no *right* to

do such a thing to me." Do you think there was any question of rights when Jesus suffered the injuries which were so unrighteously inflicted on Him?

ST. TERESA OF ÁVILA
(*The Way of Perfection*)

He that complains or murmurs is not perfect, nor is he even a good Christian.

ST. JOHN OF THE CROSS
(*Spiritual Sentences and Maxims*)

Be patient with everyone, but above all with yourself. Do not lose courage in considering your own imperfections but instantly set about remedying them — every day begin the task anew.

ST. FRANCIS DE SALES

Restraining my impatience cost me so much that I was bathed in perspiration.

ST. THÉRÈSE OF LISIEUX

We must wait for God long, meekly, in the wind and wet, in the thunder and lightning, in the cold and the dark. Wait, and he will come. He never comes to those who do not wait.

F. W. FABER

Patience is a poultice for all wounds.

IRISH PROVERB

No matter how early you get up, you can't hasten the dawn.

SPANISH PROVERB

PEACE

O God, make us children of quietness, and heirs of peace.

ST. CLEMENT OF ALEXANDRIA

Lord, make me an instrument of your peace.
    Where there is hatred, let me sow love;
    Where there is injury, pardon;
    Where there is doubt, faith;
    Where there is despair, hope;
    Where there is darkness, light;
    And where there is sadness, joy.
    O Divine Master,
    grant that I may not so much seek to be consoled
    as to console;
to be understood as to understand;
    to be loved as to love.
    For it is in giving that we receive;
    It is in pardoning that we are pardoned,
    and it is in dying that we are born to eternal life.

ST. FRANCIS OF ASSISI

If they want peace, nations should avoid the pinpricks that precede cannon shots.

NAPOLEON BONAPARTE

For centuries now we've tried everything else; the power of wealth, of mighty armies and navies, machinations of diplomats. All have failed. Before it's too late, and time is running out, let us turn from trust in the chain reactions of exploding atoms to faith of the chain reaction of God's love. Love — love of God and fellow men.

That is God's formula for peace. Peace on earth to men of good will.

CARDINAL RICHARD J.CUSHING

Those who are serving their country in the armed forces should regard themselves as servants of the people's security and liberty. While they are fulfilling this duty they are genuinely contributing to the establishment of peace.

SECOND VATICAN COUNCIL
(*The Church in the Modern World*)

Peace is not the product of terror or fear. Peace is not the silence of cemeteries. Peace is not the silent result of violent repression. Peace is the generous, tranquil contribution of all to the good of all. Peace is dynamism. Peace is generosity. It is right and it is duty.

ARCHBISHOP OSCAR ROMERO

Come Lord, do not smile and say you are already with us. Millions do not know you, and to us who do, what is the difference? What is the point of your presence if our lives do not alter? Change our lives, shatter our complacency. Make your word our life's purpose. Take away the quietness of a clear conscience. Press us uncomfortably. For only thus that other peace is made, your peace.

ARCHBISHOP HELDER CAMARA

Peace begins with a smile — smile five times a day at someone you really don't want to smile at . . . do it for peace.

BLESSED MOTHER TERESA
(*Prayer, Seeking the Heart of God*)

PEACE OF SOUL

I am serene because I know you love me.
Because you love me, nothing can move me from my
 peace.
Because you love me, I am one to whom all good has
 come.

ANCIENT SCOTTISH PRAYER

How can a man remain in peace if he is getting involved in other people's affairs, and with things outside himself, meanwhile taking little notice of his inner self? Blessed are the single-hearted, for they shall have abundance of peace.

THOMAS À KEMPIS
(*The Imitation of Christ*)

He has great tranquility of heart who cares neither for the praises nor the fault-finding of men. He will easily be content and pacified, whose conscience is pure. You are not holier if you are praised, nor the more worthless if you are found fault with. What you are, that you are; neither by word can you be made greater than what you are in the sight of God.

THOMAS À KEMPIS
(*The Imitation of Christ*)

Don't lose your inner peace for anything whatsoever, even if your whole world seems upset.

ST. FRANCIS DE SALES

Resign every forbidden joy; restrain every wish that cannot be referred to God's will; banish all eager desires, all anxiety, desiring the will of God; seek him alone and supremely, and you will find peace.

ARCHBISHOP FRANÇOIS FÉNELON

Who except God can give you peace? Has the world ever been able to satisfy the heart?

ST. GERARD MAJELLA

It is a splendid habit to laugh inwardly at yourself. It is the best way of regaining your good humor and finding God without further anxiety.

ABBÉ HENRI DE TOURVILLE
(*Letters of Direction*)

Your foolish fears about the future come from the devil. Think only of the present, abandon the future to Providence. It is the good use of the present that assures the future.

JEAN-PIERRE DE CAUSSADE, S.J.
(*The Flame of Divine Love*)

If we examine the source of our trouble and agitations, we find that they almost invariably spring from a desire of approval, or a fear of contempt.

CARDINAL JAMES GIBBONS
(*The Ambassador of Christ*)

It is implied in . . . true peace that we shall never be wholly submerged by the vortex of successive tensions which we have to endure. We shall never so forget the true and perennial order of things as to overestimate the task of the moment merely because we are caught in the tension of our effort to realize it.

DIETRICH VON HILDEBRAND

Thinking about interior peace destroys interior peace. The patient who constantly feels his pulse is not getting any better.

HUBERT VAN ZELLER, O.S.B.
(*Considerations*)

If you yourself are at peace, then there is at least some peace in the world.

THOMAS MERTON

Many people have asked me why I am at peace, or how I can be at peace. First of all, you have to put yourself totally in the hands of the Lord. Secondly, you have to begin seeing death not so much as an enemy but as a friend. And thirdly, you have to begin letting go. And if you can do these three things, then you experience peace.

CARDINAL JOSEPH BERNADIN
(*shortly before his death from cancer*)

It is not by escaping from our problems that we shall find peace. No, it is by facing up to them, bravely and in a straightforward manner, that we shall discover peace deep down. The wind lashes the surface of the sea and makes it rough and turbulent, but in the deep there is calm. The wind can only strike the surface.

CARDINAL BASIL HUME, O.S.B.
(*The Mystery of the Cross*)

PEDOPHILIA

Celibacy is not the real issue when dealing with this problem, as child abusers are not interested in or capable of adult sexual relations. The real issue is the need to understand the true meaning of pedophilia and ephebophilia, remove priests with these sexual orientations from active ministry and heighten seminary requirements so that persons with these orientations will not be admitted to formation programs and will be dismissed if this orientation is discovered or seriously suspected.

MELVIN C. BLANCHETTE AND GERALD D. COLEMAN
(*"Priest Pedophiles," America, April 25, 2002*)

PENANCE

My friend, when you want to write on a blackboard, you must first wipe off what is written there. I have, I assure you, a great deal to wipe off my board!

VENERABLE CHARLES DE FOUCAULD
(*when accused of excessive fasting*)

PERFECTION

He who climbs never stops going from beginning to beginning; through beginnings that have no end. He never stops desiring what he already knows.

ST. GREGORY OF NYSSA
(*Homily on the Song of Songs*)

Do not wish to be anything but what you are, and try to be that perfectly.

ST. FRANCIS DE SALES

The greatest thing for us is the perfection of our own soul; and the saints teach us that this perfection consists in doing our ordinary actions well.

ARCHBISHOP WILLIAM BERNARD ULLATHORNE, O.S.B.
(*Humility and Patience*)

PERSECUTION

To flee from persecution implies no fault in him who flees, but in him who persecutes.

ST. BERNARD OF CLAIRVAUX

We are asking pardon for the divisions among Christians, for the use of violence that some have committed in the service of truth, and for attitudes of mistrust and hostility assumed toward followers of other religions.

POPE JOHN PAUL II (*Rome, March 12, 2000*)

PERSEVERANCE

If there be anywhere on earth a lover of God who is always kept safe from falling, I know nothing of it — for it was not shown to me. But this was shown — that in falling and rising again we are always held close in one love.

JULIAN OF NORWICH
(*Revelations of Divine Love*)

Nothing great was ever done without much enduring.

ST. CATHERINE OF SIENA

It is constancy that God wants.

MATT TALBOT

Another fall . . . and what a fall! Despair? No! Humble yourself and through Mary, your mother, have recourse to the merciful love of Jesus. A *miserere* — "have mercy on me" — and lift up your heart! And now, begin again.

ST. JOSEMARÍA ESCRIVÁ
(*The Way*)

PIETY

Devotion that has not a tent on Calvary and one near the tabernacle, will not result in solid piety and will never accomplish anything great. I find that we do not preach enough on this Mystery of Love par excellence. As a result, souls suffer, become sensual and material in their piety, and are inordinately attached to creatures because they fail to find their consolation and strength in the Lord.

ST. PETER JULIAN EYMARD

There is little piety in big churches.

ITALIAN PROVERB

PILGRIMAGE

They that go much on pilgrimage are seldom thereby made perfect and holy.

THOMAS À KEMPIS
(*The Imitation of Christ*)

PLAGUE

There are some persons in the number of those afflicted who, notwithstanding they were wellborn and bred, have been constrained by extremity of want to sell or pawn all they had, remain shut up within the bare walls of a poor chamber, having not wherewithal to allay the pangs of hunger, nor scarcely cover nakedness. There are others who, for the space of three days together, have not gotten a morsel of bread to put into their mouths. We have just cause to fear that some do perish for want of food, others for want of tendance; others for want of helps and remedies. . . .

ST. HENRY MORSE AND ST. JOHN SOUTHWORTH,
BOTH LATER MARTYRED
(*Appeal for London plague victims, October 9, 1636*)

POETRY

Science is for those who learn; poetry, for those who know.

JOSEPH ROUX
(*Meditations of a Parish Priest*)

POLITICS

Politics are a part of morals.

CARDINAL HENRY EDWARD MANNING

The whole art of the political speech is to put "nothing" into it. It is much more difficult than it sounds.

HILAIRE BELLOC

Let those who are suited for it, or can become so, prepare themselves for the difficult but most honorable art of politics. Let them work to exercise this art without thought of personal convenience and without benefit of bribery. Prudently and honorably let them fight against injustice and oppression, the arbitrary rule of one person or one party, and lack of tolerance. Let them devote themselves to the welfare of all sincerely and fairly, indeed with charity and political courage.

SECOND VATICAN COUNCIL
(*The Church in the Modern World*)

POLITICIANS

Blessed the politician who well understands his role in the world.

Blessed the politician who personally exemplifies credibility.

Blessed the politician who works for the common good and not for his own interests.

Blessed the politician who is true to himself, his faith and his electoral promises.

Blessed the politician who works for unity and makes Jesus the fulcrum of its defense.

Blessed the politician who works for radical change, refusing to call good that which is evil and using the Gospel as a guide.

Blessed the politician who listens to the people before, during and after the elections, and who listens to God in prayer.

Blessed the politician who has no fear of the truth or the mass media, because at the time of judgment he will answer only to God.

CARDINAL FRANÇOIS XAVIER NGUYEN VAN THÛAN

POOR (see also SOCIAL JUSTICE)

You are not making a gift of your possessions to the poor person. You are handing over to him what is his. For what has been given in common for the use of all, you have arrogated to yourself. The world is given to all, and not only to the rich.

ST. AMBROSE

God has no need of your money, but the poor have. You give it to the poor, and God receives it.

SAINT AUGUSTINE

The bread which you do not use is the bread of the hungry; the garment hanging in your wardrobe is the garment of him who is naked; the shoes you do not wear are the shoes of the one who is barefoot; the acts of charity that you do not perform are so many injustices that you commit.

ST. BASIL

The needy are our neighbors, if we note rightly;
As prisoners in cells, or poor folk in hovels,
Charged with children and overcharged by landlords.
What they may spare in spinning they spend on rental,
On milk, or on meal to make porridge
To still the sobbing of the children at meal time.
Also, they themselves suffer much hunger.
They have woe in winter-time and wake at midnight
To rise and rock the cradle at the bedside,
To card and to comb, to darn clouts and to wash them,
To rub and to reel and to put rushes on the paving.
The woe of these women who dwell in hovels
Is too sad to speak of or say in rhyme.
And many other men have much to suffer
From hunger and from thirst; they turn the fair side
    outward,
For they are abashed to beg, lest it should be
    acknowledged
At their neighbors what they need at noon and even.
I know all this well; for the world has taught me
What befalls a mother who has many children,

With no claim but his craft to feed and clothe them,
When the mouths are many and the money scarce.
They have bread and penny ale in place of a pittance,
And cold flesh and venison from the butcher.
On Fridays and fast days a farthing worth of mussels
Would be a feast for such folk, with a few cockles.
It were an alms to help with such burdens,
And to comfort such cottagers and crooked men and
    blind folk.

WILLIAM LANGLAND
(*The Vision of Piers Plowman*)

If you want God to hear your prayers, hear the voice of
the poor. If you wish God to anticipate your wants,
provide those of the needy without waiting for them to
ask you. Especially anticipate the needs of those who
are ashamed to beg. To make them ask for alms is to
make them buy it.

ST. THOMAS OF VILLANOVA

A small number of very rich men have been able to lay
upon the teeming masses of the laboring poor a yoke
little better than that of slavery itself.

POPE LEO XIII (*Rerum Novarum*)

The trouble with us in the past has been that we were too
often drawn into an alliance with the wrong side. Selfish
employers have flattered the Church by calling it the
great conservative force, and then called upon the police
to act while they paid but a pittance of wages to those
who worked for them ... our place is beside the poor.

CARDINAL GEORGE MUNDELEIN,
ARCHBISHOP OF CHICAGO (*1938*)

When I give bread to the poor, they call me a saint. When I ask why the poor have no bread, they call me a Communist.

ARCHBISHOP HELDER CAMARA

I don't think the poor ever get used to cockroaches, bedbugs, body lice, flees, rats and such like vermin that go with poverty. They simply endure them, sometimes with patience, sometimes with a corroding bitterness that the comfortable and pious stigmatize as envy. Someone asked Peter once why God had created bedbugs, and he said: "For our patience, probably."

DOROTHY DAY (*About Peter Maurin*)

If a free society cannot help the many who are poor, it cannot save the few who are rich.

PRESIDENT JOHN F. KENNEDY
(*Inaugural Address, January 20, 1961*)

Commitment to the poor is based on the Gospel: it does not have to rely on some political manifesto.

POPE JOHN PAUL II (*Conference of
Latin American Bishops, Puebla, 1979*)

Today it is fashionable to talk about the poor. Unfortunately it is not fashionable to talk with them.

BLESSED MOTHER TERESA

POOR IN SPIRIT

"Poor in spirit" refers, not precisely to humility, but to an attitude of dependence on God and detachment from earthly supports.

RONALD KNOX

POVERTY

All the wise men that ever were, by aught that I can
    witness,
Praise poverty as the best of life, if patience follow it,
As by far the more blessed, and better than riches.
Although it is sour to suffer, sweet comes after,
there is a rough rind round the walnut,
But after that bitter bark has been shelled away
There is a kernel of comfort which conduces health –
So after poverty or penance patiently suffered;
For that makes man mindful of God, and more truly
    willing
To weep and to pray well, whence mercy arises.
And thus Christ is the kernel and comfort of the spirit.
The poor man sleeps more soundly and safely than
    the others.
He dreads death, darkness and robbers
Less than he who is rich. . . .

WILLIAM LANGLAND
(The Vision of Piers Plowman)

To appreciate the true usefulness of poverty, how far it
really has a place among the means suitable to attain our
final end, we should reflect on the many sins from
which we are preserved by holy poverty, since it does
away with the stuff of which they are made. . . . It slays
pride, that worm of the rich, and cuts out those infer-
nal leeches of excess and gluttony, and of so many other
sins. And should we fall, through weakness, it helps us
to get up quickly, because there is none of that amorous
attachment which, like glue, binds the heart to the earth
and to the things of the earth, and leaves no freedom to

get up again, to come to one's senses and to turn to God. Poverty makes it easier in every case to hear better the voice, that is, the inspiration of the Holy Spirit, removing any obstacles in its way. It also makes prayer more effective in the sight of God. "The Lord heard the prayer of the poor." It speeds us along the way of the virtues like the traveler relieved of every burden. It frees us from that slavery common to so many of the great of this world, in which "all things obey or serve money."

JUAN DE POLANCO, S.J.,
SECRETARY TO ST. IGNATIUS LOYOLA
(*Letter to members of the
Society of Jesus, August 7, 1547*)

The real advantage of poverty lies in this: It makes us raise our hearts to God.

ST. VINCENT DE PAUL

God does not create poverty. We do, because we do not share.

BLESSED MOTHER TERESA

POWER

Power tends to corrupt and absolute power corrupts absolutely.

LORD ACTON

PRAYER

As far as you can, when you pray, make a deaf-mute of your intellect.... Renounce everything and you will obtain everything.

ABBA EVAGRIUS (*Of Prayer*)

The thinking soul has a forecourt, namely sense; it has a temple, namely reason; and it has a priest, the intellect. An intellect pillaged by harmful thoughts is to be found in the forecourt; an intellect plundered by permitted thoughts is in the temple; an intellect that escapes both is judged fit to enter the sanctuary.

ELIAS EKDIDOS (*Philokalia*)

Pray simply. Do not expect to find in your heart any remarkable gift of prayer. Consider yourself unworthy of it. Then you will find peace. Use the empty cold dryness of your prayer as food for your humility. Repeat constantly: I am not worthy; Lord, I am not worthy! But say it calmly, without agitation.

ST. MACARIUS OF OPTINA

In your prayer, shun grace-notes and flowery excesses; one word was enough to reconcile the thief and the prodigal son with God. . . . Often the mere babblings of a child will touch his father in heaven.

ST. JOHN OF THE LADDER (*Philokalia*)

Lord, teach me to seek you, and reveal yourself to me as I look for you. For I cannot seek you unless you first teach me. Nor find you unless you first reveal yourself to me.

ST. AMBROSE

Prayer is the place of refuge for every worry, a foundation for cheerfulness, a source of constant happiness, a protection against sadness.

ST. JOHN CHRYSOSTOM

Pray with your whole being even though you think it has no savor for you. For such prayer is very profitable even though you feel nothing, though you see nothing, even though it seems impossible to you. It is in dryness and barrenness, in sickness and feebleness that your prayer is most pleasing to me, even though you think that it has little savor for you.

JULIAN OF NORWICH
(*Revelations of Divine Love*)

Souls without prayer are like bodies, palsied and lame, having hands and feet they cannot use.

ST. TERESA OF ÁVILA (*The Interior Castle*)

However softly we speak, he is near enough to hear us. Neither is there any need for wings to go to find him. All one need do is go into solitude and look at him within oneself. . . . Since he does not force our will, he takes what we give him; but he does not give himself completely unless we give ourselves completely.

ST. TERESA OF ÁVILA (*The Way of Perfection*)

Prayer reveals to souls the vanity of earthly goods and pleasures. It fills them with light, strength and consolation; and gives them a foretaste of the calm bliss of our heavenly home.

ST. ROSE OF VITERBO

You need not cry very loud; he is nearer to us than we think.

BROTHER LAWRENCE

I would have no desire other than to do your will. Teach me to pray; pray yourself in me.

ARCHBISHOP FRANÇOIS FÉNELON

Do not distress yourself about your prayers. It is not always necessary to employ words, even inwardly, it is enough to raise your heart and let it rest in our Lord, to look lovingly up toward this divine Lover of our souls for between lovers the eyes speak more eloquently than the tongue.

ST. FRANCIS DE SALES

Those who pray are certainly saved; those who do not pray are certainly damned.

ST. ALPHONSUS LIGUORI

We must pray literally without ceasing — without ceasing; in every occurrence and employment of our lives. You know I mean that prayer of the heart which is independent of place or situation, or which is, rather, a habit of lifting up the heart to God, as in a constant communication with Him.

ST. ELIZABETH SETON

The wish for prayer is a prayer itself.

GEORGES BERNANOS
(*The Diary of a Country Priest*)

Do I want to pray or only to think about my human problems? Do I want to pray or simply kneel there contemplating my sorrow? Do I want to direct my prayer towards God or let it direct itself towards me?

HUBERT VAN ZELLER, O.S.B. (*Considerations*)

Fortunate is he for whom children pray.

J. B. MORTON
(*Hilaire Belloc, a Memoir*)

God only comes to those who ask him to come; and he cannot refuse to come to those who implore him long, often and ardently.

SIMONE WEIL

You don't know how to pray? Put yourself in the presence of God, and as soon as you have said, "Lord, I don't know how to pray!" you can be sure you have already begun.

ST. JOSEMARÍA ESCRIVÁ (*The Way*)

To pray well you must think of Jesus on the cross. Surely you can see how impossible it is to be distracted when you see your Brother crucified?

BLESSED BROTHER ANDRÉ, C.S.C.

When people today speak of "adult" Christians in prayer, sometimes they exaggerate. Personally, when I speak alone with God or Our Lady, I prefer to feel myself as a child; the miter, the skull-cap and the ring all disappear. I send the grown-up on vacation, and even the bishop, with all the grave dignity and ponderousness due to his rank! And I abandon myself to the spontaneous tenderness that a child has for his mom and dad.

ALBINO LUCIANI, LATER POPE JOHN PAUL I
(*My Rosary*)

Prayer is the best weapon we possess, the key that opens the heart of God.

ST. PADRE PIO

Change your hearts . . .
Unless we change our hearts we are not converted.
Changing places is not the answer.

The answer is to change our hearts.
And how do we change?
By praying.

BLESSED MOTHER TERESA
(*Prayer, Seeking the Heart of God*)

Prayer is both a gift of grace and a determined response on our part. It always presupposes effort.

CATECHISM OF THE CATHOLIC CHURCH, 2725

It is very difficult to be a praying person and then go and be beastly to your neighbor.

CARDINAL BASIL HUME, O.S.B.

How to pray? This is a simple matter. I would say: Pray any way you like, so long as you do pray.

POPE JOHN PAUL II

No prayer, no power.
    A little prayer, a little power.
    A lot of prayer, a lot of power!
    Never forget this.

ANONYMOUS

PRAYERS FOR THE DEAD

May the angels lead you into paradise: may the martyrs welcome you at your coming, and lead you into the heavenly city, Jerusalem. May the choir of angels receive you, and with Lazarus, who is poor no longer, may you have eternal rest.

THE ROMAN MISSAL (*In Paradisum*)

O God, the Creator and Redeemer of all the faithful, grant to the souls of thy servants departed the remission of all their sins, that, by our devout prayers, they may obtain that pardon for their sins which they have always desired.

THE ROMAN MISSAL
(*Collect for First Mass of All Souls*)

Deliver me, O Lord, from eternal death on that awful day: when the heavens and the earth shall be moved: when you shall come to judge the world by fire. Fear and trembling have laid hold of me, and I am greatly afraid because of the wrath to come when the heavens and the earth shall be shaken.... Eternal rest grant unto them, O Lord, and let perpetual light shine upon them.

ROMAN RITUAL (*Burial Service Responsory*)

You see me lying speechless before you. Weep over me, O brethren, friends, relatives and acquaintances. For yesterday I was conversing with you, but the dread hour of death came upon me all of a sudden. But now, all my friends who have loved me and held me dear, give me your last farewell kiss; for I shall no longer walk with you, or talk with you. I go before the Judge who knows no favorites. Both slave and master stand before him, king and soldier, rich and poor, equal in all respects. Each shall be rewarded with glory or shame according to his deeds. So I beseech you all, pray to Christ our God for me without ceasing, that I may not be sentenced to the place of punishment for my sins, but that I may be established in the light of eternal life.

BYZANTINE LITURGY
(*Prayer at the Grave*)

Where is earthly endeavor? Where is the vanity of temporal things? Where is gold and silver? Where is the crowd and tumult of household servants? All is dust, all ashes, all shadows! But come, let us cry to the King: O Lord, endow with your eternal goods him who has departed from our midst and grant him rest in everlasting bliss.

BYZANTINE LITUURGY
(*Funeral Service*)

O Christ, rest the souls of thy servants with the saints, where there is no sickness, nor sadness, nor sighing, but life without ending.

BYZANTINE LITURGY (*Compline*)

PREDESTINATION

When I am told (by those who confuse predestination with God's providence) that God already knows who will be saved and who will be damned, and therefore anything we do is useless, I usually answer with four truths that the bible spells out for us:

God wants that everyone be saved;

No one is predestined to go to hell;

Jesus died for everyone;

and everyone is given sufficient graces for salvation.

GABRIELE AMORTH
(*An Exorcist Tells His Story*)

PRESIDENCY

I am not the Catholic candidate for President. I am the Democratic Party's candidate for President, who happens also to be a Catholic.

JOHN F. KENNEDY

PRIDE

Pride is out and pride is in,
And pride is root of every sin,
And pride will always fight to win,
Till he has brought a man to woe.
Man, beware, or fall in woe:
Consider pride, and let it go.
Lucifer was angel-bright,
A conqueror of power and might;
But through his pride he lost his light,
And fell to everlasting woe.
Man, beware, or fall in woe:
Consider pride, and let it go.
If you think that swear-words roared
Or fashionable clothes afford
You rights to be a king or Lord
Little it shall avail you so.
Man, beware, or fall in woe:
Consider pride, and let it go.
When at last to church you glide,
Worms shall burrow through your side,
And little shall avail your pride
Or any other vice you show.
Man, beware, or fall in woe:
Consider pride, and let it go.
Pray to Christ with bloody side
And other gashes cruel and wide,
That so he may forgive your pride
And all your sinning here below.
Man, beware, or fall in woe:
Consider pride, and let it go.

ANONYMOUS (*15th century*;
Translated by Brian Stone)

You must ask God to give you power to fight against the sin of pride which is your greatest enemy — the root of all that is evil, and the failure of all that is good. For God resists the proud.

ST. VINCENT DE PAUL

Pride dies twenty minutes after death.

ST. FRANCIS DE SALES

PRIESTHOOD

The priest by nature is like all other men; by dignity he surpasses every other man on earth; by his conduct he ought to compare with the angels.

ST. BERNARD OF CLAIRVAUX

O priest! Take care lest what was said to Christ on the cross be said to you: "He saved others, himself he cannot save."

ST. NORBERT

A good man was ther of religioun,
And was a poorë Parson of a town;
But riche was of holy thought and werke
He was also a learnèd man, a clerk
That Cristës gospel gladly woldë preach;
His parisshens devoutly wolde he teach. . . .
Wyd was his parish, and houses far asonder,
But yet he laftë not for reyne or thonder,
In sickness and in mischief to visite
The ferthest in his parish, smal and great,
Uppon his feet, and in his hand a staf,
This noble ensample to his sheep he gaf,
That first he wroughte, and after that he taughte,

Out of the gospel he those wordës caughte,
And this figure he added yet thereto,
That if gold rustë, what should iron do?

Laftë not: ceased not

GEOFFREY CHAUCER
(*Canterbury Tales, Prologue*)

To live in the midst of the world with no desire for its pleasures; to be a member of every family, yet belonging to none; to share all sufferings; to penetrate all secrets, to heal all wounds; to daily go from men to God to offer him their homage and petitions; to return from God to men to bring them his pardon and hope; to have a heart of fire for charity and a heart of bronze for chastity; to bless and to be blest forever. O God, what a life, and it is yours O Priest of Jesus Christ!

JEAN-BAPTISTE LACORDAIRE, O.P.

It is necessary to pray for priests because they are often forgotten by the living, since Christians often consider that priests do not need prayers.

ST. JOSEPH MOSCATI

It is not a priest's business to impose his own ideas, but to aid the workings of grace.

ABBÉ HENRI HUVELIN

It doesn't matter so much my being a coward – and the rest. I can put God into a man's mouth just the same – and I can give him God's pardon. It wouldn't make any difference to that if every priest in the Church was like me.

GRAHAM GREENE
(*The Power and the Glory*)

The priest is not an angel sent from heaven.
He is a man, a member of the Church, a Christian.
Remaining man and Christian, he begins to speak to you the word of God.

This word is not his own. No, he comes to you because God has told him to proclaim God's word. Perhaps he has not entirely understood it himself. Perhaps he adulterates it. Perhaps he falters and stammers. How else could one speak God's word, ordinary man that he is? But must not some one of us say something about God, about eternal life, about the majesty of grace in our sanctified being; must not some one of us speak of sin, judgment and the mercy of God?

KARL RAHNER, S.J.

Tonight, Lord, I am alone.
Little by little the sounds died down in the church,
The people went away,
And I came home,
Alone.
I passed people who were returning from a walk.
I went by the cinema that was disgorging its crowd.
I skirted the terraces where tired strollers were trying to
    prolong the pleasure of a Sunday holiday.
I bumped into youngsters playing on the footpath,
Youngsters, Lord,
Other people's youngsters who will never be my own.
Here I am, Lord,
Alone.
The silence troubles me,
The solitude oppresses me.
Lord, I'm 35 years old,
A body made like others,

ready for work,
A heart made for love,
But I've given you all.
It's true, of course, that you needed it.
I've given you all, but it's hard, Lord.
It's hard to give one's body; it would like to give itself
    to others.
It's hard to love everyone and to claim no one.
It's hard to shake a hand and not want to retain it.
It's hard to inspire affection, to give it to you.
It's hard to be nothing to oneself in order to be
    everything to others.
It's hard to be like others, among others, and to be of
    them.
It's hard always to give without trying to receive.
It's hard to seek out others and to be unsought oneself.
It's hard to suffer from the sins of others, and yet be
    obliged to hear and bear them.
It's hard to be told secrets, and be unable to share
    them.
It's hard to carry others and never, even for a moment,
    be carried.
It's hard to sustain the feeble and never be able to lean
    on one who is strong.
It's hard to be alone,
Alone before everyone,
Alone before the world,
Alone before suffering,
    death,
    sin. . . .
Lord tonight, while all is still and I feel sharply the
    sting of solitude,

While men devour my soul and I feel incapable of
  satisfying their hunger,
While the whole world presses on my shoulders with
  all its weight of misery and sin,
I repeat to you my "yes" — not in a burst of laughter,
  but slowly, clearly, humbly,
Alone, Lord, before you,
In the peace of the evening.

MICHEL QUOIST (*"The Priest:
A prayer on Sunday night," Prayers of Life*)

At times loneliness will weigh heavily on the priest, but
not for that reason will he regret having generously
chosen it. He who has chosen to belong completely to
Christ will find, above all, in intimacy with him and in
his grace, the power of spirit necessary to banish sadness
and regret and to triumph over discouragement.

POPE PAUL VI

You are priests, not social or political leaders. Let us not
be under the illusion that we are serving the Gospel
through an exaggerated interest in the wide field of
temporal problems.

POPE JOHN PAUL II

There is a deep contradiction between priesthood and
depression. You can be a good and depressed banker or
taxi-driver, a gloomy but effective accountant or lawyer.
But one cannot be a preacher of the gospel and be
plunged in gloom. It makes no sense. We can only be
credible bearers of the good news if we are fundamen-
tally, if not always, joyful . . . there is a deep joy that
belongs to our vocation as priests. This joy is deeply

linked with sorrow and even with anger. These are the passions of those who are alive with the gospel.

TIMOTHY RADCLIFFE, O.P.
(*Address to National Conference of Priests,*
England and Wales, 2002)

PRISON

In prison there are two possible solutions. You can rebel against your situation, or you can regard yourself as a monk.

JACQUES FESCH
(*Letter to Brother Thomas, O.S.B.*)

PROBLEM OF EVIL

In the final analysis, the questions of why bad things happen to good people transmutes itself into some very different questions, no longer asking why something happened, but asking how we will respond, what we intend to do now that it happened.

PIERRE TEILHARD DE CHARDIN, S.J.

PROFESSION OF FAITH

I am a Catholic. As far as possible I go to Mass every day. As far as possible I kneel down and tell these beads every day. If you reject me on account of my religion, I shall thank God that he has spared me the indignity of being your representative.

HILAIRE BELLOC
(*to the electors of South Salford, 1907*)

PROSTITUTION

While it is always gravely sinful to engage in prostitution, the imputability of the offense can be attenuated by destitution, blackmail or social pressure.

CATECHISM OF THE CATHOLIC CHURCH, 2355

PROVIDENCE

For, if the providence of God does not preside over human affairs, there is no point in busying oneself about religion.

ST. AUGUSTINE (*De Utilitate Credendi*)

Man proposes, and God disposes.

ST. AUGUSTINE

Many a man curses the rain that falls upon his head, and knows that it brings abundance to drive away hunger.

ST. BASIL

All events that take place in this world, even those apparently fortuitous or casual, are comprehended in the order of divine providence, on which fate depends.

ST. THOMAS AQUINAS (*Summa Theologica*)

Commit every particle of your being in all things, down to the smallest details of your life, eagerly and with perfect trust to the unfailing and most sure providence of God.

JEAN-PIERRE DE CAUSSADE, S.J.
(*Abandonment to Divine Providence*)

It is a perfectly correct view of things – and strictly consonant with the Gospel – to regard providence across the ages as brooding over the world in ceaseless effort to spare that world its bitter wounds and to bind up its hurts. Most certainly it is God himself who, in the course of the centuries, awakens the great benefactors of mankind, and the great physicians, in ways that agree with the general rhythm of progress. He it is who inspires, even among those furthest from acknowledging his existence, the quest for every means of comfort and every means of healing.

PIERRE TEILHARD DE CHARDIN, S.J.

Circumstances are the sacraments of God's will.

EDEL QUINN

Often place your confidence in Divine Providence and be assured that sooner Heaven and earth shall pass away than that the Lord neglect to protect you.

ST. PADRE PIO

PRUDENCE

If according to times and needs you should be obliged to make fresh rules and change certain things, do it with prudence and good advice

ST. ANGELA MERICI

Prudence is the cause of the other virtues being virtues at all.

JOSEPH PIEPER

PUBLIC LIFE

If you can't completely eradicate wrong ideas, or deal with inveterate vices as effectively as you wish, that's no

reason for turning your back on public life altogether.
You wouldn't abandon ship in a storm just because you
couldn't control the winds.

ST. THOMAS MORE (Utopia)

PURITY

Without charity, purity is fruitless and its sterile waters
turn the soul into a swamp, a stagnant marsh, from
which rises the stench of pride.

ST. JOSEMARÍA ESCRIVÁ (The Way)

R

RACISM

Many times the new face of racism is the computer printout, the graph of profits and losses, the pink slip, the nameless statistic. Today's racism flourishes in the triumph of private concern over public responsibility, individual success over social commitment and personal fulfillment over authentic compassion.

UNITED STATES CATHOLIC BISHOPS
(*Brothers and Sisters to Us*)

RATIONALISTS

Rationalists renounce reason in their attempt to solve the problem of Christ. Either Christ was God or he was mad. The rationalist will not accept the former alternative, he dare not suggest the latter.

ARNOLD LUNN (*Now I See*)

REASON

It is the will of God that you occupy yourself in writing books: such is your vocation. There is no way more useful to influence people than to start from reason and by this means to lead to religion.

POPE PIUS VIII
(*to Antonio Rosmini*)

RECOLLECTION

Come, now, insignificant man! Fly for a moment from your affairs, escape for a little while from the tumult of your thoughts. Put aside now your weighty cares and leave your wearisome toils. Abandon yourself for a brief space to God and rest for a little in him. Go into the inner chamber of your mind, shut out everything save God and whatever may help you in seeking God. Then, having barred the door of your chamber, seek him.

St. Anselm (*Prosologion*)

It is better to say one Our Father fervently and devoutly than a thousand with no devotion and full of distraction.

St. Edmund

A monk met the handmaids of God upon a certain road, and at the sight of them he turned out of the way, and the abbess said to him: "If you had been a perfect monk you would not have looked so closely as to see that we were women."

The Desert Fathers

When a person is set down before God, is trying hard to be recollected, is even trying to think of God and Christ, and all that happens is that there is a blank, an emptiness, a pain, it is not easy to get across to that person that all is well and this is as it should be!

Michael Hollings

REDEMPTION

The efficacy of the divine blood is such that a single true impulse of charity, however imperceptible, may in the divine justice balance thousands of crimes.

LÉON BLOY

REFORM

The reformer is always right about what is wrong. He is generally wrong about what is right.

G. K. CHESTERTON
(*Illustrated London News article, 1928*)

As long as the Church lasts, it will feel the need for reform, for a more perfect assimilation of its actuality to the ideal which illumines its path.

KARL ADAM
(*The Spirit of Catholicism*)

REFORMATION

It is of first importance to appreciate this historical truth. Only a few of the most bitter or ardent Reformers set out to destroy Catholicism as a separate existing thing of which they were conscious and which they hated. Still less did most of the Reformers set out to erect some other united counter-religion. They set out (as they themselves put it and as it had been put for a century and a half before the great upheaval) "to reform." They professed to purify the Church and restore it to its original virtues of directness and simplicity. They professed in their various ways (and the various groups of them differed in almost everything except their increasing reaction against unity) to get rid of excrescences, superstitions and historical falsehoods of which, heaven knows, there was a multitude for them to attack.

HILAIRE BELLOC
(*The Great Heresies*)

RELIGION

Religion is the act of man — the whole man, soul and body. It is not the act of the soul only, for man is not only soul. . . . The supernatural does not ignore the natural or substitute something else for it. It is built upon or built into the natural. Sanctifying grace does not provide us with a new soul; it enters into the soul we already have. Nor does it give the soul new faculties but elevates the faculties that are already there, giving intellect and will new powers of operation. God-as-Sanctifier does not destroy or bypass the work of God-as-Creator. What God has created, God sanctifies.

FRANK SHEED
(*Theology and Sanity*)

What a travesty to think religion means saving my little soul by my little good deeds and letting the rest go hang.

GERALD VANN, O.P. (*The Heart of Man*)

Religion is the world in its journey toward God. Christianity is God journeying toward the world, and people who believe in him taking the same direction as he.

CARDINAL HANS URS VON BALTHASAR

RELIGIOUS EXERCISES

The time that really matters is the time between our
religious exercises.

R. H. BENSON (*The Light Invisible*)

RELIGIOUS LIFE

I have desired to go
Where springs not fail,
To fields where flies no sharp and sided hail
And a few lilies blow.
And I have asked to be
Where no storms come,
Where the green swell is in the havens dumb,
And out of the swing of the sea.

GERARD MANLEY HOPKINS, S.J.
(*Heaven-Haven: A nun takes the veil*)

One of the sure signs of fervor and progress in religious
life is joy and contentment. When we are satisfied with
God and with His way of dealing with us, it reflects on
the countenance. The face is aglow with joy.

BLESSED CYPRIAN TANSI, O.C.S.O. (*Retreat Notes*)

RENEWAL

Co-operate with others to bring about a new spring in
the Church. Prepare people to welcome a new Pente-
cost. Become that open door which permits the cool
breeze to enter and renew the Church. . . .

The most disastrous scandal of our time is the
separation between the practice of religion within

church buildings and the practice of religion outside in society.

CARDINAL FRANÇOIS XAVIER NGUYEN VAN THÛAN
(*Thoughts of Light from a Prison Cell*)

REPENTANCE

Repentance is deep understanding.

ANONYMOUS
(*The Shepherd of Hermas*)

We make a ladder for ourselves out of our vices if we trample the vices themselves under foot.

ST. AUGUSTINE

Even though there is only one baptism for the whitening of stains, yet there are two eyes which, when filled with tears, provide a baptismal font for the limbs. For the Creator knew well beforehand that sins multiply in us at all times, and though there is only a single baptism, he fixed in the single body two fonts that give absolution.

ST. EPHRAIM THE SYRIAN
(*Hymns on the Ascetic Abraham*)

When you attack the roots of sin, fix your thought on the God whom you desire rather than upon the sin which you hate.

WALTER HILTON
(*The Ladder of Perfection*)

I would much rather feel penitence than know how to define it.

THOMAS À KEMPIS (*The Imitation of Christ*)

Our repentance is not so much regret for the evil we have done, as a fear of what may happen to us because of it.

FRANÇOIS DUC DE LA ROCHEFOUCAULD (*Maxims*)

It can take less than a minute to commit a sin. It takes not as long to obtain God's forgiveness. Penitence and amendment should take a lifetime.

HUBERT VAN ZELLER, O.S.B. (*Considerations*)

REPRESSION

I want to make a special appeal to soldiers, national guardsmen and policemen: each of you is one of us. The peasants you kill are your own brothers and sisters. When you hear a man telling you to kill, remember God's words, "thou shalt not kill." No soldier is obliged to obey a law contrary to the law of God. In the name of God, in the name of our tormented people, I beseech you, I implore you, in the name of God I command you to stop the repression.

ARCHBISHOP OSCAR ROMERO
(*in his last broadcast sermon*)

REPUTATION

He that has an ill name is half hanged.

15TH-CENTURY PROVERB

RESIGNATION

When his life's work was threatened, St. Ignatius Loyola was asked what he would do if Pope Pius IV dissolved or otherwise acted against the Society of Jesus, to which he had devoted his energy and gifts; and he replied: "I would pray for fifteen minutes, then I would not think of it again."

ALAN PATON

REVOLUTION

I have felt for a long time — in fact ever since I first knew and loved Christ, and I still feel — that the Church is the total Revolution.

CARDINAL JULES GERARD SALIÈGE

ROSARY

When you say the rosary, say after each mystery: O my Jesus, forgive us our sins, save us from the fires of hell, and lead all souls to heaven, especially those in most need of thy mercy.

THE BLESSED VIRGIN MARY
(FÁTIMA, JULY 13, 1917)

The rosary is an impoverished prayer? What, then, would be a "rich" prayer? The rosary is a procession of Paters, the prayer taught by Jesus; of Aves, the salutation of God to the Virgin by means of an angel; of Glorias, the praise of the Most Holy Trinity.

ALBINO LUCIANI, LATER POPE JOHN PAUL I
(*My Rosary*)

The rosary has accompanied me in moments of joy and in moments of difficulty. To it I have entrusted any number of concerns; in it I have always found comfort. . . . The rosary is my favorite prayer. A marvelous prayer!

POPE JOHN PAUL II
(*Rosarium Virginis Mariae*)

Moving on from the infancy and the hidden life in Nazareth to the public life of Jesus, our contemplation brings us to those mysteries which may be called in a special way "mysteries of light.". . . In proposing to the Christian community five significant moments – "luminous" mysteries – during this phase of Christ's life, I think that the following can be fittingly singled out: (1) his baptism in the Jordan, (2) his self-manifestation at the wedding of Cana, (3) his proclamation of the Kingdom of God, with his call to conversion, (4) his Transfiguration, and (5) his institution of the Eucharist, as the sacramental expression of the Paschal mystery.

POPE JOHN PAUL II
(*Rosarium Virginis Mariae*)

RUSSIA

I shall come to ask for the consecration of Russia to my Immaculate Heart and the communion of reparation on the first Saturdays. If people attend to my requests, Russia will be converted and the world will have peace. If not, Russia will spread its errors throughout the world, stirring up war and the persecution of the Church. The good will be martyred, and the Holy Father will have much to suffer, and various nations will be annihilated. In the end, my Immaculate Heart will triumph.

THE BLESSED VIRGIN MARY
(*Fátima, July 13, 1913*)

S

SACRAMENTS

What was visible in Christ has now passed over into the sacraments of the Church.

POPE ST. LEO THE GREAT (*Sermons*)

Christ's death is the worldwide cause of salvation. All the same, any universal cause needs to be applied to produce particular effects; consequently determinate remedies need to be applied to men if they are to be brought into the blessings flowing from Christ's death. These remedies, which are the sacraments of the Church, come to us in portions and are bound up with what we can experience.

ST. THOMAS AQUINAS (*Contra Gentes*)

A sacrament is a remembrance of the past [Christ's Passion], a proof of the present [grace], and a promise of the future [eternal life].

ST. THOMAS AQUINAS (*Summa Theologica*)

SACRED HEART

Behold this Heart which so loved men that it spared nothing, even to the exhausting of itself and wearing itself out, in order to show them its love.... Instead of acknowledgment I receive from the greater number nothing but ingratitude, by their irreverences and sacrileges, and by the coldness and contempt with which they treat me in this sacrament of love. But what I feel most deeply is that there are hearts consecrated to me which treat me so. It is on this account that I make this demand of you: that the first Friday after the Octave of the Blessed Sacrament [Corpus Christi] be devoted to a special feast in honor of my Heart; that you will go to communion on that day and give it a reparation of honor by an act of amendment to repair the insults it has received during the time of its being exposed on the altar. I promise you, also, that my Heart will expand itself that it may pour forth, with abundance, the influence of its divine love upon those who shall thus honor it, and shall do their best to have such honor paid to it.

CHRIST TO ST. MARGARET MARY ALACOQUE

I need the closest possible union with Jesus, as if I were spending my whole life before his tabernacle . . . I must think of myself as living solely for the Sacred Heart of Jesus.

BLESSED POPE JOHN XXIII

SACRIFICE

The sacrifice most acceptable to God is complete renunciation of the body and its passions. This is the only real piety.

CLEMENT OF ALEXANDRIA (*Stromateis*)

I left Oxford for good on Monday, February 23rd, 1846. On the Saturday and Sunday before, I was in my house at Littlemore simply by myself, as I had been for the first day or two when I had originally taken possession of it. I slept on Sunday night at my dear friend's,

Mr. Johnson's, at the Observatory. Various friends came to see the last of me . . . and I called on Dr. Ogle, one of my very oldest friends, for he was my private tutor when I was an Undergraduate. In him I took leave of my first college, Trinity, which was so dear to me, and which held on its foundation so many who have been kind to me both when I was a boy, and all through my Oxford life. Trinity had never been unkind to me. There used to be much snap-dragon growing on the walls opposite my freshman's rooms there, and I had for years taken it as the emblem of my own perpetual residence even unto death in my University.

On the morning of the 23rd I left the Observatory. I have never seen Oxford since, excepting its spires, as they are seen from the railway.

VENERABLE JOHN HENRY NEWMAN
(*Apologia pro Vita Sua*)

I saw Jesus moving through the world, laden with his Cross, searching for souls to bear it with him; but they all ran away at his approach . . . so once more I offered myself.

MARTHE ROBIN, FRENCH MYSTIC (*1902-1981*)

SAINTS

Everything that Brigid would ask of the Lord was granted her at once. For this was her desire: to satisfy the poor, to expel every hardship, to spare every miserable man.

She was abstemious, she was innocent, she was prayerful, she was patient. She was glad in God's commandments; she was firm, she was humble, she was forgiving, she was loving; she was a consecrated casket for keeping Christ's body and His blood: she was a temple of God. Her heart and mind were a throne of rest for the Holy Spirit. She was simple to God; she was compassionate to the wretched; she was splendid in miracles and marvels.

Wherefore her name among created things is dove among birds, vine among trees, sun among stars. . . .

THE BOOK OF LISMORE

The saints are like the stars. In his providence Christ conceals them in a hidden place that they may not shine before others when they might wish to do so. Yet they are always ready to exchange the quiet of contemplation for the works of mercy as soon as they perceive in their heart the invitation of Christ.

ST. ANTHONY OF PADUA

Every saint is a pattern, but no saint is a pattern of everything.

ABBÉ HENRI DE TOURVILLE (*Letters of Direction*)

To most, even good people, God is a belief. To the saints, he is an embrace.

FRANCIS THOMPSON

There is only one sorrow, the sorrow of not being a saint.

LÉON BLOY

Consult any of those saints whom the world calls mad. You will immediately be struck by the moderation and wisdom of his advice. . . . You will notice with astonishment that he understands human affairs a thousand times better than those who spend their lives in transacting them. He knows the world a thousand times better than men know it.

ERNEST HELLO
(*Life, Science and Art*)

The Catholic Church has a way of growing saints which is shared by no other communion. They are not turned out all alike as by a machine, but have the most startling individualities, so that the world has constantly counted them as mad. In a well-managed garden flowers are healthier, larger, brighter than in the fields, precisely because their idiosyncrasies are protected, encouraged, assisted to develop. And for this reason "individualism" in the truest sense flourishes far more luxuriantly in the enclosed garden of the Catholic Church than in the uncultivated woods and meadows without.

ABBOT JOHN CHAPMAN, O.S.B.
(*Bishop Gore and the Catholic Claims*)

Behind every saint stands another saint.

BARON FRIEDRICH VON HÜGEL
(*The Mystical Element in Religion*)

It is a wonderful experience to discover a new saint. For God is greatly magnified and marvelous in each one of his saints, differently in each individual one. There are no two saints alike; but all of them are like God; like him in a different and special way.

THOMAS MERTON
(*The Seven Storey Mountain*)

The mediocre Christian allots himself a measure that seems appropriate to him and considers anyone who gives more to be a professional saint. It is important to realize that the genuine saint never sees his offer to God as something beyond the norm, as a work beyond what is required.

CARDINAL HANS URS VON BALTHASAR
(*In of the Fullness Faith: On the Centrality of the Distinctively Catholic*)

The saints have always been the source and origin of renewal in the most difficult moments in the Church's history.

POPE JOHN PAUL II

Great saints have great defects, just as tall trees cast long shadows.

ALEX REBELLO

SALVATION

There is no salvation outside the Church.

ST. CYPRIAN

And to be like Our Lord perfectly is our very salvation and our full bliss. And if we do not know how we shall do all this, ask Our Lord and he will teach us.

JULIAN OF NORWICH
(*Revelations of Divine Love*)

Now, therefore, we declare, say, determine and pronounce that for every human creature it is necessary for salvation to be subject to the authority of the Roman Pontiff.

POPE BONIFACE VIII (*Unam Sanctam*)

Man is created to praise, reverence and serve God our Lord, and by this means to save his soul. The other things on the face of the earth are created for man's sake, to help him to pursue the end for which he is created. It follows, therefore, that a man must make use of them insofar as they help him to attain his end, and withdraw himself from them insofar as they hinder him. For this reason we must make ourselves indifferent to all created things, so far as we are permitted to do so and not forbidden. In other words, we should not prefer health to sickness, wealth to poverty, honor to dishonor, a long life to a short life. In all other things, likewise, we should desire and choose only those which most lead to the end for which we were created.

ST. IGNATIUS LOYOLA (*Spiritual Exercises*)

Virtue may unlock hell, or even,
A sin turn in the wards of heaven . . .
There is no expeditious road
To pack and label men for God
And save them by the barrel-load,
Some may, perchance, with strange surprise,
Have blundered into Paradise.

FRANCIS THOMPSON (*Epilogue*)

Father Conmee thought of the souls of black and brown and yellow men and of his sermon on St. Peter Claver, S.J., and the African mission and the propagation of the faith and of the millions of black and brown and yellow souls that had not received the baptism of water when their last hour came like a thief in the night. That book by the Belgian Jesuit *Le Nombre des Élus,* seemed to Father Conmee a reasonable plea.

Those were millions of human souls created by God in His Own likeness to whom the faith had not (DV) been brought. But they were God's souls created by God. It seemed to Father Conmee a pity that they should all be lost, a waste, if one might say.

JAMES JOYCE (*Ulysses*)

A poor thing was dying, a London butterfly, broken on the wheel. They used her and cast her aside. She was now dying — hardly out of her teens. She had been drugging, trying to keep herself up to the level of that life. I was called in. She was conscious but speechless. There was no hope, poor child. I had infinite pity for her in my soul. . . .

She didn't want a priest. But I was sent by the Shepherd. I didn't care two straws whether she wanted me or didn't. God wanted her.

VINCENT MCNABB, O.P.
(*God's Way of Mercy*)

Those who, through no fault of their own, do not know the Gospel of Christ or his Church, but who nevertheless seek God with a sincere heart, and, moved by grace, try in their actions to do his will as they know it through the dictates of their conscience – these too may achieve eternal salvation.

SECOND VATICAN COUNCIL
(*Dogmatic Constitution on the Church*)

. . . And the salvation of souls, which must always be the supreme law in the Church, is to be kept before one's eyes.

CODE OF CANON LAW
(*1752 – the final Canon*)

SAME-SEX MARRIAGE

There are absolutely no grounds for considering homosexual unions to be in any way similar or even remotely analogous to God's plan for marriage and family. Marriage is holy, while homosexual acts go against the natural moral law. . . .

In those situations where homosexual unions have been legally recognized or have been given the legal status and rights belonging to marriage, clear and emphatic opposition is a duty. One must refrain from any kind of formal cooperation in the enactment or application of such gravely unjust laws and, as far as possible, from material cooperation on the level of their application. In this area, everyone can exercise the right to conscientious objection.

CONGREGATION FOR THE DOCTRINE OF THE FAITH
(*Considerations Regarding Proposals to give Legal Recognition to Unions·between Homosexual Persons*)

SCANDAL

For no one does more harm in the Church than he who, having the title or rank of holiness, acts evilly.

POPE ST. GREGORY THE GREAT
(*Pastoral Care*)

At the present time nearly everywhere the name of religious is a synonym for rogue. . . . we, therefore, who last of all have enrolled ourselves as religious under the most holy name of Jesus are under an obligation to be the light of the world by the modesty of our behavior, the fervor of our charity, the innocence of our lives, and the example of our virtues.

Thus shall we be able to raise the lowered prestige of the Catholic Church, and to build up again the ruins that others by their vices have caused.

ST. ROBERT SOUTHWELL, S.J.

I do not believe that there was ever a time when the gravest scandals did not exist in the Church, and act as impediments to the success of its mission. Those scandals have been the occasion of momentous secessions and schisms. . . . It is also a fact that, in spite of them still, the Church has ever got on and made way, to the surprise of the world; as an army may fight a series of bloody battles, and lose men, and yet go forward from victory to victory.

VENERABLE JOHN HENRY NEWMAN
(*Letter to Lady Chatterton*)

When I have done wrong, I may imagine that I alone suffer the penalties, whereas in reality by my very act I may have started others also along a like career of wrong. Or even it may be that my wrong actions do not so much lead others to copy me, but raise in their minds thoughts against the value of the sacraments or against the divinity of the faith. People looking on may well say to themselves that if I, who go daily or weekly to my duties, am no better than I am, they had better not attempt to improve their own negligence; or if Catholics do no more than I, then there could be no reason for converting men to it. . . . It is quite possible that without considering the effect of what I am doing or saying, I am really and effectively "corrupting youth."

BEDE JARRETT, O.P.
(*Meditations for Layfolk*)

If you say that the Church is a long succession of scandals, you are telling the truth, though if that is all you say, you are distorting the truth.

GERALD VANN, O.P.

The scandalous behavior of a few has undermined the credibility of many.

POPE JOHN PAUL II (*Address to Philippine Bishops of Caceres, Capiz, Cebu, Jaro and Palo*)

SCIENCE

... Science without conscience is but the ruin of the soul.

FRANÇOIS RABELAIS

A science which does not bring us nearer to God is worthless.

SIMONE WEIL

Physics does not change the nature of the world it studies, and no science of behavior can change the essential nature of man, even though both sciences yield technologies with a vast power to manipulate the subject matters.

POPE PAUL VI

Dozing through tomorrow's strange new world just isn't good enough for the human race.

CARDINAL CORMAC MURPHY-O'CONNOR

SCIENCE AND RELIGION

It is the Holy Spirit's intention to teach us how to go to heaven, not how the heavens go.

CARDINAL CESARE BARONIUS

Reason teaches that the truths of divine revelation and those of nature cannot really be opposed to one another, and that whatever is at variance with them must be false.

POPE LEO XIII (*Libertas Praestantissimum*)

SCRIPTURE

The holy and inspired Scriptures are sufficient of themselves for the preaching of the Truth.

ST. ATHANASIUS (*Contra Gentiles*)

The Bible is a letter from Almighty God to his creatures.

POPE ST. GREGORY THE GREAT

Ignorance of scripture is ignorance of Christ.

ST. JEROME

Reading the scriptures is a wonderful thing. The mind of the scriptures can never be exhausted. It is a well without a bottom.

ST. JOHN CHRYSOSTOM

The whole series of the divine scriptures is interpreted in a fourfold way. In all holy books one should ascertain what everlasting truths are therein intimated, what deeds are narrated, what future events are foretold, and what commands or counsels are there contained.

THE VENERABLE BEDE
(*De Tabernaculo*)

The Church was gathered and the faith was believed before any part of the New Testament was put into writing. And which writing was or is the true scripture neither Luther nor Tyndale knoweth but by the credence they give to the Church.

ST. THOMAS MORE (*Apology*)

Come to the Bible, not to study the history of God's divine action, but to be its object; not to learn what it has achieved throughout the centuries and still does, but simply to be the subject of its operation.

JEAN-PIERRE DE CAUSSADE, S.J.

A competent religious guide must be clear and intelligible to all, so that everyone may fully understand the true meaning of the instructions it contains. Is the Bible a book intelligible to all? Far from it; it is full of obscurities and difficulties not only for the illiterate, but even for the learned.

CARDINAL JAMES GIBBONS
(*The Faith of Our Fathers*)

The claim of many Christians that it is the Bible which fully guides them and provides the final say in matters of their faith is inconsistent and cannot stand in the face of reason:

In fact ... the Protestant had no conceivable right to base any arguments on the inspiration of the Bible, for the inspiration of the Bible was a doctrine which had been believed, before the Reformation, on the mere authority of the Church; it rested on exactly the same basis as the doctrine of Transubstantiation. Protestantism repudiated Transubstantiation, and in doing so repudiated the authority of the Church; and then, without a shred of logic, calmly went on believing in the inspiration of the Bible, as if nothing had happened! Did they suppose that Biblical inspiration was a self-evident fact, like the axioms of Euclid?

RONALD KNOX
(*The Belief of Catholics*)

Without guidance we are at first confused, then discouraged. Even those who persevere do not get a tithe of what there is to be got. One can, of course, read Scripture in a state of pious coma, feeling that the general experience is uplifting and not expecting any very specific meaning – rather like listening to a lovely voice singing in a language we do not know. But this is fooling oneself. To read the Bible without external aids is to fail to take it seriously. "The word of God is living and effectual and more piercing than any two-edged sword": is Scripture so to us? A two-edged sword is not meant for playing with. Aid in using scripture we must indeed have: the Bible read without commentary is like a landscape before sunrise; it is all there, of course, but not to the eye. . . .

FRANK SHEED
(*God and the Human Condition*)

The Church has always venerated the divine Scriptures just as it venerates the Body of the Lord, since from the table both of the Word of God and of the Body of Christ it unceasingly receives and offers to the faithful the Bread of Life. It has always regarded the Scriptures together with sacred Tradition as the supreme rule of faith, and will ever do so.

SECOND VATICAN COUNCIL
(*Dogmatic Constitution on Divine Revelation*)

SCRUPLES

Do not scrutinize so closely whether you are doing much or little, ill or well, so long as what you do is not sinful and that you are heartily seeking to do everything for God. Try as far as you can to do everything well, but when it is done, do not think about it. Try, rather, to think of what is to be done next. Go on simply in the Lord's way, and do not torment yourself. We ought to hate our faults, but with a quiet, calm hatred; not pettishly and anxiously.

ST. FRANCIS DE SALES

Get rid of those scruples that deprive you of peace. What robs you of your peace of soul cannot come from God. . . .

Still those scruples! Talk simply and clearly with your director.

Obey . . . and don't belittle the most loving heart of our Lord.

ST. JOSEMARÍA ESCRIVÁ (*The Way*)

SEARCH FOR GOD

Late have I loved Thee, O Beauty so ancient and so new; late have I loved Thee! For behold Thou wert within me, and I outside; and I sought Thee outside and in my unloveliness fell upon those lovely things that Thou hast made. Thou wert with me and I was not with Thee. I was kept from Thee by those things, yet had they not been in Thee, they would not have been at all. . . . I taste Thee and now hunger and thirst for

Thee: Thou didst touch me, and I have burned for
Thy peace.

St. Augustine (*Confessions*)

There is scarcely anything which the understanding
can know about God, but the will can love him most
deeply. Let a man imprison himself within himself, in
the center of his soul, where the image of God is, and
there let him wait upon God, as one listens to another
speaking from some high tower, or as though one had
him within his heart, and as if in all creation there were
nothing to save the soul and God. He should even forget himself and what he is doing, for as one of the
Fathers said "perfect prayer is that in which he who is
praying is unaware that he is praying at all."

St. Peter of Alcántara

In the measure you desire him, you will find him.

St. Teresa of Ávila
(*The Way of Perfection*)

Withold your heart from all things: seek God and you
will find him.

St. Teresa of Ávila (*Maxims*)

There are three kinds of people: those who have sought
God and found him, and these are reasonable and
happy; those who seek God and have not yet found
him, and these are reasonable and unhappy; and those
who neither seek God nor find him, and these are
unreasonable and unhappy.

Blaise Pascal (*Pensées*)

God is always with us, why should we not always be
with God?

Archbishop William Bernard
Ullathorne, O.S.B.(*Humility and Patience*)

There is but one thing in the world worth pursuing – the knowledge of God.

R. H. BENSON
(*Introduction to Lady Lovat's Life of St. Teresa*)

Our knowledge of God is paradoxically not of him as the object of our scrutiny, but of ourselves as utterly dependent on his saving and merciful knowledge of us. It is in proportion, as we are known to him that we find our real being and identity in Christ. We know him in and through ourselves in so far as his truth is the source of our being and his merciful love is the very heart of our life and existence.

THOMAS MERTON

I suddenly saw that all the time it was not I who had been seeking God, but God who had been seeking me. I had made myself the center of my own existence and had my back turned to God. All the beauty and truth which I had discovered had come to me as a reflection of his beauty, but I had kept my eyes fixed on the reflection and was always looking at myself. But God had brought me to the point at which I was compelled to turn away from the reflection, both of myself and of the world which could only mirror my own image. During that night the mirror had been broken, and I had felt abandoned because I could no longer gaze upon the image of my own reason and the finite world which it knew. God had brought me to my knees and made me acknowledge my own nothingness, and out of that knowledge I had been reborn. I was no longer the center of my life and therefore I could see God in everything.

BEDE GRIFFITHS, O.S.B. (*The Golden String*)

If there is any path at all on which I can approach you, it must lead through the very middle of my ordinary daily life. If you have given me no single place to which I can flee and be sure of finding you, then I must be able to find you in every place in each and every thing I do. In your love all the diffusion of the day's chores comes home again to the evening of your unity, which is eternal life.

KARL RAHNER, S.J. (*Meditations and Prayers*)

SELF-ABNEGATION

The more we empty ourselves, the more room we give God to fill us.

BLESSED MOTHER TERESA

SELF-CONTROL

That man is rightly called a king who makes his own body an obedient subject, and by governing himself with suitable rigor, refuses to let his passions breed rebellion in his soul, for he exercises a kind of royal power over himself. And because he knows how to rule his own person as king, so too does he sit as its judge. He will not let himself be imprisoned by sin, or thrown headlong into wickedness.

ST. AMBROSE (*Exposition of the Psalms*)

There is no higher rule than that over oneself, over one's impulses; there is the triumph of free will.

BALTHASAR GRACIÁN, S.J.
(*The Art of Wordly Wisdom*)

Get used to saying No.

ST. JOSEMARÍA ESCRIVÁ (*The Way*)

Each of us makes his own weather, determines the color of the skies in the emotional universe which he inhabits.

ARCHBISHOP FULTON J. SHEEN

SELF-DECEPTION

It is amusing to see souls who, while they are at prayer, fancy they are willing to be despised and publicly insulted for the love of God, yet afterwards do all they can to hide their small defects; if anyone unjustly accuses them of a fault, God deliver us from their outcries!

ST. TERESA OF ÁVILA (*The Interior Castle*)

Self-love is cunning, it pushes and insinuates itself into everything, while making us believe it is not there at all.

ST. FRANCIS DE SALES
(*Letters to Persons in Religion*)

Men, not having been able to cure death, misery, and ignorance, have imagined to make themselves happy by not thinking about these things.

BLAISE PASCAL (*Pensées*)

Religious talk is a very feast to self-deceit.

F. W. FABER (*Spiritual Conferences*)

SELF-KNOWLEDGE

All our trials and disturbances come from not understanding ourselves.

ST. TERESA OF ÁVILA

SELF-LIBERATION

Indeed, an awareness of the need for self-liberation is essential to a correct understanding of the liberation process. It is not a matter of "struggling for others", which suggests paternalistic and reformist objectives, but rather of becoming aware of oneself as not completely fulfilled and living in an alienated society.

GUSTAVO GUTIERREZ
(*A Theology of Liberation*)

SELF-LOVE

First learn to love yourself, and then you can love me.

ST. BERNARD OF CLAIRVAUX

SELFISHNESS

He who lives only to benefit himself confers a benefit on the world when he dies.

TERTULLIAN

There is no room in the Society [of Jesus] for the man who desires only his own salvation and consecration.

ST. IGNATIUS LOYOLA

SERMONS

To me it is nothing when I am applauded and well spoken of. There is only one thing I ask of you — to prove your approval of me through your works. That is how you can speak well of me, and that is what is going to do you good. This, to me, is the greatest honor. . . .

This is not a theater. You don't sit here in order to admire actors and to applaud them. This is a place where you must learn the things of God.

ST. JOHN CHRYSOSTOM

The test of a preacher is that his congregation goes away saying, not "What a lovely sermon!" but "I will do something."

ST. FRANCIS DE SALES

A good sermon should be like a woman's skirt: short enough to arouse interest but long enough to cover the essentials.

RONALD KNOX

SERVICE

There is something I dread for you more than any sword or poison. It is the lust for power. Why have you been set above men? Not to rule over them, I am sure of that! A burden of service is our lot, not the privilege of power.

ST. BERNARD OF CLAIRVAUX
(*to Pope Eugene III*)

SEX

Sex has become one of the most discussed subjects of modern times. The Victorians pretended it did not exist: the moderns pretend that nothing else exists.

ARCHBISHOP FULTON J. SHEEN

SHAKESPEARE

... Shakespeare grew up in a community saturated with Catholic sympathies. Several of his teachers and fellow pupils were devout Catholics; some left England to seek ordination, some returned to martyrdom. As we have seen, his mother grew up in a conspicuously Catholic family, and his father, a conformist during the 1560s and early 1570s, experienced a profound conversion or reconversion in the early 1580s. Shakespeare himself was probably a conformist – his plays show familiarity with the so-called Bishops' Bible, the version used in church for most of Elizabeth's reign. But the evidence from Southwark suggests that he may have avoided taking communion in the Church of England, which would mean that he was what his father had been for much of his adult life, a "church-papist," outwardly conforming but inwardly rejecting Protestant teaching.

There is much in the plays to support this view. Several of them, especially *Hamlet,* show an extensive familiarity with Catholic teachings, such as purgatory, and no hint of disapproval. Indeed, Shakespeare's treatment of Catholic themes is remarkably sympathetic. Friars, nuns and the religious life get a remarkably good press from him. Anglican clergy, by contrast, a bad one. The sensibility which evoked in sonnet 73 "bare ruin'd choirs, where late the sweet birds sang," was certainly receptive to the beauty of the old faith, alert to the tragedy and loss involved in Reformation.

EAMON DUFFY (*Was Shakespeare Catholic?:*
The Tablet, April 27, 1994)

SHAME

There smites nothing so sharp, nor smelleth so sour as shame.

WILLIAM LANGLAND
(*The Vision of Piers Plowman*)

SICKNESS AND DEATH

Felix Randal, the farrier, O he is dead then? my duty
    all ended,
Who have watched his mould of man, big-boned and
    hardy-handsome,
Pining, pining, till time when reason rambled in it
    and some
Fatal four disorders, fleshed there, all contended?

Sickness broke him. Impatient he cursed at first, but
    mended,
Being anointed and all; though a heavenlier heart
    began some
Months earlier, since I had our sweet reprieve and
    ransom
Tendered to him. Ah well, God rest him all road ever
    he offended!

This seeing the sick endears them to us, us too it
    endears.
My tongue had taught thee comfort, touch had
    quenched thy tears,
Thy tears that touched my heart, child Felix, poor
    Felix Randal;

How far from then forethought of, all thy more
    boisterous years,
When thou at the random grim forge powerful
    amidst peers,
Didst fettle for the great gray drayhorse his bright and
    battering sandal!

GERARD MANLEY HOPKINS, S.J.
(*Felix Randal*)

SIGN OF PEACE

The baptized shall embrace each other, men with men
and women with women. But let not men embrace
women.

ST. HIPPOLYTUS (*The Apostolic Tradition*)

SIGN OF THE CROSS

In all our actions, when we come in or go out, when we
dress, when we wash, at our meals, before retiring to
sleep, we make on our foreheads the sign of the cross.
These practices are not enjoined by a formal law of
scripture, but tradition teaches them, custom confirms
them, faith observes them.

TERTULLIAN (*De Corona*)

SIGNS OF CONTRADICTION

We are not set on this earth to help a fallen world function smoothly. We are Signs of Contradiction: or we are
nothing.

CATHOLIC HERALD
(*editorial, July 11, 2003*)

SILENCE

The fruit of silence is prayer, the fruit of prayer is faith, the fruit of faith is love, and the fruit of love is silence

BLESSED MOTHER TERESA

SIN

There is only one calamity — sin.

ST. JOHN CHRYSOSTOM

Love the sinner but hate the sin.

ST. AUGUSTINE

What destroys us is forgetfulness of God, which shrouds the commandments in darkness and despoils us of all good.

GREGORY OF SINAI (*Philokalia*)

There is in some of us a very bad habit. We treat our sins against God, however appalling, with gentle indulgence: but when by contrast it is a matter of sins against ourselves, albeit tiny ones, we exact reparation with ruthless severity.

ST. JOHN CASSIAN
(*On the Lord's Prayer*)

Christian, remember your dignity, and now that you share in God's own nature, do not return by sin to your former base condition. Bear in mind who is your head and of whose body you are a member. Do not forget that you have been rescued from the power of darkness and brought into the light of God's Kingdom.

POPE ST. LEO THE GREAT
(*Second Sermon on the Nativity*)

If you can find a place where God is not, go there and sin with impunity.

ST. ANSELM

Everyone is his own enemy.

ST. BERNARD OF CLAIRVAUX

What good is a fruitless repentance ruined almost immediately by new faults?

ST. BERNARD OF CLAIRVAUX

Nor did demons crucify him, it is you who have crucified him and crucify him still, when you delight in your vices and sins.

ST. FRANCIS OF ASSISI (*Admonition*)

God is none other than the Savior of our wretchedness. So we can only know God well by knowing our iniquities. . . . Those who have known God without knowing their wretchedness have not glorified him, but have glorified themselves.

BLAISE PASCAL (*Pensées*)

I would give my life a thousand times that God might not be offended.

ST. GERARD MAJELLA

No man can break any of the Ten Commandments. He can only break himself against them.

G. K. CHESTERTON

There is only one thing more dangerous than sin – the murder of a man's sense of sin.

POPE JOHN PAUL II

This is the mission entrusted to the Church, a hard mission: To uproot sins from history; to uproot sins from the political order; to uproot sins from the economy; to uproot sins wherever they are.

ARCHBISHOP OSCAR ROMERO

Now there is an eighth Cardinal Sin.

CARDINAL JAIME SIN
(*on receiving the red hat*)

SINNERS

Pray. Pray and sacrifice yourselves for sinners, for many souls go to hell because they have no one to sacrifice or pray for them.

THE BLESSED VIRGIN MARY
(*Fátima, August 13, 1917*)

SLOWNESS

There is a slowness in affairs which ripens them, and a slowness which rots them.

JOSEPH ROUX
(*Meditations of a Parish Priest*)

SOCIALISM

Whether considered as a sacrifice, or as an historical fact, or as a movement, socialism, if it really remains socialism, cannot be brought into harmony with the dogmas of the Catholic Church.... Religious socialism,

Christian socialism, are expressions implying a contradiction in terms.

POPE PIUS XI
(*On the Reconstruction of the Social Order*)

SOCIAL JUSTICE

It is not the institution or structures of society that the priest has to transform, but the people, and they themselves will do the rest.

FREDERICO SUAREZ, S.J.

There are many people who possess too much and want to possess more; there are far many more others who do not possess enough, who possess nothing and who are ready to take it if they are given nothing. Between these two classes of men a struggle is brewing, and this struggle threatens to be terrible: with the power of gold on the one side and the power of despair on the other. We should throw ourselves between these two enemy armies at least to soften the impact if not to prevent it.

BLESSED FREDERIC OZANAM

Let Catholic writers take care when defending the cause of the proletariat and the poor not to use language calculated to inspire among the people aversion to the upper classes of society.

POPE LEO XIII
(*On Capital and Labor*)

Therefore everyone has the right to possess a sufficient amount of the earth's goods for themselves and their family. This has been the opinion of the Fathers and Doctors of the church, who taught that people are bound to come to the aid of the poor and to do so not merely out of their superfluous goods. Persons in extreme necessity are entitled to take what they need from the riches of others.

Faced with a world today where so many people are suffering from want, the council asks individuals and governments to remember the saying of the Fathers: "Feed the people dying of hunger, because if you do not feed them you are killing them," and it urges them according to their ability to share and dispose of their goods to help others, above all by giving them aid which will enable them to help and develop themselves.

SECOND VATICAN COUNCIL
(*The Church in the Modern World*)

... The superfluous wealth of rich countries should be placed at the service of poor nations. The rule which up to now held good for the benefit of those nearest to us, must today be applied to all the needy of this world. Besides, the rich will be the first to benefit as a result. Otherwise their continued greed will certainly call down upon them the judgment of God and the wrath of the poor, with consequences no one can foretell.

SECOND VATICAN COUNCIL
(*On the Development of Peoples*)

Many would like a preaching so spiritualistic that it leaves sinners unbothered and does not call idolaters those who kneel before money and power. A preaching that says nothing of the sinful environment... is not the Gospel.

ARCHBISHOP OSCAR ROMERO

The Christian has not done enough in this area of conversion of the neighbor to social justice, to history. He has not perceived clearly enough yet that to know God is to do justice.

GUSTAVO GUTIERREZ
(*A Theology of Liberation*)

Jesus and the Church are not fighting against poverty, but against injustice and for human beings. Poverty as a style of life in which human needs are adequately satisfied, and no trust is put in economic wealth, is quite different from the poverty which is a result of vast injustices which impoverish others. The former is liberating; the latter leaves people marginalized, ignorant, hungry, unhealthy or insecure: conditions which characterize vast sections of the Latin American people. These conditions... may be looked on as the result of chance by those who are free of them, and even as unchangeable destiny by those who suffer them. But for the Christian who sees them with the eyes of faith – as for all those with right judgment – they are not the product of the natural order, but the result of human disorder or laziness, and therefore an injustice which cries to heaven.

STATEMENT BY THE BISHOPS OF CHILE (*1980*)

As followers of Christ, we are challenged to make a fundamental "option for the poor" — to speak for the voiceless, to defend the defenseless, to assess life styles, policies, and social institutions in terms of their impact on the poor. This "option for the poor" does not mean pitting one group against another, but rather, strengthening the whole community by assisting those who are the most vulnerable. As Christians, we are called to respond to the needs of all our brothers and sisters, but those with the greatest needs require the greatest response....

The needs of the poor take priority over the desires of the rich; the rights of workers over the maximization of profits; the preservation of the environment over uncontrolled industrial expansion; production to meet social needs over production for military purposes.

ECONOMIC JUSTICE FOR ALL:
PASTORAL MESSAGE OF US BISHOPS (*1986*)

It is manifestly unjust that a privileged few should continue to accumulate excess goods, squandering available resources, while masses of people are living in conditions of misery at the very lowest level of subsistence. Today, the dramatic threat of ecological breakdown is teaching us the extent to which greed and selfishness — both individual and collective — are contrary to the order of creation, an order which is characterized by mutual interdependence.

POPE JOHN PAUL II

Love for others, and in the first place love for the poor, in whom the Church sees Christ himself, is made concrete in the promotion of justice.

POPE JOHN PAUL II (*On the Hundredth Anniversary of On Capital and Labor, 1991*)

SOLITUDE

One must cross the desert and live there to receive God's grace. It is there that one can drive away from oneself everything that is not God.

VENERABLE CHARLES DE FOUCAULD

If you cannot go into the desert, you must nonethless "make some desert" in your life, every now and then leaving men and looking for solitude to restore, in prolonged silence and prayer, the stuff of your soul. This is the meaning of "desert" in your spiritual life.

One has to be courageous not to let oneself be carried along by the world's march; one needs faith and willpower to go cross-current towards the Eucharist, to stop, to be silent, to worship.

CARLO CARRETTO
(*Letters from the Desert*)

Not all of us are called to be hermits, but all of us need enough silence and solitude in our lives to enable the deeper voice of our own self to be heard at least occasionally.

THOMAS MERTON

SOUL

Our Lord does not come down from heaven every day to lie in a golden ciborium. He comes to find another heaven which is infinitely dearer to him – the heaven of our souls, created in his image, the living temples of the adorable Trinity.

ST. THÉRÈSE OF LISIEUX

To be rooted is perhaps the most important and least recognized need of the human soul.

SIMONE WEIL

SOUL AND BODY

It is true, whoever said it, that the soul and the body are two enemies that cannot be separated, and two friends that cannot get along.

ST. JOSEMARÍA ESCRIVÁ (*The Way*)

SPEAKING IN TONGUES

Our Lord sometimes gives the soul feelings of jubilation and a strange prayer it doesn't understand. I am writing about this favor so that if he grants it to you, you may give him such praise and know what is taking place.... It seems like gibberish, and certainly the experience is like that, for it is a joy so excessive that the soul wouldn't want to enjoy it alone but wants to tell everyone about it so that they might help this soul to praise our Lord.

ST. TERESA OF ÁVILA
(*The Interior Castle*)

SPIRITUAL DIRECTION

Spiritual directors are not the chief workers, but rather the Holy Spirit; they are mere instruments, only to guide souls by the rule of faith and the law of God according to the spirit which God gives to each. Their object, therefore, should be not to guide souls by a way of their own, suitable to themselves; but to ascertain if they can, the way in which God himself is guiding them.

ST. JOHN OF THE CROSS
(*The Ascent of Mount Carmel*)

Do you want to walk earnestly towards devotion? Then get a good spiritual director to guide you, that is the best of all advice.

ST. FRANCIS DE SALES

SPIRITUAL DRYNESS

God of our life, there are days when the burdens we carry chafe our shoulders and weigh us down; when the road seems dreary and endless, the skies grey and threatening; when our lives have no music in them, and our hearts are lonely, and our souls have lost their courage. Flood the path with light, run our eyes to where the skies are full of promise; tune our hearts to brave music; give us the sense of comradeship with heroes and saints of every age; and so quicken our spirits that we may be able to encourage the souls of all who journey with us on the road of life, to Your honor and glory.

ST. AUGUSTINE

One single act done with dryness of spirit is worth more than many done with sensible devotion.

ST. FRANCIS DE SALES
(*Spiritual Conferences*)

There is a difference between possessing the presence of God and having the feeling of his presence.

ST. FRANCIS DE SALES
(*Spiritual Conferences*)

SPIRITUAL EXERCISES

Just as walking, marching and running are bodily exercises, so the methods of preparing and devoting the soul . . . can be called spiritual exercises.

ST. IGNATIUS LOYOLA (*Spiritual Exercises*)

SPIRITUAL FLIGHT

I fled Him, down the nights and down the days;
I fled Him down the arches of the years;

I fled Him, down the labyrinthine ways
Of my own mind, and in the midst of tears
I hid from Him, and under running laughter,
Up vistaed hopes I sped
And shot, precipitated,
Adown Titanic glooms of chasmèd fears,
From those strong Feet that followed, followed after.
But with unhurrying chase,
And unperturbèd pace,
Deliberate speed, majestic instancy,
They beat – and a Voice beat
More instant than the Feet –
"All things betray thee, who betrayest Me."
I pleaded, outlaw-wise,
By many a curtained casement, curtained red,
Trellised with intertwining charities
(For, though I knew His love who followèd,
Yet I was sore adread
Lest, having Him, I must have naught beside). . . .

FRANCIS THOMPSON
(*The Hound of Heaven*)

SPIRITUAL QUEST

Most men prefer and strive for the present, we for the
future.

ST. AMBROSE
(*On the Duties of the Clergy*)

It is not what you are, nor what you have been, that
God looks at with his merciful eyes, but what you
would wish to be.

THE CLOUD OF UNKNOWING

Grant us, O Lord, not to mind earthly things, but to love things heavenly; and even now, while we are placed among things that are passing away, to cleave to those that shall abide.

LEONINE SACRAMENTARY (*Collect*)

God does not despise these hidden struggles with ourselves, so much richer in merit because they are unseen: "The patient man is better than the valiant and he that ruleth his spirit than he that taketh cities" (Prov. xvi. 32). By our little acts of charity practiced in the shade we convert souls far away, we help missionaries, we win for them abundant alms, and by that means build actual dwellings both spiritual and material for our Eucharistic Lord.

ST. THÉRÈSE OF LISIEUX

To discover God is not to discover an idea but to discover oneself. It is to awake to that part of one's existence which has been hidden from sight and which one has refused to recognize. The discovery may be very painful; it is like going through a kind of death. But it is the one thing that makes life worth living.

BEDE GRIFFITHS, O.S.B.
(*The Golden String*)

We are all pilgrims on the wearisome roads of our life. There is always something ahead of us that we have not yet overtaken. When we do catch up with something it immediately becomes an injunction to leave it behind us and go onwards. Every end becomes a beginning.

KARL RAHNER, S.J.
(*Meditations and Prayers*)

STATE OF GRACE

If I am not, may it please God to put me in it; if I am, may it please God to keep me there.

ST. JOAN OF ARC (*at her trial*)

STATE OF LIFE

Some people, because of their state of life, cannot be without wealth and position. They must at least keep their heart free of love for such things.

ST. ANGELA MERICI

The value of life does not depend upon the place we occupy. It depends upon the way we occupy that place.

ST. THÉRÈSE OF LISIEUX

STATE OWNERSHIP

Certain forms of property must be reserved to the State, since they carry with them a power too great to be left to private individuals without danger to the community at large.

POPE PIUS XI
(*Quadragesimo Anno*)

STEM CELL RESEARCH

No objective, even though noble in itself, such as a foreseeable advantage to science, to other human beings, or to society, can in any way justify experimentation on living human embryos or fetuses, whether viable or not, either inside or outside the mother's body.

CONGREGATION FOR THE
DOCTRINE OF FAITH (*Vatican Instruction on Respect for Human Life in Its Origins and on the Dignity of Procreation*)

Recent scientific developments have demonstrated that the destruction of embryos may be completely unnecessary to achieve the benefits that stem cell research provides.

BISHOP JOHN J. NEVINS

Human life must be respected and protected absolutely from the moment of conception. From the first moment of his existence, a human being must be recognized as having the rights of a person – among which is the inviolable right of every innocent being to life.

CATECHISM OF THE CATHOLIC CHURCH, 2270

STERILIZATION

You have been advocating the sterilization of moral degenerates. Well, I am a moral expert and I certify *you* as moral degenerates. Good afternoon.

VINCENT MCNABB, O.P. (*to a group of eugenicists*)

STIGMATA

Do you think that the Lord gave them to me for a decoration?

ST. PADRE PIO
(*asked if the stigmata were painful*)

SUBMISSION

Blessed are they who do not their own will on earth, for God will do it in heaven above.

ST. FRANCIS DE SALES

SUFFERING

Nothing, however little, that is suffered for God's sake, can pass without merit in God's sight.

THOMAS À KEMPIS
(*Imitation of Christ*)

We may not look at our pleasure to go to Heaven in feather beds. It is not the way. For Our Lord himself went there with great pain and many tribulations. The servant may not look to be in better case than the master.

ST. THOMAS MORE

The more suffering for Christ in this world, the more glory with Christ in the future.

ST. PHILIP HOWARD

Many people would be glad to have afflictions, so long as they were not inconvenienced by them.

ST. FRANCIS DE SALES
(*Introduction to the Devout Life*)

If God causes you to suffer much, it is a sign that He has great designs for you, and that he certainly intends to make you a saint.

ST. IGNATIUS LOYOLA

You can advance farther in grace in one hour during a time of affliction than in many days during a time of consolation.

ST. JOHN EUDES

The chief pang of most trials is not so much the actual suffering itself as our own spirit of resistance to it.

JEAN NICOLAS GROU, S.J.

The more I am crucified, the more I rejoice.

ST. BERNADETTE

Suffering passes, but the fact of having suffered never leaves us.

LÉON BLOY

From the first [Father Damien] never doubted that he would take the leprosy in time as how – constantly living with the contagion, dressing the patients' sores, washing their bodies, even digging their graves, could he escape it? But he fell to work with a cheerful heart. He had lived with them about ten years when he began to suspect it. In his letters home he made no mention of his fate, but to his bishop he wrote: "I cannot come to Honolulu, for leprosy has attacked me. There are signs of it on my left cheek and ear, and my eyebrows are beginning to fall, I shall soon be quite disfigured. . . ."

Henceforward, in preaching to his flock, he never said "My brethren" but "We lepers."

A. T. QUILLER-COUCH
(*The Roll Call of Honour*)

Jesus did not come to explain suffering, but to fill it with his presence.

PAUL CLAUDEL

We shouldn't always pray for miseries to be removed. Sometimes we should pray for the strength to bear them better.

BLESSED BROTHER ANDRÉ, C.S.C.

Sickness is a wonderful grace, an incomparable richness.

MARTHE ROBIN

SUNDAY

The Lord's day, the day of Resurrection, the day of Christians, is our day. It is called the Lord's day because on it the Lord rose victorious to the Father. If pagans call it "the day of the sun" we willingly agree, for today the light of the world is raised, today is revealed the sun of justice with healing in his rays.

ST. JEROME
(*Homily on Easter Sunday*)

Blessed is Sunday, for on it began creation. . . . On Sunday heaven and earth rejoiced and the whole universe was filled with light. Blessed is Sunday, for on it were opened the gates of paradise so that Adam and all the exiles might enter it without fear.

SYRIAC OFFICE OF ANTIOCH

T

TECHNOLOGY

The Church welcomes technological progress and receives it with love, for it is an indubitable fact that technological progress comes from God and, therefore, can and must lead to him.

POPE PIUS XII
(*Christmas Message, 1953*)

TEMPTATION

If in Christ we have been tempted, in him we overcome the devil. Do you think only of Christ's temptations and fail to think of his victory? See yourself as tempted in him, and see yourself as victorious in him. He could have kept the devil from himself; but if he were not tempted he could not teach you how to triumph over temptation.

ST. AUGUSTINE
(*Commentary on the Psalms*)

When a man comes to know that he can fall away from God as a dry leaf falls from a tree, then he knows the power of his soul.

ST. ISAAK OF SYRIA

There is a certain usefulness to temptation. No one but God knows what our soul has received from him, not even we ourselves. But temptation reveals it in order to teach us to know ourselves, and in this way we discover our evil inclinations and are obliged to give thanks for the benefits that temptation has revealed to us.

ORIGEN (*On Prayer*)

Another way to defeat these temptations is not to be afraid of them. Do not equate the temptation to despair or blaspheme or doubt the sacraments with the sin of despair or blasphemy or doubting the sacraments. Going through these temptations does not defile the soul any more than if your soul should hear a hound bark or feel a flea biting. They irritate the soul but they do not damage it. You must despise temptation and not give it a place of unwarranted importance in your life. The more you become preoccupied with the temptation the more likely you are to give in to it. Keep your minds away from temptation and concentrate on living your life. If temptations still will not go away, do not become upset or heavy in your spirit. Out of your love for God put up with the temptation as you place your trust in God. Temptations are like other sicknesses which attack the body. They may be allowed by our Lord so that we have our sins cleansed by them. Jesus was prepared to be whipped and die on the cross out of his love for us.

WALTER HILTON
(*The Ladder of Perfection*)

There is no order so holy, nor place so retired, where there are not temptations and adversities.

THOMAS Á KEMPIS
(*The Imitation of Christ*)

All great amusements are a danger to the life of the Christian; but of all those which the world has invented there is none more to be feared than the play.

BLAISE PASCAL (*Pensées*)

In the war of the senses, the conquerors are the cowards who fly.

ST. PHILIP NERI

Now is the way clear, now is the meaning plain:
Temptation shall not come in this kind again.
The last temptation is the greatest treason:
To do the right thing for the wrong reason.

T. S. ELIOT (*Murder in the Cathedral*)

You tell me that in your heart you have fire and water, cold and heat, empty passions and God: one candle lit to St. Michael and the other to the devil.
Calm yourself. As long as you are willing to fight there are not two candles burning in your heart. There is only one: the archangel's.

ST. JOSEMARÍA ESCRIVÁ (*The Way*)

I have often been asked . . . "When does the lust of the flesh disappear? When does anyone become calm?" I am 72 — and I don't know yet.

CARDINAL RICHARD J. CUSHING

TERRORISM

History shows that the recruitment of terrorists is more easily achieved in areas where human rights are trampled on and where injustice is a part of daily life.

POPE JOHN PAUL II (*September 7, 2002*)

Terrorism can never be defended as a protest against poverty; but neither can it be defeated simply by force of arms.

CARDINAL CORMAC MURPHY-O'CONNOR
(*article, The Times, September 2002*)

In the end, the world will not live with such injustice. A world in which every European cow receives $2 a day in subsidy and 1.2 billion people have to live on less. A world where, last year, the inflated US subsidy on cotton took $300 million from the pockets of the poor in sub-Saharan Africa. . . . Unless the war on terrorism is accompanied by a war on injustice, peace can never be assured.

JOHN GUMMER, BRITISH POLITICIAN
(*Catholic Herald, October 18, 2002*)

THANKSGIVING

No duty is more urgent than that of returning thanks.
ST. AMBROSE

If the only prayer you say in your whole life is "thank you" that would suffice.

MEISTER ECKHART

We should spend as much time in thanking God for his benefits as we do in asking him for them.
ST. VINCENT DE PAUL

Oh, how can we ever be grateful enough for His making use of us!

CORNELIA CONNOLLY

TIME

Time goes by turns, and chances change by course,
From fair to foul, and better hap to worse.

ST. ROBERT SOUTHWELL, S.J.
(*Time Goes By Turns*)

Let us especially regret the smallest amount of time
that we waste or fail to use in loving God.

ST. JOHN OF THE CROSS

Lord, you must have made a mistake in your
    calculations.
    There is a big mistake somewhere.
    The hours are too short,
    The days are too short,
    Our lives are too short.
Lord, I have time,
    I have plenty of time,
    All the time that you give me,
    The years of my life,
    the days of my years,
    the hours of my days,
    They are all mine.
    Mine to fill, quietly, calmly,
    But to fill completely, up to the brim,
    To offer them to you, that of their insipid water
    You may make a rich wine such as you made
    once in Cana of Galilee.
I am not asking you tonight, Lord, for the time to do
    this and then that,
    But your grace to do conscientiously, in the time
    that you give me, what you want me to do.

MICHEL QUOIST (*Prayers of Life*)

TOLERANCE

The Church reproves, as foreign to the mind of Christ, any discrimination against men or harassment of them because of their race, color, condition of life, or religion.

SECOND VATICAN COUNCIL
(*Non-Christian Religions*)

We are asking pardon for the divisions among Christians, for the use of violence that some have committed in the service of truth, and for attitudes of mistrust and hostility assumed toward followers of other religions.

POPE JOHN PAUL II
(*Rome, March 12, 2000*)

TRADITION

Tradition means giving votes to the most obscure of all classes — our ancestors. It is the democracy of the dead. Tradition refuses to submit to the small and arrogant oligarchy who merely happen to be walking about.

G. K. CHESTERTON (*Orthodoxy*)

TRANSUBSTANTIATION

People say that the doctrine of transubstantiation is difficult to believe; I did not believe the doctrine till I was a Catholic. I had no difficulty in believing it as soon as I believed the Catholic Roman Church was the oracle of God, and that she had declared this doctrine to be part of the original revelation. It is difficult, impossible to imagine, I grant – but how is it difficult to believe?

VENERABLE JOHN HENRY NEWMAN
(*Apologia pro Vita Sua*)

TRAVEL

I have wandered all my life, and I have traveled; the difference between the two is this — we wander for distraction, but we travel for fulfillment.

HILAIRE BELLOC

TRIDENTINE RITE

The Holy See urges bishops to be extremely tolerant to those of Christ's faithful who wish to participate in the sacred liturgy in accordance with the previous liturgical books and to keep their sensibilities constantly before their eyes.

CARDINAL JORGE ARTURO MEDINA ESTEVEZ
PREFECT OF THE CONGREGATION FOR
DIVINE WORSHIP (*October 1999*)

TRUST

Say nothing good of yourself, you will be distrusted; say nothing bad of yourself, you will be taken at your word.

JOSEPH ROUX
(*Meditations of a Parish Priest*)

TRUST IN GOD

I bind unto myself today
The strong Name of the Trinity,
By invocation of the same
The Three in One and One in Three.
I bind this today to me forever
By power of faith, Christ's incarnation;

His baptism in Jordan river,
His death on Cross for my salvation;
His bursting from the spicèd tomb,
His riding up the heavenly way,
His coming at the day of doom
I bind unto myself today.

I bind unto myself the power
Of the great love of cherubim;
The sweet "Well done" in judgment hour,
The service of the seraphim,
Confessors' faith, Apostles' word,
The Patriarchs' prayers, the prophets' scrolls,
All good deeds done unto the Lord
And purity of virgin souls.

I bind unto myself today
The virtues of the star lit heaven,
The glorious sun's life giving ray,
The whiteness of the moon at even,
The flashing of the lightning free,
The whirling wind's tempestuous shocks,
The stable earth, the deep salt sea
Around the old eternal rocks.

I bind unto myself today
The power of God to hold and lead,
His eye to watch, His might to stay,
His ear to hearken to my need.
The wisdom of my God to teach,
His hand to guide, His shield to ward;
The word of God to give me speech,
His heavenly host to be my guard.

Against the demon snares of sin,
The vice that gives temptation force,
The natural lusts that war within,
The hostile men that mar my course;
Or few or many, far or nigh,
In every place and in all hours,
Against their fierce hostility
I bind to me these holy powers.

Against all Satan's spells and whiles,
Against false words of heresy,
Against the knowledge that defiles,
Against the heart's idolatry,
Against the wizard's evil craft,
Against the death wound and the burning,
The choking wave, the poisoned shaft,
Protect me, Christ, till Thy returning.

Christ be with me, Christ within me,
Christ behind me, Christ before me,
Christ beside me, Christ to win me,
Christ to comfort and restore me.
Christ beneath me, Christ above me,
Christ in quiet, Christ in danger,
Christ in hearts of all that love me,
Christ in mouth of friend and stranger.

I bind unto myself the Name,
The strong Name of the Trinity,
By invocation of the same,
The Three in One and One in Three.
By Whom all nature hath creation,
Eternal Father, Spirit, Word:

Praise to the Lord of my salvation,
Salvation is of Christ the Lord.

ST. PATRICK
(*Lorica – Breastplate of Faith*)

Trust the past to God's mercy, the present to God's love
and the future to God's providence.

ST. AUGUSTINE

God is not a deceiver, that he should offer to support
us, and then, when we lean upon Him, should slip
away from us.

ST. AUGUSTINE

All shall be well and all shall be well and all manner of
things shall be well.

JULIAN OF NORWICH
(*Revelations of Divine Love*)

Fly we to Our Lord and we shall be comforted; touch
we him and we shall be made clean; cleave to him and
we shall be secure and safe from all manner of peril.

JULIAN OF NORWICH
(*Revelations of Divine Love*)

This is our Lord's will . . . that our prayer and our trust
be, alike, large. For if we do not trust as much as we
pray, we fail in full worship to our Lord in our prayer;
and also we hinder and hurt ourselves. The reason is
that we do not know truly that our Lord is the ground
from which our prayer springs; nor do we know that it
is given us by his grace and his love. If we knew this, it
would make us trust to have of our Lord's gifts all that
we desire. For I am sure that no man asks mercy and

grace with sincerity, without mercy and grace being given to him first.

JULIAN OF NORWICH
(*Revelations of Divine Love*)

God is omnipotent. Aim high, be high. . . . Ardent desire and abject humility work wonders.

MEISTER ECKHART

Let nothing disturb thee,
Nothing affright thee;
All things are passing;
God never changeth;
Patient endurance
Attaineth to all things;
Who God possesseth
In nothing is wanting;
Alone God sufficeth..

ST. TERESA OF ÁVILA
(*Poems, translated by H.W. Longfellow*)

An Act of Perfect Acceptance to the will of God unites us more to Him than a hundred other acts of virtue.

ST. ALPHONSUS LIGUORI

It sometimes comes into my head to wonder whether I have ever properly confessed my sins, whether I am in a good or bad spiritual state. What progress have I made in prayer or the interior life? When this happens I say to myself at once, God has chosen to hide all this from me, so that I may just blindly abandon myself to his mercy. So I submit myself and I adore his decision. . . . He is the Master; may all that he wills be accomplished in me; I want no grace, no merit, no perfection, but that which will please him. His will alone is sufficient for me and that will always be the measure of my desires.

JEAN-PIERRE DE CAUSSADE, S.J.
(*The Flame of Divine Love*)

Where I sow, others will reap.

VENERABLE CHARLES DE FOUCAULD

My Lord God, I have no idea where I am going. I do not see the road ahead of me. I cannot know for certain where it will end. Nor do I really know myself, and the fact that I think I am following your will does not mean that I am actually doing so. But I believe that the desire to please you does in fact please you. And I hope that I have that desire in all that I am doing. I hope that I will never do anything apart from that desire. And I know that if I do this you will lead me by the right road though I may know nothing about it. Therefore I will trust you always though I may seem to be lost and in the shadow of death. I will not fear, for you are ever with me, and you will never leave me to face my perils alone.

THOMAS MERTON (*Thoughts in Solitude*)

We do very little good when we embark on our own. We do much good when we allow God to direct us and direct our enterprises.... We must learn to avoid worrying ourselves about anything, to leave ourselves, our concerns, in the hands of God; learn to do away with anxieties of all sorts.... And whilst doing whatever we have to do, we should do it at a pace and a speed that will allow us time continually to turn to God for guidance... our conversation with God should be continual.

BLESSED CYPRIAN TANSI, O.C.S.O.
(*Retreat Notes*)

Life becomes an unbearable burden whenever we lose touch with the presence of a loving Savior and we see only hunger to be alleviated, injustice to be addressed, violence to be overcome, wars to be stopped, and loneliness to be removed. All these are critical issues, and Christians must try to solve them; however, when our concern no longer flows from our personal encounter with the living Christ, we feel oppressive weight.

HENRI J. M. NOUWEN
(*The Only Necessary Thing*)

I know God won't give me anything I can't handle. I just wish he didn't trust me so much.

BLESSED MOTHER TERESA

My past, O Lord, to your mercy; my present, to your love; my future, to your Providence!

ST. PADRE PIO

Pray, trust, and don't worry.

ST. PADRE PIO

God never shuts one door but he opens another.

IRISH PROVERB

TRUTH

Truth may be stretched, but it cannot be broken, and always gets above falsehood, as oil does above water.

MIGUEL DE CERVANTES

He who does not bellow the truth, when he knows the truth, makes himself the accomplice of liars and forgers.

CHARLES PEGUY (*Basic Verities*)

I have consecrated my life to the service of truth. I have loved the truth and I still love it, as one loves a person.
CARDINAL YVES CONGAR, O.P.

TYRANNY

Tyranny is always better organized than freedom.
CHARLES PEGUY (*Basic Verities*)

U

UNION WITH GOD

Utterly at home, he lives in us for ever.

JULIAN OF NORWICH
(*Revelations of Divine Love*)

Whatever you do, think not of yourself, but of God.

ST. VINCENT FERRER

Not the goods of the world, but God. Not riches, but God. Not honors, but God. Not distinction, but God. Not dignities, but God. Not advancement, but God. God always and in everything.

ST. VINCENT PALLOTTI

Why don't you give yourself to God once and for all . . . really . . . *now!*

ST. JOSEMARIÁ ESCRIVÁ (*The Way*)

V

VATICAN II

We have to conclude that the meaning of the Council will become clearer in the course of time and that even those who participated in it are less likely to understand its full significance than later generations. If we are too close to something we may not see it as it really is.

IAN KER (*"What Did the Second Vatican Council Do For Us?" The Catholic Herald, October 11, 2002*)

VERBOSITY

Let us have a reason for beginning, and let our end be within due limits. For a speech that is wearisome only stirs up anger.

ST. AMBROSE

The more you say, the less people remember.

ARCHBISHOP FRANÇOIS FÉNELON (*Dialogues*)

VIOLENCE

The God of peace is never glorified by human violence.

THOMAS MERTON

The religions should not be used as a tragic excuse for enmities which have their origins elsewhere. No one has the right to call upon God to satisfy their own selfish interests. I ask all religious leaders to reject all violence as offensive to the name of God and to be tireless promoters of peace and harmony.

POPE JOHN PAUL II
(*Azerbaijan, May 22, 2002*)

VIRTUE

Lord and Master of my life, take far from me the spirit of laziness, discouragement, domination and idle talk; grant to me, thy servant, a spirit of chastity, humility, patience, love. Yea, my Lord and King, grant me to see my sins and not to judge my neighbor, for thou art blessed forever and ever. Amen.

ST. EPHRAIM OF SYRIA

Where there is charity and wisdom, there is neither fear nor ignorance. Where there is patience and humility, there is neither wrath nor disturbance. Where there is poverty with gladness, there is neither cupidity nor avarice.... Where there is fear of the Lord to guard the entrance hall, there the enemy can have no place to enter

ST. FRANCIS OF ASSISI

Would that we had spent one whole day well in this world!

THOMAS À KEMPIS
(*The Imitation of Christ*)

Well, brothers, and when shall we begin to do good?

ST. PHILIP NERI

Think well. Speak well. Do well. These three things, through the mercy of God, will make a man go to heaven.

ST. CAMILLUS DE LELLIS

We do not very often come across opportunities for exercising strength, magnanimity, or magnificence; but gentleness, temperance, modesty, and humility, are graces which ought to color everything we do. There may be virtues of a more exalted mold, but . . . these are the most continually called for in daily life.

ST. FRANCIS DE SALES

Now let us do something beautiful for God.

BLESSED MOTHER TERESA

Yesterday is gone. Tomorrow has not yet come. We have only today. Let us begin.

BLESSED MOTHER TERESA

VOCATION

When we are whom we are called to be, we will set the world ablaze.

ST. CATHERINE OF SIENA

May 5. Cold. Resolved to be a religious.

May 6. Fine but rather thick and with a very cold N.E. wind.

May 7. Warm; misty morning; then beautiful turquoise sky. Home, after having decided to be a priest and religious but still doubtful [between] St. Benedict and St. Ignatius. . . .

GERARD MANLEY HOPKINS, S.J.
(*Journal, 1868*)

So few men have the courage to question themselves in order to ascertain what they are really capable of becoming. And so few men have the will to become it.

CARDINAL DESIRÉ JOSEPH MERCIER

God seeks himself in us, and the aridity and sorrow of our heart is the sorrow of God who is not known to us, who cannot yet find himself in us because we do not dare to believe or trust the incredible truth that he could live in us, and live there out of choice, out of preference. But indeed we exist solely for this, to be the place he has chosen for his presence, his manifestation in the world, his epiphany.

THOMAS MERTON
(*A Letter on the Contemplative Life*)

No human being is meant to be a carbon copy. . . . Each must be his own man, much as this may mean resembling someone else. This is not egocentricity or independence of the herd. It is the incommunicable response to the particular summons of God.

HUBERT VAN ZELLER, O.S.B.
(*Considerations*)

W

WAR

In order for a war to be just, three things are necessary.
First, the authority of the sovereign by whose command the war is to be waged. . . .

Secondly, a just cause is required, namely that those
who are attacked, should be attacked because they
deserve it on account of some fault. . . .

Thirdly, it is necessary that the belligerents should
have a rightful intention, so that they intend the
advancement of good, or the avoidance of evil.

ST. THOMAS AQUINAS
(*Summa Theologica*)

Every act of war directed to the indiscriminate destruction of whole cities or vast areas with their inhabitants
is a crime against God and man, which merits firm
and unequivocal condemnation.

SECOND VATICAN COUNCIL
(*The Church in the Modern World*)

Today the scale and horror of modern warfare –
whether nuclear or not – makes it totally unacceptable
as a means of settling differences between nations.

POPE JOHN PAUL II
(*Coventry, England, 1982*)

In this world, Christians will always have to cope with the
evil in the human breast that sows division, destruction
and devastation. . . . The aim of a just war is the blocking

of great evil, the restoration of peace and the defense of minimum conditions of justice and world order.

MICHAEL NOVAK

I say: NO TO WAR! War is not always inevitable. It is always a defeat for humanity.

POPE JOHN PAUL II (*January 13, 2003*)

WEALTH

Every evil, harm and suffering in this life comes from the love of riches.

ST. CATHERINE OF SIENA

All bow down before wealth. Wealth is that to which the multitude of men pay an instinctive homage. They measure happiness by wealth and by wealth they measure respectability.

VENERABLE JOHN HENRY NEWMAN
(*Discourses to Mixed Congregations*)

WISDOM

He is not wise to me who is wise in words only, but he who is wise in deeds.

POPE ST. GREGORY THE GREAT

Wisdom does not enter a malicious mind.

FRANÇOIS RABELAIS

Jesus needs neither books nor doctors of divinity to instruct souls; he, the Doctor of Doctors, he teaches without the noise of words.

ST. THÉRÈSE OF LISIEUX

Accumulated knowledge does not make a wise man. Knowledgeable people are found everywhere, but we are cruelly short of wise people.

MICHEL QUOIST
(*With Open Heart*)

Everyone is wise until he speaks.

IRISH PROVERB

The good Lord set definite limits on man's wisdom, but set no limits on his stupidity – and that's just not fair!

KONRAD ADENAUER

WITNESS

To be a witness does not consist in engaging in propaganda or even stirring people up, but in being a living mystery. It means to live in such a way that one's life would not make sense if God did not exist.

DOROTHY DAY

WOMEN

All women of us suld have honoring,
Service and love above all other thing.

Suld: should

WILLIAM DUNBAR
(*In Praise of Women*)

It is most laudable in a married woman to be devout, but she must never forget that she is a housewife and sometimes she must leave God at the altar to find him in her housekeeping.

ST. FRANCES OF ROME

But whenever you can, my comrades, avoid women. Especially if they are young, beautiful, of doubtful reputation or low rank. Conduct religious conversations only with aristocratic women, and then never with the door shut! Dispatch a female penitent who powders or primps with a quick exhortation. If she continues to be vain, let her find another confessor.

ST. IGNATIUS LOYOLA

If the man is the head of the family, the woman is the heart, and as he occupies the chief place in ruling, so she may and ought to claim for herself the chief place in love.

POPE PIUS XI
(*Casti Connubii*)

The house does not rest upon the earth, but upon a woman.

ITALIAN PROVERB

Adam must have an Eve to blame for his faults.

ITALIAN PROVERB

The Catholic Church has never really come to terms with women. What I object to is being treated either as Madonnas or Mary Magdalenes.

SHIRLEY WILLIAMS, BRITISH POLITICIAN
(*newspaper interview*)

WOMEN'S DRESS

What value is given to cloth by adulteration with false colors? God likes not that which he did not himself produce. Had he not the power to order that sheep should be born with purple or sky-blue fleeces? He had the power but he did not wish; and what God did not wish certainly ought not to be produced artificially.

TERTULLIAN (*Women's Dress*)

WONDER

Wonder is especially proper to childhood; it is the sense of wonder above all that keeps us young.

GERALD VANN, O.P.

WORK

The thing to love in an active life is not honor or power, for all things are vanity under the sun, but the work itself.

ST. AUGUSINE (*The City of God*)

Laborare est Orare
To work is to pray.

MOTTO OF THE BENEDICTINE ORDER

Whatsoever good work you undertake, pray earnestly to God that He will enable you to bring it to a successful conclusion.

ST. BENEDICT (*The Holy Rule*)

Each small task of everyday life is part of the total harmony of the universe.

ST. THÉRÈSE OF LISIEUX

All life demands struggle. Those who have everything given to them become lazy, selfish, and insensitive to the real values of life. The very striving and hard work that we so constantly try to avoid is the major building block in the person we are today.

POPE PAUL VI

WORKING CLASS

The great scandal of the 19th century is that the Church lost the working class.

POPE PIUS XI

WORLD

As the years go by Lord, I come to see more and more clearly, in myself and in those around me, that the greatest secret preoccupation of modern man is much less to battle for possession of the world than to find a means of escaping from it.

PIERRE TEILHARD DE CHARDIN, S.J.
(*Hymn of the Universe*)

The world has become a global village.

MARSHALL MCLUHAN

I am not afraid that God will destroy the world, but I am afraid that he may abandon it to wander blindly in the sophisticated wasteland of contemporary civilization.

CARLO CARRETTO (*In Search of the Beyond*)

Much advance publicity was made for the address the Master would deliver on "The Destruction of the World" and a large crowd gathered at the monastery grounds to hear him.

The address was over in less than a minute. All he said was:

These things will destroy the human race:
politics without principle,
progress without compassion,
wealth without work,
learning without silence,
religion without fearlessness
and worship without awareness.

ANTHONY DE MELLO, S.J.

WORLDLINESS

The simplicity of the just man is laughed to scorn. This is the wisdom of this world: to hide one's feelings by artifice, to veil one's thoughts in words; to make false-hood appear truth, and the truth falsehood. Certainly, this prudence young men learn by experience and boys pay to learn it. Those who know it take pride in it, looking down on the others: those who know it not, humbly and timidly admire those who know it; this evil of duplicity, veiled under an honorable name, is esteemed by them, and perversity of mind is called good breeding.

POPE ST. GREGORY THE GREAT
(*Book of Morals*)

Our labor here is brief, but the reward is eternal. Do not be disturbed by the clamor of the world which passes like a shadow. Do not let the false delights of a deceptive world deceive you.

ST. CLARE OF ASSISI

You cannot please both God and the world at the same time, They are utterly opposed to each other in their thoughts, their desires, and their actions.

ST. JOHN VIANNEY

Woe unto them that keep God like a silk hat,
that believe not in God but in a god.
Woe unto them that are pompous
for they will sooner or later be ridiculous.
Woe unto them that are tired of everything,
for everything will certainly be tired of them.
Woe unto them that cast out everything,
for out of everything they will be cast out.
Woe unto the flippant,
for they shall receive flippancy.
Woe unto them that are scornful
for they shall receive scorn.

G. K. CHESTERTON

Our minds are like crows. They pick up everything that glitters, no matter how uncomfortable our nests get with all that metal in them.

THOMAS MERTON

Z

ZEAL

Zeal without knowledge is always less useful and effective than regulated zeal, and very often it is highly dangerous.

ST. BERNARD OF CLAIRVAUX

We are sometimes stirred by emotion, and mistake it for zeal.

THOMAS À KEMPIS (*The Imitation of Christ*)

Mistrust your zeal for doing good to others.

ABBÉ HENRI HUVELIN

It is possible to have the faith, and to do nothing about it. It is far commoner to have the faith and do next to nothing about it.

RONALD KNOX (*Retreats for Lay People*)

Catholics and Communists have committed great crimes, but at least they have not stood aside, like an established society, and been indifferent. I would rather have blood on my hands than water, like Pilate.

GRAHAM GREENE (*The Comedians*)

If you are what you should be, you will set the world ablaze!

POPE JOHN PAUL II
(*World Youth Day, Rome 2000*)

INDICES

INDEX OF SOURCES